ALPHABETICAL REFERENCE GUIDE

THE MODERN WRITER'S HANDBOOK

Frank O'Hare
The Ohio State University

Macmillan Publishing Company
New York

To my parents
Frank O'Hare
and
Theresa Sutherland O'Hare
for their encouragement and support
and
for their love

Macmillan Publishing Company
866 Third Avenue, New York, New York 10022

Collier Macmillan Canada, Inc.

Library of Congress Cataloging-in-Publication Data

O'Hare, Frank.
    The modern writer's handbook.

    Includes index.
    1. English language—Rhetoric—Handbooks, manuals,
etc. 2. English language—Grammar—1950   —
Handbooks, manuals, etc. I. Title.
PE1408.O37 1986   808'.042   85-23948
ISBN   0-02-389100-9

Printing: 1 2 3 4 5 6 7 8 9   Year: 6 7 8 9 0 1 2 3 4 5

ISBN   0-02-389100-9

PREFACE

Whether produced for the academic community or for the world at large, discourse usually involves someone writing to others about a matter of mutual concern. *The Modern Writer's Handbook* is designed to facilitate communication between writers and their readers, to help writers, in the words of Kenneth Burke, to "identify" with, to become "consubstantial" with, their readers, and thus to win their respect.

The Modern Writer's Handbook assumes commitment on the part of the developing writer. We are not interested in the individual who dashes down the first thing that comes into his or her head, checks for superficial errors in mechanics, usage, or spelling, and produces a final draft that earns a yawning *So what?* from its readers. For this book to be useful, the user must be prepared to spend time examining a topic, generating information about that topic in a variety of ways, carefully analyzing the needs of the potential audience, finding the best organizational frame, and then working through several drafts en route to a final draft that must be edited and proofread with care.

The Modern Writer's Handbook is based on the premise that eventually, at the final draft or proofreading stage of the writing process, maturing writers will be energetically concerned with the surface features of their papers and will, out of respect for themselves and their potential readers, work strenuously to ensure that their prose conforms to the conventions of modern edited written English. The first half of this book, therefore, presents a comprehensive survey of those generally accepted principles we call grammar, usage, and mechanics.

Although the organization of the book follows a sequence that allows the user to learn progressively—the parts of the sentence precede the parts of speech because an understanding of the former gives functional meaning to the latter—the primary consideration in planning the organization was to make the book convenient as a reference. Each section covers its topic thoroughly so that the user seeking an explanation can be confident of finding it under one heading. In some instances, the policy of gathering related topics together has led to repetitions, but the result is ready access to a solution.

Points of grammar, mechanics, and usage are explained as clearly as possible and demonstrated by numerous examples. The examples have been selected with particular care in the realization that the user cannot always associate the stated principle with his or her immediate problem but can usually discover a parallel construction or similar problem in the examples. Many examples are from published sources in a variety of disciplines because an actual usage is often more eloquent than a fabricated one. Following each section of explanation is a brief set of exercises applying the principle discussed. These exercises are designed to help users familiarize themselves with the principle and gain confidence in putting it to work. Where modern usage clearly shows ambiguity in the application of a principle, the explanation includes all the options, as in the case of the serial comma before the conjunction.

The second half of *The Modern Writer's Handbook* summarizes the writing process and offers guidance in invention, drafting, and revision. It ends with an analysis of the library research paper, including directions on using the library, taking notes, styling source references (in accordance with the most recent *MLA Handbook* prescriptions), and preparing a bibliography.

In the back of the book are a glossary of usage, which addresses common confusions and misuses, and a glossary of grammatical terms for convenient reference.

In order to become a confident, competent writer, the inexperienced writer should develop two complementary habits: intensive, thoughtful reading and discussion of the best prose available and abundant practice with the composing process, ideally in a writing workshop. *The Modern Writer's Handbook*

CONTENTS

Grateful acknowledgment is given authors and publishers
for permission to reprint excerpts from the following:

is designed to help the inexperienced writer grow. It is not an alternative to writing but an aid to writing. If it is studied as though it were a compendium of basic information, it will fail its user, for it is, in essence, a reference tool designed to build confidence. Paradoxically, the more diligently this book is used, the less it will be needed.

Acknowledgments

Many individuals helped in the preparation of this book. The quality of the result is my responsibility alone, but I am particularly indebted to the following reviewers for their detailed examination of various drafts and their excellent advice for improving the work: Professor Barbara Carson, University of Georgia; Professor Joan Cunningham, Meridian Junior College; Professor Joseph K. Davis, Memphis State University; Professor Kathleen E. Dubs, University of San Francisco; Professor Nevin K. Laib, Texas Tech University; Professor Richard K. Larson, Herbert H. Lehman College; Professor Thomas E. Martinez, Villanova University; and Professor George Miller, University of Delaware.

I also wish to express my gratitude to Eileen Thompson, whose energy and intelligence were invaluable in the preparation of the manuscript; to John Elliott, Senior Editor, for his meticulous editorial work; to Tony English, Editor-in-Chief, the most truly civilized person I have encountered in the world of publishing, for his many creative contributions to the text; and to my wife, Moira, and my children, Frank, Greg, and Angela, for their support of my work.

FRANK O'HARE

PUNCTUATION AND MECHANICS   121

INTRODUCTION

This book will not teach you to write. Writing is a complex creative process that you must learn by your own system of trial and error, and unless you try—and keep trying—no volume of advice and information is going to make you proficient. But this book does have a purpose. It will help you direct your writing efforts in two ways: first, by providing you with the ground rules of writing, which are the conventions of grammar, punctuation, and usage, and second, by describing the writing process itself—the numerous options facing writers as they think about, plan, draft, and revise their work.

To understand how the contents of this book relate to your writing, think back to the time you were learning to drive. Probably one of the first things you did was to learn the rules of the road; indeed, you had to pass a written test on the rules before you could get behind the wheel. The rules did not teach you to drive a car, but they did give you guidelines by which you could operate your car on the road in a way other drivers expected. The principles of grammar, punctuation, and usage are analogous to the rules of the road. They establish a common ground of conduct between writer and reader so that writers may make themselves understood and that readers may understand.

When you began to drive, you learned by getting the feel of the car how to make it respond as you wanted it to. You were not taught that feel; you acquired it through intensive practice, through trial and error. However, you were probably told by an experienced driver what you should do to get the car moving—how to turn on the ignition and start the engine, how to shift into gear, and where the brake pedal was. This book contains the advice of experienced writers and instructors on how to get writing started, on how to approach revising a draft, on how to analyze and improve paragraphs and sentences, and on what steps to follow in writing a library research paper.

None of this advice will give you the feel of writing, but it may help you find the feel with a little less fumbling and frustration.

The principles of grammar, sentence form, punctuation, spelling, and diction constitute the first half of the book. Because many of these principles have been imposed on the language over centuries by people trying to produce an orderly system, the principles consist not only of the logical but also of the arbitrary, the foreign, the dated, and the debatable. They are complicated, and most of us need occasional reminders of the accepted code. The first half of this book is a compilation of reminders for your reference.

Some of these principles reflect commonsense logic. The sentence *My sister handed Harriet her keys* contains an ambiguous pronoun. Are the keys my sister's or Harriet's? Under "Pronoun reference" (Section 10b) in this book, you will find instructions for recognizing and avoiding such ambiguities. Other principles are—or at least seem—entirely arbitrary. Why, for example, should a period or comma come inside a closing quotation mark and a colon or semicolon outside the quotation mark? (See Section 24, "Quotation marks.") The only answer is that convention has it so. Many other principles derive from the histories of the languages from which English is descended, languages in which a word ending changed according to the relation of the word to other words. From this heritage we preserve a distinction between *who* and *whom* (see Section 11, "Pronoun case") and the practice of adding *s* to a verb with a third-person singular subject (see Section 9, "Subject-verb agreement"). And still other principles are today under debate or in a state of change—whether, for example, the pronoun *he* alone is appropriate in reference to a noun that could apply to a man or a woman (see Section 10a, "Pronoun-antecedent agreement) and whether there really is a difference between *that* and *which* (see Glossary of Usage).

The second half of the book consists of suggestions for writing. These suggestions are not principles. It is not wrong to write a draft without outlining first (see Section 40, "The process of writing: first draft"), but you, individually, may find outlining helpful, and we therefore explain it as an option. Do not regard this half of the book as some sort of prescription for success in writing. We recommend, instead, that you note what is there and see if anything strikes you as a method you would like to try. You may also find the second half helpful in the case of a specific writing task facing you.

Most sections of the book are followed by brief exercises involving application of the principle discussed. If you are aware of particular weak spots in your writing, we suggest you round out your review of the points in question by trying the exercises to fix the principles in your mind.

Finally, if we have not said enough here about the need to practice writing to be successful at writing, we recommend that you look at Section 39, "Preparation for writing." This book is only one element in a long-term commitment that will require your dedication and persistence. The result will, we believe, be worth the effort. The competent writer achieves not only a better standard of communication but a better understanding of how thoughts become ideas that ultimately influence action. Writing is a way of knowing: a means of growing emotionally and intellectually and of understanding yourself and your world.

GRAMMAR

GRAMMAR

Grammar is the formal study of the features and constructions of language. The word *grammar* comes from the ancient Greek word *grammatiké*, which meant the study of literature, in the broad sense of "the way written language is put together." The purpose of studying grammar is to gain an understanding of language so that you can use it effectively.

The basic pattern for writing is the sentence. A useful definition of a sentence is "a word or group of words that expresses a complete thought." A sentence may be as short as one word or as long as fifty words or more.

Here are five sentences. Notice that each begins with a capital letter and ends with an end punctuation mark (a period, a question mark, or an exclamation point).

> Frank Lloyd Wright, considered by many to be the founder of modern architecture, profoundly influenced American life.
> Did you know that sharks, unlike human beings, grow set after set of teeth?
> Alcoholism is a disease, not an indulgence!
> Snow fell.
> Stop!

1 The parts of a sentence

Regardless of its length, a sentence always contains at least one **clause,** consisting of a subject and its matching predicate. (Sometimes the subject is implied rather than stated.) Study the parts of the sentences below.

               subject   predicate
                   ↓   ↓
The scientist's research won.

                           direct object
                             ↓
The scientist's research won recognition.

                         indirect object
                            ↓
The scientist's research won her recognition.

  subject predicate   predicate nominative
    ↓   ↓   ↓
The scientist is Barbara McClintock.

               predicate adjective
                   ↓
Her research is remarkable.

Notice how the following sentences grow from the basic subject-verb pattern.

The scientist investigated.
In her laboratory the scientist investigated.
In her laboratory at Cold Spring Harbor, the scientist investigated.
In her laboratory at Cold Spring Harbor, the scientist investigated gene development.
In her laboratory at Cold Spring Harbor, the scientist investigated gene development in maize.
In her laboratory at Cold Spring Harbor, the scientist investigated gene development in maize, and her discovery won.
In her laboratory at Cold Spring Harbor, the scientist investigated gene development in maize, and her discovery of jumping genes won.
In her laboratory at Cold Spring Harbor, the scientist investigated gene development in maize, and her discovery of jumping genes won recognition.

In her laboratory at Cold Spring Harbor, the scientist investigated gene development in maize, and her discovery of jumping genes won her recognition.

In her laboratory at Cold Spring Harbor, the scientist investigated gene development in maize, and her discovery of jumping genes won her recognition by the scientific community.

The award was the Nobel Prize.

The award won by Barbara McClintock was the Nobel Prize.

The award won by Barbara McClintock, who is a distinguished cytogeneticist, was the Nobel Prize.

The award won in 1983 by Barbara McClintock, who is a distinguished cytogeneticist, was the Nobel Prize.

1a Subjects

The **subject** of the sentence answers the question "who?" or "what?" about the predicate, or verb. The subject is the part of the sentence about which something is being said.

How can you identify the subject of a sentence? Form a question by putting "who" or "what" before the verb. In some sentences, the subject *performs* the action expressed by the verb.

Halfway through her performance, the **soprano** *hit* a flat note.

Captain Cook *searched* for a northwest passage to China.

Mass extinctions *mark* the boundaries between eras on the geological time scale.

Who hit a flat note? The *soprano.* Who searched for a northwest passage to China? *Captain Cook.* What marks the boundaries between eras? *Mass extinctions.*

In other sentences, the subject *receives* the action of the verb; that is, it is acted upon.

The **deer** *was wounded* by the hunters.

Lyndon Johnson *was educated* at Southwest Texas State Teachers College.

The first modern bank in the United States *was established* by Robert Morris, a Philadelphia financier.

What was wounded by the hunters? *The deer.* Who was educated at Southwest Texas State Teachers College? *Lyndon Johnson.* What was established by Robert Morris? *The first modern bank in the United States.*

If the verb is a linking verb, such as *be* or *seem*, the subject is the person or thing identified or described.

> **James Boswell** was both the friend and the biographer of Samuel Johnson.
> **George Eliot** was the pseudonym of Mary Anne Evans.
> **Aaron Burr's reputation as a traitor** seems unjustified.

Who was both the friend and the biographer of Samuel Johnson? *James Boswell.* What was the pseudonym of Mary Anne Evans? *George Eliot.* What seems unjustified? *Aaron Burr's reputation as a traitor.*

The second way to identify the subject of a sentence is to pay attention to word order. In most English sentences, the subject appears before the predicate. However, there are exceptions. Sometimes word order is reversed for effect.

> On his head sits **a crown.**
> Through the ice-covered streets walked **the funeral cortege.**
> From these schools will come **tomorrow's leaders.**

Sometimes word order is altered to ask a question.

> Did **Miró's art** influence Pollock and Motherwell?
> Should **reporters** be required to disclose their sources?
> Does **classical music** have an audience among the young?

Sometimes one of the expletives *there* and *here* appears at the beginning of the sentence. These words are never the subject but simply serve to postpone the appearance of the subject.

The word *it* is also sometimes used as an expletive. In each of the following sentences, the subject is printed in **boldface.**

> There are **six books** in this series.
> Here are **four ways to increase productivity at this plant.**
> It is necessary **to read the instructions before starting.**

Sometimes the sentence is a command. In a command, the subject *you* is implied rather than stated.

> Help me with this word-processing program.
> Please read this chapter before the next class.
> List five twentieth-century American composers.

The simple subject

The **simple subject** is the main noun or noun substitute in the subject.

> In 1984 **Michael Jackson** won eight Grammy awards.
> The young **singer** accepted the awards graciously.
> **He** was applauded for his originality and creativity.
> **Winning awards** is a thrilling experience.

A simple subject may consist of two or more nouns or noun substitutes that take the same predicate.

> **Nicaragua and El Salvador** are much in the news today.
> In ancient Greece, **war and athletics** were believed to be influenced by Nike, the winged goddess of victory.
> **Desire, anger, and pain** must be annihilated in order to reach Nirvana.

Since a prepositional phrase ends with a noun or noun substitute, people sometimes look to it for the subject of the sentence. However, the simple subject is never found in a prepositional phrase. In each of the following sentences, the simple subject is printed in **boldface** and the prepositional phrase is in *italics*.

> **Each** *of the states* chooses delegates to the convention.
> **Neither** *of the pandas* is a female.
> **One** *of Charlemagne's achievements* was the development of an effective administrative system.

The complete subject

The **complete subject** consists of the simple subject and all the words that modify it. In each of the following sentences, the simple subject is printed in **boldface** and the complete subject is in *italics*.

> *The extremely talented **Darryl Strawberry*** played as a right fielder for the New York Mets.
> *The surprise **winner** of the New Hampshire primary* was Gary Hart.
> *A hot **bath** and a vigorous **massage*** are good remedies for aching muscles.

From now on in this book, the term *subject* will mean the simple subject.

Exercise. First identify the simple subject in each of the following sentences. Then identify the complete subject.

1. Are the wives of the early presidents too often overlooked and underrated?

2. The unpretentious Martha Washington is credited with having had a humanizing effect on her more austere husband.

3. The gifted Abigail Adams should be better known for the breadth of her intellectual interests than for her hanging of the presidential laundry in the White House.

4. The detailed letters and memoirs of Dolley Madison provide an excellent source of information about the time.

5. Through the efforts of Abigail Fillmore, Congressional funds were secured to set up a small library in the White House.

1b Predicates

The **predicate** of a sentence tells what the subject does or is. It is the part of the sentence that comprises what is said about the subject. The predicate consists of a verb (a word that expresses action or a state of being) and all the words that complete the meaning of the verb.

How can you identify the predicate of a sentence? Form a question by putting "does what?" or "is what?" after the subject.

The pianist **played a complicated piece.**
The amateur treasure hunters **found a few valuable pieces.**
The bald eagle **is the symbol of the United States.**

The pianist did what? *Played a complicated piece.* The amateur treasure hunters did what? *Found a few valuable pieces.* The bald eagle is what? *Is the symbol of the United States.*

The simple predicate

The **simple predicate** is the verb, which may consist of more than one word.

The town meeting **is** the epitome of a democratic society in action.
Early in her reign Elizabeth **had reestablished** the Church of England.
The Cultural Revolution in China **was headed** by Mao Zedong.
Many accidents **could have been prevented.**

A simple predicate may include two or more verbs that take the same subject.

The small group of colonists **boarded** the British ships and **threw** their cargoes of tea overboard.
Poe **fell** in love with his cousin Virginia and **married** the thirteen-year-old child.
Thoreau **opposed** the poll tax and **had been speaking** against it for years but **had** never before **broken** the law.

The complete predicate

The **complete predicate** consists of the simple predicate and all the words that modify it and complete its meaning. In each of the following sentences, the simple predicate is printed in **boldface** and the complete predicate is in *italics*.

A jet flying overhead ***broke*** *the stillness of the night.*
The Connecticut River ***divides*** *the state into two almost equal regions.*
The goal of landing Americans on the moon and returning them to Earth ***was accomplished*** *by Apollo 11.*

1c Complements

A **complement** completes the meaning of a verb. The four major types of complements are the direct object, the indirect object, the predicate nominative, and the predicate adjective.

Direct objects

A **direct object** is a noun or noun substitute that specifies the person or thing directly *receiving* the action of a transitive verb. To identify the direct object, form a question by putting "whom?" or "what?" after the verb.

> Darwin accepted a **position** aboard H.M.S. *Beagle.*
> In addition to his other accomplishments, William James achieved a **reputation** as a literary figure.
> The congresswoman greeted **us** warmly and then opened the **discussion.**

Darwin accepted what? *A position.* William James achieved what? *A reputation.* The congresswoman greeted whom? *Us.* She opened what? *The discussion.*

Indirect objects

An **indirect object** is a noun or noun substitute that tells to whom or what or for whom or what the action of the verb is performed. A sentence can have an indirect object only if it has a direct object; the indirect object always comes just before the direct object.

> The director gave the **plans** her approval.
> He wrote **her** a poem expressing his admiration.
> In one of Aesop's fables, a mouse does a **lion** a favor.

Usually, sentences containing indirect objects can be rewritten by putting *to* or *for* before the indirect object.

> The director gave her approval **to the plans.**
> He wrote a poem **for her** expressing his admiration.
> In one of Aesop's fables, a mouse does a favor **for a lion.**

Predicate nominatives

A **predicate nominative** is a noun or noun substitute that follows a verb and renames the subject.

> The culprit is **he.**
> Martha Graham became **one** of the principal innovators of modern dance.
> E. B. White's closest companion at the *New Yorker* was **James Thurber.**

The pronoun *he* renames *culprit*. The pronoun *one* renames *Martha Graham*. The noun *James Thurber* renames *companion*.

In a construction of this type, the linking verb serves as an equal sign. The noun on the left-hand side of the linking verb equals the noun on the right-hand side.

Predicate adjectives

A **predicate adjective** is an adjective that follows a verb and describes the subject.

> Isadora Duncan's style of dancing seemed **revolutionary** to her contemporaries.
> The drama critic's review was especially **acrimonious.**
> Halfway through their journey over the mountains, the pioneers felt too **weary** to travel on.

Exercise. First identify the complete subject and the complete predicate in each of the following sentences. Then identify any complements. Classify each complement as a direct object, an indirect object, a predicate nominative, or a predicate adjective.

1. The new employee incentive plan caused a thirty percent increase in productivity.

2. Camp counseling and clerking are two summer jobs available to most college students.

3. Richard Nixon's involvement in Watergate was unacceptable to both Democrats and Republicans.

THE PARTS OF SPEECH **2**

4. These schools of broadcasting do not find even their best students jobs.

5. The Swedish-born Jenny Lind was one of the finest sopranos of her time.

2 The parts of speech

Words have traditionally been classified into eight categories, called **parts of speech**—noun, verb, adjective, adverb, pronoun, preposition, conjunction, and interjection. The function a word performs in a sentence determines which part of speech it is. A word may function as more than one part of speech, as shown in the following examples.

> The committee is seeking ways to make a **ride** on the bus more comfortable. (*noun*)
> Thousands of commuters **ride** the bus to work every day. (*verb*)

> For many years **New England** dominated literary life in America. (*noun*)
> Emily Dickinson's poems carry traces of other **New England** writers. (*adjective*)

> Some scholars feel that the story of Jason and the Argonauts reflects trading expeditions that occurred **before** the Trojan War. (*preposition*)
> **Before** Schliemann excavated the ruins of ancient Troy, most people believed that the story of the Trojan War was pure myth. (*conjunction*)

2a Nouns

A **noun** is a word that names. Nouns may name persons.

Shakespeare	actor	women
Margaret Mead	citizen	scholars

Nouns may name places.

Pittsburgh	prairie	suburbs
Pacific Ocean	camp	Great Lakes

Nouns may name animate or inanimate objects.

reindeer	Bunsen burner	cassettes
baboon	veranda	word processors

Nouns may name events, ideas, or concepts.

meeting	freedom	frustration
French Revolution	honor	philanthropy

In the following sentences, the nouns are printed in **boldface.**

> While in his **bath, Archimedes,** a Greek **mathematician** and **inventor,** worked out the **principle** of **buoyancy.**
> **Barbara Tuchman** argues that the **acceptance** of the **Wooden Horse** by the **Trojans** was the **epitome** of **folly.**
> The **discovery** of the **Rosetta stone** led to an **increase** in **knowledge** of the ancient **world.**

Nouns can be classified in other ways: as proper or common nouns, and as concrete or abstract nouns. **Proper nouns** name particular persons, places, objects, or ideas. Proper nouns are capitalized.

Milton	Chevrolet	Martin Luther King, Jr.
San Francisco	Hinduism	Argentina

Common nouns are less specific. They name people, places, objects, and ideas in general, not in particular. Common nouns are not capitalized.

historian	manuscript	file cabinet
library	religion	presidency

Concrete nouns name things that can be seen, touched, heard, smelled, or tasted.

landscape	granite	symphony
chocolate	perfume	beaker

Abstract nouns name concepts, ideas, beliefs, and qualities. Unlike concrete nouns, abstract nouns name things that cannot be perceived by the five senses.

love	justice	creativity
inspiration	kindness	monotheism

When you read the preceding lists, you probably noticed that some nouns are made up of more than one word. Nouns that consist of more than one word are called **compound nouns.** Some compound nouns are written as one word, some are hyphenated, and some are written as two or more separate words.

bedroom	floppy disk	cathode-ray tube
heartland	democratic socialism	father-in-law

Nouns are characterized by several features.

1. Nouns show **number.** Most nouns can be either singular or plural. (For guidelines on forming the plural of nouns, see pages 178–181.)

Singular:	computer	success	criterion	woman	sheep
Plural:	computers	successes	criteria	women	sheep

2. Nouns have **gender.** They are either masculine, feminine, or neuter (sometimes called indeterminate).

Masculine:	Abraham Lincoln	waiter	boy
Feminine:	Harriet Tubman	waitress	girl
Neuter:	human being	attendant	child
	Eiffel Tower	chair	justice

3. Nouns have **case.** Case refers to the structural function of a noun in a sentence. Although English has three cases—subjective (nominative), objective, and possessive—the form of the noun changes only when it is used in the possessive case. (For more information on forming the possessive case, see pages 194–197.)

   The subjective case is used for subjects and predicate nominatives. The objective case is used for direct and indirect objects and for objects of prepositions. The possessive case is used to show possession.

Subjective: **Harrison** worked late.
Objective: The boss trained **Harrison.**
Possessive: **Harrison's** proposal was accepted by the trustees.

2b Verbs

A **verb** is a word that expresses action or a state of being. In the following sentences, the verbs are printed in **boldface.**

> Isaac Bashevis Singer **writes** his stories and novels in Yiddish.
> Plato **outlived** his teacher, Socrates.
> The Constitution **is** the keystone of our democracy.

Action and linking verbs

An **action verb** expresses an action, which may be physical or mental.

> During the 1920's many blacks **moved** from the rural South to the industrial North. (*physical*)
> Gwendolyn Brooks **received** many awards and honors for her poetry. (*physical*)
>
> Dorothy Parker **delighted** her companions with her ready wit. (*mental*)
> The Puritans **valued** plainness and simplicity. (*mental*)

A **linking verb** connects the subject to a word that identifies or describes the subject. A linking verb expresses a state of being or a condition rather than an action. The most common linking verb is *be.*

> Radiotherapy **is** the treatment of disease with radiation.
> Woody Guthrie **was** a popular folksinger.
> Americans **were** aghast at the sinking of the *Lusitania.*

Other common linking verbs are *appear, become, feel, grow, look, remain, seem, smell, sound,* and *taste.*

> Compared to other warm-blooded animals, hummingbirds **appear** extravagant in their use of energy.
> Houdini **became** world-famous for his daring escapes.
> The fate of Amelia Earhart **remains** a mystery.

Many linking verbs can also be used as action verbs.

> During the campaign, the arguments over prayer in the schools **grew** heated. (*linking*)
> Gregor Mendel **grew** his plants in the monastery garden. (*action*)

In 1974 the fate of the kangaroo in its natural habitat **appeared** uncertain. (*linking*)

One night in New South Wales, a number of kangaroos **appeared** at my campsite. (*action*)

A linking verb connects the subject to a predicate nominative or to a predicate adjective. A predicate nominative identifies the subject, while a predicate adjective describes the subject.

Napoleon was a brilliant **general.** (*predicate nominative*)

After his defeat at Waterloo, *Napoleon* was **disconsolate.** (*predicate adjective*)

The *macadamia* is Australia's only edible **nut.** (*predicate nominative*)

The macadamia's *shell* is nearly **impregnable.** (*predicate adjective*)

The *bobcat* remains North America's most common native **cat.** (*predicate nominative*)

Despite the trainer's efforts, the *bobcat* remains **wild.** (*predicate adjective*)

A linking verb may also connect the subject to a word that answers the question "where?"

We were **upstream** from their camp.

The *plane* was directly **overhead** when it burst into flames.

Unfortunately, *they* were **downwind** of the skunk when it sprayed.

Transitive and intransitive verbs

A **transitive verb** is an action verb that takes an object. An object is a word that is necessary to complete the idea expressed by the verb.

Marie and Pierre Curie successfully **isolated** *radium*.

During the Civil War, Union forces **blockaded** *Charleston Harbor*.

Several of Hawthorne's characters **know** *guilt* intimately.

Professor Higgins **introduced** *Eliza Doolittle* to society.

An **intransitive verb** is an action verb that does not take an object. In other words, an intransitive verb does not need an object to complete its meaning.

Sometimes even good old Homer **nods**.
HORACE

People **hate**, as they **love**, unreasonably.
WILLIAM THACKERAY

Consider the lilies of the field, how they **grow**; they **toil** not, neither **do** they **spin**.
MATTHEW 6:28

Many verbs can be either transitive or intransitive.

The narrator **mourned** the *loss* of his beautiful Annabel Lee. (*transitive*)
After the death of the President, the nation **mourned**. (*intransitive*)

The audience **howled** its *derision* at the speaker. (*transitive*)
Out on the tundra, the wolves **howled**. (*intransitive*)

Queen Victoria **ruled** *Great Britain, Ireland, and India*. (*transitive*)
In the midst of battle, death **ruled**. (*intransitive*)

Auxiliary verbs and modals

A verb has four basic forms, called **principal parts:** the present infinitive, the past tense, the past participle, and the present participle.

Present infinitive	Past tense	Past participle	Present participle
(to) compute	computed	computed	computing
(to) analyze	analyzed	analyzed	analyzing
(to) fall	fell	fallen	falling
(to) bring	brought	brought	bringing

The present infinitive is the dictionary form of the verb. For example, if you wanted to know the meaning of the first verb in the chart above, you would look up *compute*, the present infinitive form, in your dictionary. The present participle of all verbs is formed by adding *-ing* to the present infinitive. The past tense and past participle of most verbs, called **regular verbs,** are formed by adding *-d* or *-ed* to the present infinitive. Verbs like *fall* and *bring* are **irregular verbs;** their past tense and past participle are formed in some other way. (For more information on irregular verbs, see pages 60–63.)

A **verb phrase** is made up of the present infinitive, the present participle, or the past participle preceded by one or more auxiliary verbs or modals. As discussed in the following pages, the two **auxiliary verbs,** *be* and *have*, are used to form the perfect tenses, progressive forms of tenses, and the passive voice. In the following sentences, the verb phrase is printed in *italics* and the auxiliary is in **boldface.**

> Several movies *are popularizing* a street form of dance called break dancing.
> Edna St. Vincent Millay's first book of poems *was published* in 1917.
> Jacobo Timerman *has called* attention to the violation of human rights in Argentina.

Modals are used to form questions, to help express a negative, to emphasize, to show future time, and to express such conditions as possibility, certainty, or obligation. The words *do, does, did; can, could; may, might, must; will, shall; would, should;* and *ought to* are modals. A verb phrase may include both auxiliaries and modals. In each of the following sentences, the verb phrase is printed in *italics* and the modal is in **boldface.**

> For a democracy to work, its citizens **must** *participate.*
> You **should** *practice* at least an hour a day.
> The election **may** *be decided* on the basis of personality.

Sometimes an auxiliary or modal is separated from the main part of the verb.

> **Do** you *know* the full name of the Imagist poet H.D.?
> The price of gold **has** not *been falling.*
> The teacher **is** now *computing* her students' grade-point averages.

Verbs display three characteristics: tense, voice, and mood.

Tense

Tense is the time expressed by the form of the verb. The six tenses are the simple present, present perfect, simple past, past perfect, simple future, and future perfect. Each of these tenses has a progressive form that indicates continuing action.

	Basic form	**Progressive form**
Simple present:	compose(s)	is (are) composing
Present perfect:	has (have) composed	has (have) been composing
Simple past:	composed	was (were) composing
Past perfect:	had composed	had been composing
Simple future:	will (shall) compose	will (shall) be composing
Future perfect:	will (shall) have composed	will (shall) have been composing

Usually, the simple present, the simple past, and the simple future are referred to as the present, the past, and the future tense, respectively.

The time of an action does not always correspond exactly with the name of the tense used to write about the action. For example, in special situations the present tense can be used to write about events that occurred in the past or will occur in the future as well as events that are occurring in the present.

In general, the **present tense** is used to write about events or conditions that are happening or existing now.

> She **lives** in Austin, Texas.
> An accountant **is preparing** our tax returns.
> They **are** dissatisfied with their grades.

The present tense is also used to write about natural or scientific laws or timeless truths, events in literature, and habitual action.

> Some bacteria **are** beneficial, while others **cause** disease.
> No one **lives** forever.
> Sherlock Holmes and his archenemy, Dr. Moriarity, apparently **perish** together.
> He always **begins** his speeches with an anecdote.
> She **goes** to work every day at eight.

The past tense can also be used to write about events in literature. Whichever tense you choose, be consistent.

The present tense can be used with an adverbial word or phrase to indicate future time.

> This flight **arrives** in Chicago at 7:30 P.M.
> In the future, **turn** in your assignment on time.
> She **begins** her campaign tomorrow.

The verb *do* is used with the present infinitive to create an emphatic form of the present tense.

> You **do know** your facts, but your presentation of them is not always clear.
> He certainly **does cover** his topic thoroughly.
> After six weeks of training, they **do look** fit.

The **present perfect tense** is used to write about events that occurred at some unspecified time in the past and about events and conditions that began in the past and may still be continuing in the present.

> The novelist **has incorporated** theories of psycholinguistics into his mysteries.

Their new line of greeting cards **has been selling** well.
The two performers **have donated** the profits from their concert to charity.

The **past tense** is used to write about events that occurred and conditions that existed at a definite time in the past and do not extend into the present.

The study **explored** the dolphin's ability to communicate.
The researchers **were studying** the effects of fluoridation on tooth decay.
The patient **was relieved** when the doctor **told** him the results of the tests.

The word *did* (the past tense of *do*) is used with the present infinitive to create an emphatic form of the past tense.

In the end he **did vote** against the bill.
Despite opposition, she **did make** her opinions heard.
They **did increase** voter registration, but they lost the election.

The **past perfect tense** is used to write about a past event or condition that ended before another past event or condition began.

She voted for passage of the bill because she **had seen** the effects of poverty on the young.
The researchers **had tried** several drugs on the microorganism before they found the right one.
He **had been painting** for ten years before he sold his first canvas.

The **future tense** is used to write about events or conditions that have not yet begun.

Her next book **will continue** the saga of the Anderson family.
The voters **will be deciding** the role of religion in the schools.
We **shall stay** in London for two weeks.

The **future perfect tense** is used to write about a future event or condition that will end before another future event or condition begins or before a specified time in the future.

Before I see him again, the editor **will have read** my short story.
If he keeps to this regimen, by the end of the month the boxer **will have lost** the necessary ten pounds.

By October, she **will have been singing** with the City Opera five years.

For more information on the use of tenses, see pages 106–109.

Voice

Voice indicates whether the subject performs or receives the action of the verb. If the subject performs the action, the verb and the clause are in the **active voice.**

The President **announced** his decision.
The journal **offers** insights into contemporary poetry.
Anxiety **can cause** a rise in blood pressure.

If the subject receives the action of the verb, that is, if the subject is acted upon, the verb and the clause are in the **passive voice.** The passive voice of a verb consists of a form of *be* followed by the past participle of the verb.

The decision **was announced** by the President.
Insights into contemporary poetry **are offered** by the journal.
A rise in blood pressure **can be caused** by anxiety.
The money **has been stolen** from the safe.

Many sentences written in the passive voice, like the first three examples above, contain a phrase beginning with the word *by.* This phrase usually tells who or what actually performed the action.

Mood

Mood refers to whether a verb expresses a statement, a command, a wish, an assumption, a recommendation, or a condition contrary to fact. In English there are three moods: the indicative, the imperative, and the subjunctive.

The **indicative mood** is used to make a factual statement or to ask a question.

William Carlos Williams **lived** in Paterson, New Jersey.
Did William Carlos Williams **live** in Paterson, New Jersey?

Kublai Khan **was** the grandson of Genghis Khan.
Was Kublai Khan the grandson of Genghis Khan?

Forced from their land, the Cherokees **embarked** on the Trail of Tears.

The **imperative mood** is used to express a command or a request. In a command, the subject *you* is often not stated, but understood.

Bring me the newspaper.
Come here!
Would you please **close** that door.

The **subjunctive mood** is used to indicate a wish, an assumption, a recommendation, or a condition contrary to fact.

He wished he **were** rich. (*wish*)
If this **be** true, the validity of the collection is in doubt. (*assumption*)
It is mandatory that he **dress** appropriately. (*recommendation*)
If I **were** mayor, I would solve the problems of this city. (*condition contrary to fact*)

As you can see from these examples, the form of a verb in the subjunctive is often different from the indicative form. With most verbs the only difference is in the third-person singular form in the present tense, where the subjunctive does not have the final *s* of the indicative form.

Indicative	Subjunctive
he speaks	he speak
she manages	she manage
it works	it work

The subjunctive of the verb *to be* differs from the indicative in both the present and the past tenses.

PRESENT TENSE

Indicative		Subjunctive	
I am	we are	(if) I be	(if) we be
you are	you are	(if) you be	(if) you be
he/she/it is	they are	(if) he/she/it be	(if) they be

PAST TENSE

Indicative		Subjunctive	
I was	we were	(if) I were	(if) we were
you were	you were	(if) you were	(if) you were
he/she/it was	they were	(if) he/she/it were	(if) they were

The subjunctive is falling into disuse. However, it is still preferred for expressing a condition contrary to fact, and it is required in *that* clauses of recommendation, wish, or command and in a few idiomatic phrases.

> If she **were** in command, we wouldn't be having this problem.
> In Kipling's tale, Danny wished that he **were** king.
> He resolved that if need **be,** he would study night and day.

Exercise. Identify the nouns and the verbs in the following sentences.

1. Although people think of apples whenever the story of Adam and Eve is read, the apple is not mentioned in Genesis.

2. According to the Bible, the first man and woman ate the fruit of the tree of knowledge of good and evil, but this fruit is never identified.

3. Storytellers and writers have often used the apple as a symbol of all fruits, and the apple has figured prominently in mythology and folklore.

4. An ancient Greek myth tells how Paris, a Trojan prince, judged a beauty contest among three goddesses and gave the prize, a golden apple, to Aphrodite; this decision led to the Trojan War.

5. Most Americans know the tale of Johnny Appleseed, but many people do not know that this legend is based on the life of a real person, John Chapman.

2c Adjectives

An **adjective** is a word that modifies, or describes, a noun or pronoun. It limits or makes clearer the meaning of the noun or pronoun.

The **efficient** *secretary* organized the schedule. (*modifies a noun*)

He is **efficient.** (*modifies a pronoun*)

When Miles Davis plays, you hear a very **personal** *sound*. (*modifies a noun*)

It is, at times, also very **lonely,** very **introspective.** (*modify a pronoun*)

Writers sometimes sprinkle **their** *writing* with **foreign** *expressions*. (*modify nouns*)

This became **fashionable** in the 1550's. (*modifies a pronoun*)

An adjective modifies by answering one of three questions about the noun or pronoun. These questions are (1) "what kind?" (2) "how many?" and (3) "which one?"

By describing a quality or a condition, an adjective answers the question "what kind?"

The England of the Anglo-Saxons was not a **unified** *country*, but a land divided into **separate** *kingdoms*.

Much of the poetry of the Anglo-Saxons was in the **heroic** *tradition*.

The *riddles* in **Anglo-Saxon** *poetry* were **clever** and **humorous.**

By telling quantity, an adjective answers the question "how many?" This quantity may be definite (*one, twenty*) or indefinite (*several, few*).

When writing about literature, keep in mind **six** *features:* plot, characterization, setting, theme, point of view, and style.

The report listed **several** *reasons* for the decline of literacy.

He has **many** *questions* but **no** *answers*.

An adjective answers the question "which one?" by showing possession or by pointing out people or objects. Possessive forms of both nouns and pronouns may be considered adjectives (*girl's*, *his*), as may the demonstratives *this*, *these*, *that*, and *those* and the articles *a*, *an*, and *the*.

Bauhaus sought to correct **the** *alienation* of factory workers from

their *products*.

Asplund's *buildings* vividly revealed **the** *possibilities* of steel and glass.

These *artists* were interested in everything from designing glass-ware to planning factories.

Adjectives are characterized by several features.

1. Most adjectives have comparative and superlative forms.

	Comparative	**Superlative**
rich	richer	richest
beautiful	more beautiful	most beautiful
bad	worse	worst

Chocolate mousse is a **rich** dessert.
Chocolate mousse is a **richer** dessert than apple pie.
Chocolate mousse is the **richest** of the three desserts.

The roses are **beautiful.**
The roses are **more beautiful** than the hyacinths.
The roses are the **most beautiful** flowers in the garden.

25

(For information about the comparative and superlative forms of adjectives, see pages 94–96.)

2. Adjectives can usually be identified by their position in a sentence. For example, an adjective will fit sensibly into one of the following blanks.

The _____ object was removed.
It seems _____.
The woman, _____ and _____, left early.

3. Usually, the adverb *very* can be placed before an adjective.

The **very large** object was removed.
It seems **very odd.**
The woman, **very tired** and **very cold,** left early.

2d Adverbs

An **adverb** is a word that modifies, or limits the meaning of, a verb, an adjective, or another adverb.

During the Harbor Festival, the tall ships *sailed* **gracefully** into the bay. (*modifies a verb*)

The exhibition of art from Pompeii drew **extremely** *large* crowds. (*modifies an adjective*)

The accident at Three Mile Island demonstrated **very** *powerfully* the hazards of nuclear energy. (*modifies an adverb*)

An adverb modifies by answering one of the following questions: (1) "when?" (2) "where?" (3) "to what extent?" (4) "how?" **Adverbs of time** answer the question "when?"

The symposium *was held* **yesterday.**

Environmentalists warn that we *must* **eventually** *reach* an equilibrium with nature.

Photography *is* **now** *accorded* equal status with painting and sculpture.

Adverbs of place answer the question "where?"

As the ambassador traveled through the Middle East and North Africa, he *encountered* an Islamic revival **everywhere.**

Faith healers *look* **upward** and **inward** for cures for disease.

The ceremony *was held* **outdoors** to accommodate the large crowd.

Adverbs of degree answer the question "to what extent?" In addition, they are used to heighten, or intensify, the meaning of a verb, adjective, or adverb.

The Empire State Building is **far** *more beautiful* than the World Trade Center.

After paying her medical bills, she was left **almost** *destitute.*

In his films the **very** *talented* Charlie Chaplin was able to make people laugh at the absurdities of life.

Adverbs of manner answer the question "how?" They tell in what manner or by what means an action was done.

Disaster films *were* **enthusiastically** *embraced* by the moviegoing public.

The Beatles proved that rock music *had to be taken* **seriously.**

People *are* **strenuously** *debating* whether the lives of comatose patients *should be maintained* **artificially.**

27

Adverbs are characterized by two features.

1. Adverbs can be formed from many adjectives by adding the suffix *-ly* to the adjective. An additional spelling change is sometimes required.

   The artist's style was **delicate**. (*adjective*)
   The artist painted **delicately**. (*adverb*)

   Lech Walesa's actions seemed **heroic**. (*adjective*)
   Lech Walesa acted **heroically**. (*adverb*)

2. Most adverbs have comparative and superlative forms.

	Comparative	**Superlative**
profoundly	more profoundly	most profoundly
fast	faster	fastest
well	better	best

   The soprano is singing **well** today.
   The soprano is singing **better** than she sang yesterday.
   The soprano is singing the **best** she has in days.

   The plight of the homeless is **profoundly** moving.
   The plight of the homeless is **more profoundly** moving than I had imagined.
   The plight of the homeless is the **most profoundly** moving story in the paper today.

   (For more information about the comparative and superlative forms of adverbs, see pages 94–96.)

2e Pronouns

A **pronoun** is a word that stands for or takes the place of one or more nouns. When a pronoun refers to a specific noun, that noun is called the **antecedent** of the pronoun. In the following sentences, the arrows indicate the *italicized* antecedents of the pronouns in **boldface** type.

Because *vitamins* can have toxic side effects, **they** should be administered with care.

Megadoses of *niacin,* **which** is a B vitamin, can cause nausea and vomiting.

A pronoun may also have another pronoun as an antecedent.

Most of the records are scratched. **They** will have to be replaced.

Each of the mothers thought **her** child should receive the award.

A pronoun may lack a specific antecedent.

Who can understand the demands made upon a child prodigy?
Everyone knew that **something** was wrong.

There are seven categories of pronouns: personal, demonstrative, indefinite, interrogative, relative, intensive, and reflexive.

Personal pronouns

Personal pronouns take the place of a noun that names a person or a thing. Like nouns, personal pronouns have number, gender, and case. This means that they can be singular or plural; that they can be masculine, feminine, or neuter; and that they can function in the subjective, the objective, or the possessive case. (For more information about pronoun case, see pages 83–89.) In addition, personal pronouns are divided into three "persons": **first-person pronouns** refer to the person(s) speaking or writing, **second-person pronouns** refer to the person(s) being spoken or written *to,* and **third-person pronouns** refer to the person(s) or thing(s) being spoken or written *about.* The following is a list of all the personal pronouns.

	Singular	Plural
First person:	I, me, my, mine	we, us, our, ours
Second person:	you, your, yours	you, your, yours
Third person:	he, him, his	they, them, their, theirs
	she, her, hers	
	it, its	

Demonstrative pronouns

Demonstrative pronouns point to someone or something. The demonstrative pronouns are *this* and *that* and their plural forms *these* and *those*.

Demonstrative pronouns are usually used in place of a specific noun or noun phrase.

> The sandwiches I ate yesterday were stale, but **these** are fresh.
>
> The goddess of retributive justice was called Nemesis, and **this** is the word we use today to refer to an avenger or an unbeatable rival.
>
> James named the character Mrs. Headway, for **that** was her chief characteristic, her ability to make headway.

In addition, demonstrative pronouns are sometimes used to refer to a whole idea.

> Should we welcome the electronic age? **That** is a good question.
>
> **This** is the challenge new sergeants face: finding ways to make recruits respect you, not just fear you.

If you use a demonstrative pronoun in this way, be sure that the idea it refers to is clearly stated and not just vaguely suggested (see pages 79–80).

Indefinite pronouns

Indefinite pronouns do not take the place of a particular noun, although sometimes they have an implied antecedent. Indefinite pronouns carry the idea of "all," "some," "any," or "none." Some common indefinite pronouns are listed below.

everyone	somebody	anyone	no one
everything	many	anything	nobody

Some indefinite pronouns are plural, some are singular, and some can be either singular or plural.

> **Everything** *is* going according to plan. (*singular*)
>
> **Many** *were* certain that the war which officially started on July 28, 1914, would be over before autumn. (*plural*)

Some of the material *was* useful. (*singular*)
Some of the legislators *were* afraid to oppose the bill publicly. (*plural*)

For more information on the number of indefinite pronouns, see pages 71–72.

Interrogative pronouns

Interrogative pronouns are used to ask a question.

> who   whom   whose   what   which

Who, whom, and *whose* refer to people. *What* refers to things. *Which* refers to people or things.

> **What** were the effects of the Industrial Revolution on Europe during the first decade of the twentieth century?
>
> **Who** is Barbara McClintock and for **what** is she best known?
>
> **Which** countries were part of the Triple Entente and **which** were part of the Triple Alliance?

Relative pronouns

Relative pronouns are used to form adjective clauses and noun clauses (see pages 43–45).

who	which	whoever	whatever
whose	that	whomever	
whom	what	whichever	

Who, whom, whoever, and *whomever* refer to people. *Which, what, that, whichever,* and *whatever* refer to things. *Whose* usually refers to people but can also refer to things.

> The Black Emergency Cultural Coalition is an organization **whose** members have dedicated themselves to the elimination of racism in the arts.
>
> Betye Saar's *The Liberation of Aunt Jemima,* **which** was purchased by the University Art Museum at Berkeley, is a multidimensional work **that** uses a collage of labels from pancake-mix boxes.
>
> The food was given away to **whoever** wanted it.

For more information about relative pronouns, see page 77.

Intensive pronouns

Intensive pronouns are used to emphasize their antecedents. They are formed by adding *-self* or *-selves* to the end of a personal pronoun.

> The detectives **themselves** didn't know the solution.
> The producer wasn't sure **herself** why the show was a success.

Reflexive pronouns

Reflexive pronouns are used to refer back to the subject of the clause or verbal phrase in which they appear. They have the same form as intensive pronouns.

> During her illness Marjorie did not seem like **herself**.
> If you have young children in the house, take precautions to prevent them from electrocuting **themselves** accidentally.
> This plant can fertilize **itself**.

Exercise. Identify the adjectives, adverbs, and pronouns in each of the following sentences.

1. Recently, American cooks have become more experimental, and they have mastered many of the techniques of foreign cuisines.

2. Some have even learned to make sushi and sashimi, two Japanese delicacies prepared with raw fish.

3. Those who have experimented with Mexican dishes can now handle spices confidently.

4. What do you think of the new and lighter French cuisine which is rapidly sweeping the country?

5. Today, everyone wants to be an excellent cook, and some are even returning to school for this purpose.

2f Prepositions

across	during	near	toward
below	from	on	with

The words listed above are **prepositions,** which are words used to show the relationship of a noun or a pronoun, called the object of the preposition, to another part of the sentence. Prepositions are among the most familiar and frequently used words in the language. Some common ones are listed below.

about	concerning	past
above	despite	save (meaning
across	down	"except")
after	during	since
against	except	through
along	for	throughout
among	from	till
around	in	to
at	inside	toward(s)
before	into	under
behind	like	underneath
below	near	until
beneath	of	unto
beside	off	up
between	on	upon
beyond	onto	with
but (meaning	out	within
"except")	over	without

A **compound preposition** is made up of more than one word. Some commonly used compound prepositions are listed below.

ahead of	in addition to	on account of
as for	in back of	on top of
as well as	in case of	out of
because of	in front of	together with
by means of	instead of	with regard to

Prepositions appear at the beginning of prepositional phrases. In the following sentences, the prepositions are printed in **boldface** and the prepositional phrases are in *italics*.

> The term "metaphysical poets" was coined **by** *Samuel Johnson* **in** *the eighteenth century.*
>
> Metaphysical poets wrote **about** *human love* **in addition to** *religious love.*
>
> Often they used language normally associated **with** *human love* to tell **about** *their love* **of** *God* and religious images to tell **about** *their love* **of** *other human beings.*

Note: The *to* in the infinitive form of the verb (such as *to tell*) is not a preposition.

(For more information on prepositional phrases, see pages 39–40.)

Exercise. Identify the prepositions in each of the following sentences.

1. The word *library* comes from *liber*, the Latin word for book.

2. Aristotle had an excellent private library, and upon his death this library was given to one of his students.

3. However, the greatest library of the ancient world was established around 300 B.C. by Ptolemy I at Alexandria, which was located at the mouth of the Nile in Egypt.

4. Within this library were manuscripts from every part of the then known world.

5. Throughout the reign of the Caesars, libraries flourished in Rome, but with the rise of Christianity libraries declined in Western Europe, until the founding of the great monastic libraries during the sixth and the seventh centuries.

2g Conjunctions

and	if	until	but	or	when

The words listed above are **conjunctions,** which are words used to join other words, phrases, clauses, or sentences. There are three types of conjunctions: coordinating conjunctions, correlative conjunctions, and subordinating conjunctions.

Coordinating conjunctions

A **coordinating conjunction** joins elements that have equal grammatical rank. These elements may be single words, phrases, or clauses. The common coordinating conjunctions are the following:

and	or	for	yet
but	so	nor	

In the following sentences, the coordinating conjunctions are printed in **boldface** and the elements being joined are in *italics*.

The children of *Queen Victoria* **and** *Prince Albert* married into many of the other ruling houses of Europe.

Some enjoy Matthew Arnold primarily for his poetry, **but** *others respect him more for his criticism.*

The flax is then soaked *in tanks, in streams,* **or** *in pools.*

Words like the following, called **conjunctive adverbs,** may be used as coordinating conjunctions to join independent clauses (clauses that can stand by themselves as sentences).

accordingly	hence	otherwise
also	however	still
besides	moreover	therefore
consequently	nevertheless	thus
furthermore		

In the following sentences, the conjunctive adverbs are in **boldface** and the independent clauses are in *italics*. Notice that a semicolon precedes a conjunctive adverb that appears between independent clauses.

She wanted to photograph the building in the early morning light; **therefore,** *she got up at dawn on Saturday.*

For years the elderly have moved from the North to Florida to retire; **however,** *today many are returning to the North to be near their children.*

William Morris was a noted painter, weaver, and pattern maker; **moreover,** *he was a respected poet, novelist, and critic.*

Correlative conjunctions

Correlative conjunctions are coordinating conjunctions that are used in pairs. The most common correlative conjunctions are the following:

both . . . and	not only . . . but also
either . . . or	whether . . . or
neither . . . nor	

In the following sentences, the correlative conjunctions are in **boldface.**

Whether you succeed **or** fail depends on you.
Both exercising regularly **and** adjusting your diet are necessary
for losing weight.
Either Chick Corea **or** Gary Burton will begin the concert.

Subordinating conjunctions

Subordinating conjunctions join subordinate, or dependent,
clauses to main, or independent, clauses. The following are
some common subordinating conjunctions:

after	if	that
although	in order that	though
as	in that	unless
as if	inasmuch as	until
as long as	now that	when
as much as	once	where
because	provided that	whereas
before	since	wherever
even though	so long as	while
how	so that	whether

A clause that is structurally independent, that can stand by
itself, is called an independent clause. A clause that is structurally dependent, that cannot stand by itself, is called a
dependent clause. A subordinating conjunction is used at the
beginning of a dependent clause to show the relation between
this clause and the independent clause to which it is attached.
In the following sentences, the subordinating conjunction is
printed in **boldface** and the dependent clause is in *italics*.

The tepee was an improvement over the traditional tent, ***since*** *it
had a smoke hole at the top.*
When *a chief died*, his heir erected a totem pole to honor him.
Although *the Japan Current makes winters in the Pacific Northwest fairly easy*, it brings with it much rain.

(For more information on clauses, see pages 42–45.)

Exercise. First identify the conjunctions in each of the following
sentences. Then decide whether each is a coordinating, a
correlative, or a subordinating conjunction.

1. Neither the hippopotamus nor the rhinoceros is as large as the elephant; however, the blue whale is larger than all three.

2. Since the Asiatic elephant and the African elephant have distinctive features, they are easy to tell apart.

3. Have you noticed that Asiatic elephants have small ears and high foreheads, while African elephants have large ears and low foreheads?

4. The average African male elephant weighs about 12,000 pounds, but the average Asiatic male weighs only 10,000 pounds; furthermore, both male and female African elephants have tusks, whereas only male Asiatic elephants have tusks.

5. Although elephants are extremely large, they can walk very quietly when they want, because the soles of their feet are covered with thick elastic pads.

2h Interjections

Oh!   Wow!   Great!   Ouch!   Drat!   Whew!

The words listed above are **interjections,** words that express emotion. Grammatically, an interjection has no connection to the rest of the sentence or fragment in which it appears. In the following sentences, the interjections are in **boldface.**

Ouch! I burned my finger.   The rescuers, **alas,** arrived too late.

Well, there it is.   **What,** no kosher pizza?

Curses! Foiled again!   **Ah,** what a life!

Interjections are used much more in speech than in writing, where they are used mostly in dialogue. An interjection may be followed by an exclamation mark or by a comma. An exclamation mark indicates a strong emotional response. A comma indicates a milder response.

2i Verbals

A **verbal** is a grammatical form that is derived from a verb but does not function as a verb in a sentence. A verbal functions as a noun, an adjective, or an adverb. There are three types of verbals: participles, gerunds, and infinitives.

Participles

The present participle and the past participle of most verbs can be used as adjectives. (For more information about participles, see page 17.)

> A **dancing** bear is an image associated with Theodore Roethke.
> The peace between the two wars has been compared to a **held** breath.
> Countee Cullen used the image of **bursting** fruit as a symbol of abundance and fecundity.

Gerunds

A **gerund** is a verb form spelled in the same way as the present participle and used as a noun in a sentence.

> The problems of **parenting** were discussed at the symposium.
> The school taught **reading** and **writing** but little else.
> **Exercising** can help relieve stress.

Infinitives

The present infinitive and the present perfect infinitive of a verb can be used as a noun, an adjective, or an adverb. The **present infinitive** is the *to* form of the verb (*to go*); the **present perfect infinitive** is the *to have* form (*to have gone*).

> She wanted **to resign** at first but finally decided **to stay.** (*nouns*)
> *King Lear* is considered a difficult play **to stage.** (*adjective*)
> What he wanted most was someone **to love.** (*adjective*)
> By the end of the day I was ready **to scream.** (*adverb*)
> They were sorry **to have left** before you arrived. (*adverb*)

Sometimes the word *to* in the infinitive is understood rather than stated.

> Therapists must help their patients cope with life's problems.
> Therapists must help their patients **to** cope with life's problems.

Exercise. Identify the verbals in the following sentences. Decide whether each verbal is a participle, a gerund, or an infinitive.

1. Many people agree with the often repeated adage that seeing is believing.

2. Some agree with the statement that to see is to understand.

3. Seeking to gain insight into the ways of gorillas in the wild, Dian Fossey traveled to Africa at the request of the acclaimed scientist Louis Leakey.

4. Living among the wild gorillas and imitating their behavior, Fossey became a partially accepted member of a band of mountain apes who allowed her to sit and to eat with them.

5. Fossey's most thrilling moment occurred when a 450-pound gorilla touched her hand and then ran off, beating his chest excitedly.

3 Phrases

A **phrase** is a group of words lacking a subject and a predicate that often functions as a single part of speech. There are several types of phrases. This section discusses prepositional phrases, noun phrases, and verbal phrases.

3a Prepositional phrases

A **prepositional phrase** consists of a preposition, the object of the preposition, and all the words modifying this object. It usually begins with the preposition and ends with its object. In the following sentences, the prepositional phrases are in **boldface** and the prepositions and their objects are in *italics*.

> ***In** many **cultures*** whale meat has been an essential source ***of protein.***
>
> Some ***of** these cultural **groups*** resent efforts ***by conservationists*** to protect the whale, since these efforts would restrict the group's ability to obtain food and would conflict ***with** its **traditions.***

Conservationists, however, argue that the whale is an intelligent creature *about which* we know far too little and that if these creatures are not protected, they will disappear *from the earth.*

Note: The word *to* with the infinitive (*to obtain*) is not a preposition and does not introduce a prepositional phrase.

Usually a prepositional phrase functions as an adjective or an adverb. Occasionally it may act as a noun.

The *computer* **for the home** may become as ubiquitous as the typewriter. (*adjective*)

The phrase "fruit *fresh* **from the farm**" has become quite *popular* **in merchandising circles.** (*adverbs*)

The only reason that she wrote the book was **for the money.** (*noun*)

3b Noun phrases

A **noun phrase** consists of a noun and its modifiers. In each of the following sentences, the noun phrase is in **boldface** and the noun that is being modified is in *italics.*

> The *appearance* **of the crested iguana of Fiji and the Tongas** changes dramatically when this creature is aroused.
> Its **normally green-and-white-striped** *body* becomes black-and-white.
> The *fold* **of skin beneath its chin** lowers and becomes prominent.

3c Verbal phrases

A **verbal phrase** consists of a verbal and all its complements and modifiers. (To review verbals, see pages 37–38.) There are three types of verbal phrases: participial phrases, gerund phrases, and infinitive phrases.

Participial phrases

A **participial phrase** consists of a participle and all its modifiers and complements. It acts as an adjective in a sentence. In the following sentences, the participial phrases are in **boldface** and the participles are in *italics*.

> Throughout his life, Whitman adhered to the beliefs ***summarized* in the preface of the work.**
> A man ***curled* in the fetal position** with his arm ***covering* his head** is the subject of one of Rodin's most moving sculptures.
> Serenity is the chief quality ***embodied* in the pottery of Jade Snow Wong.**

Gerund phrases

A **gerund phrase** consists of a gerund and all its modifiers and complements. A gerund phrase acts as a noun in a sentence. In the following sentences, the gerund phrases are in **boldface** and the gerunds are in *italics*.

> For Freud, ***remaining* in Vienna** became impossible once the Nazi forces invaded Austria in 1938.
> Today we use the term loosely to mean any person who enjoys ***inflicting* pain.**
> ***Running* five miles a day** keeps a person in good condition.

Infinitive phrases

An **infinitive phrase** consists of the present infinitive or the present perfect infinitive form of the verb and all its modifiers and complements. It acts as a noun, an adjective, or an adverb. In the following sentences, the infinitive phrases are in **boldface** and the infinitives are in *italics*.

> ***To be* a pilot on the Mississippi** was young Sam Clemens's dream. (*noun*)
> ***To know* him** is ***to love* him.** (*nouns*)
> Hard work is one way ***to gain* success in business.** (*adjective*)
> She is proud ***to have dedicated* her life to music.** (*adverb*)

Exercise. Identify all the phrases in the following sentences.

41

Be prepared to tell whether each phrase is a prepositional phrase, a noun phrase, or a verbal phrase.

1. Thousands of people enjoy watching horror movies made during the 1930's and 1940's.

2. In many early horror classics the theme is fear of the unknown.

3. Some movies produced during this period featured monsters created by scientists seeking to unravel the mystery of life and death.

4. The scientists' daring to play God produced terrible consequences for both the guilty and the innocent.

5. Trying to stop the devastation, the scientists in some of these movies struggled to destroy their own creations.

4 Clauses

A **clause** is a group of words with a subject and a predicate. A clause may be independent or dependent.

4a Independent clauses

An **independent clause** is a group of words with a subject and a predicate that expresses a complete thought. In other words, an independent clause is structurally independent and can stand by itself as a simple sentence.

> The Spanish conquistadors heard the legend of El Dorado, the Man of Gold.
> The bottom of the lake was encrusted with gold.
> Some soldiers of fortune traveled down the Amazon.

4b Dependent clauses

A **dependent clause** is a group of words with a subject and a predicate that does not express a complete thought. Dependent clauses cannot stand by themselves as sentences; they must be attached to or be part of an independent clause. They are often called subordinate clauses because they are structurally subordinate to the independent clause. Usually, a dependent clause begins with a subordinating word, which may be a subordinating conjunction or a relative pronoun. There are three types of dependent clauses—adjective, adverb, and noun clauses.

Adjective clauses

An **adjective clause,** or **relative clause,** acts as an adjective and modifies a noun or pronoun. Usually, an adjective clause begins with a relative pronoun.

Jazz is a musical *form* **that originated among black Americans.**

Charlie Parker, **who was known as Bird,** played for a while with the Billy Eckstine band.

Jazz critics have extolled *John Coltrane,* **whose penetrating, raspy sound has been imitated by many other players.**

Jazz, **which began as an American art form,** is being internationalized by players such as the Argentinean Gato Barbieri.

In the first sentence above, the subject of the adjective clause is *that* and the simple predicate is *originated.* In the second sentence, the subject of the adjective clause is *who* and the simple predicate is *was known.* In the third sentence, the subject of the adjective clause is *sound* and the simple predicate is *has been imitated.* In the fourth sentence, the subject of the adjective clause is *which* and the simple predicate is *began.*

Sometimes an adjective clause modifies the entire idea expressed in the preceding clause.

On her birthday, John asked Susan to marry him, **which made her very happy.**

(For information on using commas with adjective clauses, see pages 135–136.)

Adverb clauses

An **adverb clause** acts as an adverb in a sentence. Usually, an adverb clause modifies the verb in another clause. Sometimes, though, it modifies an adjective or an adverb. An adverb clause usually begins with a subordinating conjunction that shows the relation of the adverb clause to the word or words it modifies. (To review subordinating conjunctions, turn to page 36.)

> The grandfather clock *experienced* renewed popularity **after Henry Clay Works published his song "My Grandfather's Clock."** (*modifies the verb* experienced)

> **Since hash is an inexpensive meal,** Americans *call* any cheap restaurant a hash house. (*modifies the verb* call)

> Is the Golden Gate Bridge as *long* **as the Verrazano Bridge is?** (*modifies the adjective* long)

> She speaks *more persuasively* **than I do.** (*modifies the comparative adverb* more persuasively)

Sometimes an adverb clause is elliptical, or incomplete, with the verb omitted but understood.

> Is the Golden Gate Bridge as long as the Verrazano Bridge (is)?
> She speaks more persuasively than I (speak).

(For information on using commas with adverb clauses, see pages 132–134.)

Noun clauses

A **noun clause** acts as a noun in a sentence. This means that it can function as a subject, an object, or a predicate nominative. Usually, a noun clause begins with one of the following subordinating words: *that, how, what, whatever, when, whenever, where, wherever, which, whichever, who, whoever, whose, why.*

> **That she would run for President** seemed a certainty. (*subject*)

The book explains **why the United States refused to join the League of Nations.** (*direct object*)

His home is **wherever he stops his car for the night.** (*predicate nominative*)

Exercise. Identify each dependent clause in the following sentences. For each dependent clause, be prepared to tell whether it is an adjective clause, an adverb clause, or a noun clause.

1. Many people have jobs that require them to travel.

2. Whoever has to travel frequently learns quickly how to find the best local restaurants.

3. Whenever some travelers come to a new town, they look for a restaurant that specializes in regional cooking.

4. Since these restaurants often serve food which they cannot get in their hometowns, the travelers often consider regional restaurants a special treat.

5. People who like to eat look for the sign that reads "Good Home Cooking."

5 Kinds of sentences

Sentences can be classified into four basic groups according to the number and kinds of clauses they contain. These four basic types are simple, compound, complex, and compound-complex sentences.

Simple sentences

A **simple sentence** contains only one independent clause and no dependent clause.

Hokusai and Kunisada are two important Japanese artists.

Sacajawea, a Shoshone Indian, worked as a guide and an interpreter on the Lewis and Clark expedition.

According to most authorities, Tutankhamen became pharaoh in 1361 B.C. and died in 1352 B.C.

Compound sentences

A **compound sentence** contains two or more independent clauses and no dependent clause.

> The goddess Eos granted Tithonus his request for immortality, but he forgot to ask for eternal youth.
>
> During the Crimean War, Florence Nightingale was appalled by the unsanitary conditions in British army hospitals; therefore, she introduced strict standards of cleanliness.
>
> First dice the celery; then peel and chop the onion; next brown the meat in a frying pan.

Complex sentences

A **complex sentence** contains one independent clause and one or more dependent clauses.

> Nihilists advocated the violent overthrow of all existing governments, while anarchists originally advocated freedom from governmental control through nonviolent evolution.
>
> After the museum bought one of his paintings, Cortez was interviewed on a local cable program.
>
> Because it is noted for its ability to weave intricate webs, the spider is a fitting symbol for the storyteller, or spinner of tales.

Compound-complex sentences

A **compound-complex sentence** contains two or more independent clauses and one or more dependent clauses.

> Unfortunately, the danger of crime in the cities is a bleak reality; therefore, some couples with small children choose to move to the suburbs, where they feel they can raise their children in safety.
>
> A group of painters called "neorealists" is turning back to representational styles, and the mass public, which never quite embraced abstract art, is responding enthusiastically to their work.
>
> In the last twenty years, medicine has made major advances; doctors, for example, now perform bone-marrow transplants, procedures which, though risky, offer new hope to patients whose diseases were once considered terminal.

Exercise. Identify each of the following sentences as simple, compound, complex, or compound-complex.

1. Each year Loch Ness, which is the largest lake in the Highlands of Scotland, is visited by thousands of tourists.

2. Although many come to the lake to see the legendary monster, most spot nothing, while a lucky few may catch a glimpse of a mysterious hump in the water.

3. Stories about the Loch Ness monster began to circulate widely in 1933.

4. During that year, two tourists spotted the monster crossing the road, and not long after that, a student, Arthur Grant, had a similar experience.

5. While many people scoff at the idea of a prehistoric monster living in Loch Ness, some scientific expeditions have attempted to locate the creature; however, they have as yet failed to secure incontrovertible evidence.

SENTENCE FORM

SENTENCE FORM

To write a good sentence, it is not enough to have a good idea. You have to express your idea in a form that your readers will understand. The form of a sentence has to follow certain conventions, traditional guidelines that are generally understood and accepted. The conventions of written English are much like rules of etiquette; there may be no particularly good reason for some of them, but as a whole they are essential for helping people to communicate clearly and effectively with one another. In fact, you know most of these conventions so well that you follow them without even thinking about them. Some, however, you may need to review.

6 Sentence fragments

Use sentence fragments judiciously. For formal writing avoid their use except in special situations.

A **sentence fragment** is an incomplete sentence written as a complete sentence. A sentence fragment lacks a subject, a predicate, or both, or else it doesn't express a complete thought. We use fragments all the time, especially in speech. We see them in advertising and in newspapers and magazines. In formal writing, they can be used appropriately to ask and answer questions and to emphasize a point, to record exclamations in dialogue, and to provide transition between ideas. Note the use of fragments in the following passages by professional writers. (The fragments are printed in *italics*.)

> There has been a flood of new studies of the Wild Child: historical, literary, psychological. The story is still evocative, "good to think with." But there is something new. There is a new focus for a forbidden experiment. *A new mind that is not yet a mind. A new object, betwixt and between, equally shrouded in superstition as well as science.* This is the computer.
>
> SHERRY TURKLE

> Hating to ask questions and never trusting the answers has defined the type of reporting I do. What I do is hang around. *Become part of the furniture. An end table in someone's life.* It is the art of the scavenger: set a scene, establish a mood, get the speech patterns right. What matters is that the subject bites his nails, what matters is that he wears brown shoes with a blue suit, what matters is the egg stain on his tie, the Reader's Digest Condensed Books on the shelves, the copy of *Playboy* with the centerfold torn out.
>
> JOHN GREGORY DUNNE

As you can see from these passages, fragments can be used effectively in formal writing. However, unless you have a well-thought-out reason for using fragments, avoid them in formal writing.

Fragments lacking a subject

Do not punctuate a group of words that lacks a subject as a sentence.

To eliminate a sentence fragment lacking a subject, simply add a subject to this group of words or connect it to another sentence containing its subject.

Not: Went dancing last night.
But: I went dancing last night.

Not: Jean Rhys was born in the West Indies. And evoked the magic of these islands in *Wild Sargasso Sea.*
But: Jean Rhys was born in the West Indies and evoked the magic of these islands in *Wild Sargasso Sea.*

Not: American public opinion became sharply divided. Most Americans had considered World War II a just war. Were willing to give their lives for their country. But many came to think Vietnam was an unjust war. And were repelled by the slaughter of their sons.
But: American public opinion became sharply divided. Most Americans had considered World War II a just war and were willing to give their lives for their country. But many came to think Vietnam was an unjust war and were repelled by the slaughter of their sons.

Fragments lacking a predicate

Do not punctuate a group of words that lacks a predicate as a sentence.

A predicate must be a finite, or complete, verb. Some verb forms require an auxiliary word or a modal in order to be finite. (To review auxiliary words and modals, see pages 17–18.)

To eliminate a sentence fragment that lacks a predicate, simply add a finite verb or an auxiliary word or modal to make the verb finite, or connect the fragment to another sentence that contains its verb.

Not: People of many different nationalities together on the same block.
But: People of many different nationalities live together on the same block.

Not: The sun rising over the rooftops.
But: The sun was rising over the rooftops.

Not: The alumni already given millions of dollars for the new library.
But: The alumni have already given millions of dollars for the new library.

Not: In the early twentieth century Paris was the undisputed cultural capital of the Western world. At one point, for example, Aaron Copland, one of the foremost composers of our age, Tristan Tzara, a leading Dadaist, and James Joyce, the author of *Ulysses*, all living in Paris at the same time.

But: In the early twentieth century Paris was the undisputed cultural capital of the Western world. At one point, for example, Aaron Copland, one of the foremost composers of our age, Tristan Tzara, a leading Dadaist, and James Joyce, the author of *Ulysses*, were all living in Paris at the same time.

Not: In the back of the theater were standing-room-only ticket holders. And latecomers impatient for their seats. I could hardly hear the music because of the noise they were making.

But: In the back of the theater were standing-room-only ticket holders and latecomers impatient for their seats. I could hardly hear the music because of the noise they were making.

Phrase fragments

Do not punctuate a phrase as a sentence.

To eliminate a phrase fragment, simply add it to or make it part of an independent clause.

Not: We swerved when we saw the deer. Running across the highway.

But: We swerved when we saw the deer running across the highway.

Not: To learn about police work firsthand. The professor rode with two officers in their squad car for six weeks.

But: To learn about police work firsthand, the professor rode with two officers in their squad car for six weeks.

Not: The highlight of the show was a guest appearance by Cynthia Gregory. One of this country's finest ballerinas.

But: The highlight of the show was a guest appearance by Cynthia Gregory, one of this country's finest ballerinas.

Not: Because of public opposition. The city refused to grant permission. For a skyscraper to be built on the site of the church.

But: Because of public opposition, the city refused to grant permission for a skyscraper to be built on the site of the church.

Not: Computer manufacturers use various gimmicks to attract users. In order to appeal to children. This writing program features a turtle. Instead of the ordinary cursor.

But: Computer manufacturers use various gimmicks to attract users. In order to appeal to children, this writing program features a turtle instead of the ordinary cursor.

Dependent clause fragments

Do not punctuate a dependent clause as a sentence.

Usually, a dependent clause begins with a subordinating word, which may be a subordinating conjunction or a relative pronoun. (To review dependent clauses, see pages 42–45.)

One way to eliminate a dependent clause fragment is to remove the subordinating word. Another way is to connect the dependent clause to an independent clause.

Not: Because Charlene was fluent in French.
But: Charlene was fluent in French.

Not: Before Harrison wrote his term paper. He prepared an outline.
But: Before Harrison wrote his term paper, he prepared an outline.

Not: Harold Macmillan felt it imperative for Britain to develop a firm relationship with de Gaulle. Even though the United States opposed official recognition of him.
But: Harold Macmillan felt it imperative for Britain to develop a firm relationship with de Gaulle, even though the United States opposed official recognition of him.

Not: Although John Muir is often pictured as a genial and perhaps somewhat innocent nature guide. He was actually a shrewd, strong-willed, thoughtful man. Who was an effective political lobbyist for conservation.
But: Although John Muir is often pictured as a genial and perhaps somewhat innocent nature guide, he was actually a shrewd,

strong-willed, thoughtful man who was an effective political lobbyist for conservation.

Not: Since he was avidly interested in Holmesiana. He decided to apply for membership in the Baker Street Irregulars. Where he would be able to enjoy the company of other Sherlock Holmes enthusiasts.

But: Since he was avidly interested in Holmesiana, he decided to apply for membership in the Baker Street Irregulars, where he would be able to enjoy the company of other Sherlock Holmes enthusiasts.

Exercise. Revise the following items to eliminate any sentence fragments. Two of the items contain no fragments.

1. Wrote novels, poems, and short stories.

2. Having spent the night studying.

3. James the best person for the job.

4. The bus was turning the corner.

5. After Walter had his car repaired.

6. Built on top of a cliff. The building provides unparalleled views of the harbor.

7. As the settlers pushed their way west of the Appalachians, tribes living in the Great Lakes region became alarmed.

8. When we think of the enchantment of music. We often think of Orpheus. Whose music charmed even the ruler of Hades.

9. The Constitution is often described as a living document. Since it is capable of growing and changing with the times.

10. Overlooking the sometimes-underlying violence. Many Westerners see only harmony and tranquility. When they view Japanese art.

7 Run-on sentences

Separate sentences clearly from one another.

A **run-on sentence** occurs when two or more complete sentences are written as though they were one sentence. Two types of errors result in a run-on sentence: comma splices and fused sentences.

Comma splices

Do not separate two independent clauses with only a comma, unless the clauses are very short and closely related.

A comma is sometimes used between clauses of two or three words, especially if the clauses are in parallel grammatical form.

> One sings, the other dances.
> Man proposes, God disposes.

In general, however, using only a comma between two independent clauses is considered a serious grammatical error, called a **comma splice.**

> **Not:** Researchers are attempting to program robots to see, this procedure is much more complicated than you might expect.
> **But:** Researchers are attempting to program robots to see. This procedure is much more complicated than you might expect.
> **Or:** Researchers are attempting to program robots to see, but this procedure is much more complicated than you might expect.

> **Not:** Some monasteries during the Middle Ages had fine libraries, in these libraries monks copied and illuminated manuscripts.
> **But:** Some monasteries during the Middle Ages had fine libraries; in these libraries monks copied and illuminated manuscripts.
> **Or:** Some monasteries during the Middle Ages had fine libraries, in which monks copied and illuminated manuscripts.

A comma splice also occurs when a comma (instead of a semicolon) is used between two independent clauses joined by a conjunctive adverb or a transitional phrase.

> **Not:** The exhibit at the museum was well reviewed and well promoted, consequently, there were long lines for tickets.
> **But:** The exhibit at the museum was well reviewed and well promoted; consequently, there were long lines for tickets.

Not: When the smoke alarm sounded in the middle of the night, Melissa jumped out of bed and rushed to get her family out of the house, in the meantime, her neighbor called the fire department.

But: When the smoke alarm sounded in the middle of the night, Melissa jumped out of bed and rushed to get her family out of the house; in the meantime, her neighbor called the fire department.

Fused sentences

Do not write two independent clauses without any punctuation between them.

This error is called a **fused sentence.**

Not: The school was closed because of the snowstorm not knowing this, some students showed up for classes.

But: The school was closed because of the snowstorm. Not knowing this, some students showed up for classes.

Or: Not knowing that the school was closed because of the snowstorm, some students showed up for classes.

Not: First boil the squash until it is tender then cut it open and scoop out its insides.

But: First boil the squash until it is tender; then cut it open and scoop out its insides.

Or: First boil the squash until it is tender, and then cut it open and scoop out its insides.

Although there are many ways of correcting run-on sentences, these are the four most common.

1. Make two sentences by adding a period at the end of the first clause and capitalizing the first word of the second clause.

   Not: Doctors are again using leeches these creatures can prevent the problem of clotting that occurs after reattachment surgery.

   But: Doctors are again using leeches• These creatures can prevent the problem of clotting that occurs after reattachment surgery.

2. Add a coordinating conjunction between the two clauses. Place a comma before the coordinating conjunction, unless the two clauses are very short.

   Not: Maria washed the car, Carol mowed the lawn.
   But: Maria washed the car, **and** Carol mowed the lawn.

3. Rewrite one of the independent clauses as a dependent clause.

   Not: The cat wanted her breakfast, she mewed loudly at the foot of the bed.
   But: **When** the cat wanted her breakfast, she mewed loudly at the foot of the bed.

4. If the two clauses are closely related, place a semicolon between them.

   Not: Cindy found the movie disappointing, Jayne thought it was wonderful.
   But: Cindy found the movie disappointing; Jayne thought it was wonderful.

Exercise 1. Eliminate the run-on sentence in each of the following items.

1. Years ago, all movie animation was done by hand, today, much of it is done by computer.

2. Some people consider Satchel Paige the greatest baseball player who ever lived his career spanned forty years.

3. When ancient Aztec astronomers constructed their calendar, they calculated their year as having 365 days, however, each year had a few hours left over.

4. Eugenie Clark is trying to find a shark repellent, she is experimenting with the substance excreted by the Moses sole.

5. Noah Webster changed the spelling of many words he thought words should be spelled as they are pronounced.

Exercise 2. Eliminate the fragments and run-on sentences in each of the following items.

1. Have you heard the story of Casey Jones? A brave engineer who died in a terrible railroad accident in 1900.

2. Casey Jones's real name was John Luther Jones, his story has been recounted in folk songs.

3. The original version of the folk song was composed by Wallace Saunders. A man who worked in the railroad roundhouse near the site of Casey's terrible accident.

4. Saunders put together a blues ballad that spoke not only of the tragedy of Casey Jones. But also of the pain and suffering of the many people who were injured or killed during the early, dangerous days of railroading.

5. Saunders sang about that fateful night of April 29, 1900. When Casey Jones, an engineer for the Illinois Central Railroad, drove the *Cannonball* into immortality.

6. Since the *Cannonball* was already 96 minutes late when Casey pulled out of the station at Memphis. He knew he would have to make up time to get to Canton, Mississippi, on time at first it looked as though luck was on Casey's side.

7. While his friend Sim Webb fed the fire, Casey raced the clock, pushing the *Cannonball* to do more than seventy on the straight stretches of track, Casey was unaware that disaster awaited four freight cars were stuck on the track ahead.

8. By the time Casey saw the freight cars ahead of him, it was too late to stop, however, it was not too late to save his friend Casey forced Sim to jump from the train.

9. Casey stayed with the *Cannonball*. Pulling on the brakes and jamming the engine into reverse. He cut the *Cannonball*'s speed in half.

10. Only Casey died in the terrible crash he was found with one hand on the brake and the other hand on the throttle.

8 Verb forms

Use the appropriate form of the verb.

English verbs have four principal parts, or forms. Regular verbs add -*ed* or -*d* to their present infinitive to form the past tense and past participle.

| paint | painted | cook | cooked |
| dance | danced | slice | sliced |

Irregular verbs form their past tense and past participle in a variety of other ways.

Present infinitive	Past tense	Past participle
begin	began	(has) begun
catch	caught	(has) caught
draw	drew	(has) drawn
put	put	(has) put

You can use a dictionary to find the principal parts of a verb. In most dictionaries, after the abbreviation *v.* or at the end of the definitions for the verb, the entry gives the principal parts and the third-person singular present-tense form of the verb. When the past tense and past participle are the same, the entry lists only three forms of the verb. When the past tense and past participle are different, the entry lists four forms.

> **dance** (dăns) *v.*: **danced, dancing, dances**
> **be•gin** (bĭ-gĭn′) *v.*: **began, begun, beginning, begins**
> **draw** (drô) *v.*: **drew, drawn, drawing, draws**

Most people have few problems using the proper forms of regular verbs. Many, however, do have problems with the past tense and past participle of irregular verbs. Here is a list of common irregular verbs.

Present infinitive	Past tense	Past participle
arise	arose	(has) arisen
awake	awoke	(has) awaked, awoken
be	was, were	(has) been
bear	bore	(has) borne
		(was) born
become	became	(has) become
begin	began	(has) begun
bind	bound	(has) bound
bite	bit	(has) bitten
blow	blew	(has) blown
break	broke	(has) broken
bring	brought	(has) brought

Present infinitive	Past tense	Past participle
build	built	(has) built
burst	burst	(has) burst
cast	cast	(has) cast
catch	caught	(has) caught
choose	chose	(has) chosen
cling	clung	(has) clung
come	came	(has) come
creep	crept	(has) crept
deal	dealt	(has) dealt
dig	dug	(has) dug
dive	dived, dove	(has) dived
do	did	(has) done
draw	drew	(has) drawn
drink	drank	(has) drunk
drive	drove	(has) driven
eat	ate	(has) eaten
fall	fell	(has) fallen
feel	felt	(has) felt
flee	fled	(has) fled
fling	flung	(has) flung
fly	flew	(has) flown
forbid	forbade, forbad	(has) forbidden
forget	forgot	(has) forgotten, forgot
forgive	forgave	(has) forgiven
freeze	froze	(has) frozen
get	got	(has) got, gotten
give	gave	(has) given
go	went	(has) gone
grow	grew	(has) grown
hang (objects)	hung	(has) hung
hang (people)	hanged	(has) hanged
have	had	(has) had
hit	hit	(has) hit
know	knew	(has) known
lay	laid	(has) laid
lead	led	(has) led
lend	lent	(has) lent
lie	lay	(has) lain
lose	lost	(has) lost
mean	meant	(has) meant

Present infinitive	Past tense	Past participle
pay	paid	(has) paid
prove	proved	(has) proved, proven
put	put	(has) put
ride	rode	(has) ridden
ring	rang	(has) rung
rise	rose	(has) risen
run	ran	(has) run
say	said	(has) said
see	saw	(has) seen
seek	sought	(has) sought
send	sent	(has) sent
set	set	(has) set
shake	shook	(has) shaken
shine (give light)	shone	(has) shone
shine (polish)	shined	(has) shined
shrink	shrank	(has) shrunk
sing	sang	(has) sung
sink	sank, sunk	(has) sunk, sunken
sit	sat	(has) sat
slay	slew	(has) slain
speak	spoke	(has) spoken
spin	spun	(has) spun
spit	spit, spat	(has) spit, spat
spread	spread	(has) spread
spring	sprang, sprung	(has) sprung
steal	stole	(has) stolen
sting	stung	(has) stung
stink	stank	(has) stunk
swear	swore	(has) sworn
swim	swam	(has) swum
swing	swung	(has) swung
take	took	(has) taken
teach	taught	(has) taught
tear	tore	(has) torn
think	thought	(has) thought
thrive	throve, thrived	(has) thriven, thrived
throw	threw	(has) thrown
wear	wore	(has) worn
weep	wept	(has) wept
win	won	(has) won

Over the years some irregular forms have been eliminated from the language, while others are in the process of changing. As you can see from the preceding list, the preferred past tense form of *dive* is now *dived*, not *dove*. The preferred past participle form of *prove* is *proved*, not *proven*.

The following rules will help you select the appropriate verb form.

Use the past tense form to indicate simple past time.

Not: We **seen** him in the library yesterday.
But: We **saw** him in the library yesterday.

Not: Rhonda **swum** fifteen laps.
But: Rhonda **swam** fifteen laps.

Not: His clothing **stunk** from the skunk's spray.
But: His clothing **stank** from the skunk's spray.

Use the past participle form with an auxiliary verb.

Not: **Have** you **chose** a major?
But: **Have** you **chosen** a major?

Not: If you don't lock up your bike, it **will be took.**
But: If you don't lock up your bike, it **will be taken.**

Not: Lenny **has wrote** home to his parents, asking for money.
But: Lenny **has written** home to his parents, asking for money.

Use the past participle form with a contraction containing an auxiliary verb.

Not: He's **drove** all the way from Miami.
But: He's **driven** all the way from Miami.

Not: She'd never **flew** in an airplane before.
But: She'd never **flown** in an airplane before.

Not: They've **sang** in the choir for many years.
But: They've **sung** in the choir for many years.

Master troublesome pairs of words.

The following pairs of words often give people trouble: *lie* and *lay*; *sit* and *set*; *rise* and *raise*.

Lie and *lay*

The verb *lie* means "recline." The verb *lay* means "put" or "place." Do not confuse the principal parts of these verbs.

Present infinitive	Past tense	Past participle	Present participle
lie	lay	(has) lain	(is) lying
lay	laid	(has) laid	(is) laying

The problem most people have with these verbs is using a form of *lay* when they mean *lie*. *Lie* is intransitive; it does not take an object. *Lay* is transitive; it does take an object.

Lie on the floor. (*no object*)

Lay the *book* on the table. (*object*)

Not: Why is Millie **laying** on the couch in the nurse's office?
But: Why is Millie **lying** on the couch in the nurse's office?

Not: Peter **laid** in the sun too long yesterday.
But: Peter **lay** in the sun too long yesterday.

Not: She had just **laid** down when the telephone rang.
But: She had just **lain** down when the telephone rang.

Sit and *set*

The verb *sit* means "be seated." The verb *set* usually means "place" or "put in a certain position." Do not confuse the principal parts of these verbs.

Present infinitive	Past tense	Past participle	Present participle
sit	sat	(has) sat	(is) sitting
set	set	(has) set	(is) setting

The problem most people have with these verbs is using a form of *set* when they mean *sit*. *Sit* is intransitive; it does not take an object. *Set* is usually transitive; it does take an object.

Sit in the chair by the fireplace. (*no object*)

Please **set** the table for me. (*object*)

Note: *Set* is sometimes intransitive: *The sun sets*.

Not: Some people **set** in front of the television far too much.
But: Some people **sit** in front of the television far too much.

Not: He **set** up until two in the morning, waiting for his daughter to come home from her date.
But: He **sat** up until two in the morning, waiting for his daughter to come home from her date.

Not: After **setting** in the sun for five hours, Don was burned bright red.
But: After **sitting** in the sun for five hours, Don was burned bright red.

Rise and *raise*

The verb *rise* means "go up" or "get into a standing position." The verb *raise* means "lift." Do not confuse the principal parts of these verbs.

Present infinitive	Past tense	Past participle	Present participle
rise	rose	(has) risen	(is) rising
raise	raised	(has) raised	(is) raising

Rise is intransitive; it does not take an object. *Raise* is transitive; it does take an object.

Without yeast, the bread will not **rise**. (*no object*)

After they won the game, they **raised** the school *banner*. (*object*)

Not: They **rose** the curtain before the cast was fully assembled on stage.
But: They **raised** the curtain before the cast was fully assembled on stage.

Not: Every morning they **rise** the blinds before leaving for work.
But: Every morning they **raise** the blinds before leaving for work.

Not: He **rose** his voice in order to be heard.
But: He **raised** his voice in order to be heard.

Exercise 1. Identify the inappropriate verb form in each of the following sentences. Replace it with the appropriate form.

1. In general, larger eggs are lain by older chickens and smaller eggs by younger chickens.

2. You will have to pay for the piece that you breaked.

3. In the Old West, they often hung horse thieves.

4. Nancy was awoke by a loud blast of thunder.

5. You say the light in the sky couldn't have been a UFO, but I know what I seen.

6. After he shone his shoes, he put a water repellent on them.

7. The telephone had rang fifteen times before he answered it.

8. Do you know that 284,000 tons of popcorn were ate by Americans during 1980?

9. Cynthia has never rode on a motorcycle.

10. The cheerleaders rose their pompoms over their heads.

Exercise 2. Identify the inappropriate verb form in each of the following sentences. Replace it with the appropriate form.

1. Many people have seeked the lost continent of Atlantis.

2. The moon shined like a diamond in a tiara.

3. Many people weeped when they learned of Kennedy's death.

4. Although the wolf has almost disappeared from all of the United States except Alaska, the coyote has throve.

5. Iowa's Sac County is knowed as the "Popcorn Capital of the World."

6. His belief in the kindness of human beings was shook by the war.

7. Someone's stole my class notes.

8. Lie your head on my shoulder.

9. She became a celebrity after she swum the Channel.

10. As a treasure hunter, he was always on the lookout for ships that had sank long ago.

9 Subject-verb agreement

Make a verb agree with its subject in number.

If the subject is singular, the verb form must be singular. If the subject is plural, the verb form must be plural.

Except for the verb *be*, the verb form changes to indicate number only in the present tense and only with a third-person singular subject. All other verbs except *have* add an *s* or *es* to the basic present-tense form with a third-person singular subject. *Have* changes to *has*.

The cushion **feels** soft.	The tomato **tastes** ripe.
The cushions **feel** soft.	The tomatoes **taste** ripe.
The goose **flies** south.	The baby **has** a pacifier.
The geese **fly** south.	The babies **have** pacifiers.
The woman **rushes** to class.	He **brushes** his hair.
The women **rush** to class.	They **brush** their hair.

The verb *be* changes to indicate number in both the present tense and the past tense and in both the first person and the third person.

Present tense		**Past tense**	
I am	we are	I was	we were
you are	you are	you were	you were
he/she/it is	they are	he/she/it was	they were

Some kinds of subjects present special problems with subject-verb agreement. The following rules will help you choose the appropriate verb form.

Compound subject with *and*

In general, use a plural verb form with a compound subject joined by the word *and.*

A **compound subject** consists of two or more nouns that take the same predicate.

> *Crystal and Sal* **make** films for a living.
> *History and biology* **were** his best subjects.
> *Ted and his friends* **are supporting** Greene for mayor.

Use a singular verb form with a compound subject joined by *and* if the compound is considered a single unit.

> *Pork and beans* **is** a popular dish.
> The *bow and arrow* **is** still regarded as a useful weapon.

Use a singular verb form with a compound subject joined by *and* if the parts of the compound refer to the same person or thing.

> My *friend and guest* **is** the artist Laura Anderson.
> His *pride and joy* **was** his 1962 convertible.

Compound subject with *or* or *nor*

With a compound subject joined by *or* or *nor* or by *either ... or* or *neither ... nor,* make the verb agree with the subject closer to it.

> The *cat or her kittens* **have pushed** the vase off the table.

> *Either the employees or their supervisor* **is** responsible.

> *Neither the camera nor the lenses* **were broken.**

Intervening phrases or clauses

Make the verb agree with its subject, not with a word in an intervening phrase or clause.

Intervening phrases

Several *people* in my club **subscribe** to that magazine.
The *books* by that writer **are** very popular.
The *picture* hanging between the windows at the top of the stairs **is** a portrait of the artist's mother.

Phrases introduced by *together with, as well as, in addition to, accompanied by,* and similar expressions do not affect the number of the verb.

The emerald *bracelet,* as well as her other jewels, **is** in the safe.
The *novel,* together with the plays that she wrote when she was much younger, **establishes** her reputation.
His *wit,* accompanied by his excellent grasp of the facts, **makes** him a sharp interviewer.

Intervening clauses

The *books* that are in my briefcase **are** about Russian history.
The *people* who came to the concert that was canceled **are receiving** rain checks.
The *doctor* who is attending these patients **is** Ellen Okida.

Collective nouns

A collective noun may take either a singular or a plural verb form.

Usually a collective noun refers to a group of people or things as a single unit. When this is the case, the collective noun is singular and the verb form should be singular.

The *army* **needs** the support of the civilian population.
The *flock* **is heading** toward the west end of the lake.
The *group* **is selling** tickets to raise money for charity.

Sometimes a collective noun refers to a group of things or

people as individuals. When this is the case, the collective noun is plural and the verb form should be plural.

> The *jury* **are arguing** among themselves; six feel the defendant is guilty, two feel he is innocent, and four are undecided.
> The *congregation* **disagree** about whether to keep the church open during the week.

Some people feel that using a plural verb form with a collective noun sounds awkward. You can avoid this problem by inserting "the members of" or a similar expression before the collective noun.

> The *members* of the jury **are arguing** among themselves; six feel the defendant is guilty, two feel he is innocent, and four are undecided.
> The *members* of the congregation **disagree** about whether to keep the church open during the week.

Nouns plural in form but singular in meaning

Use a singular verb form with nouns plural in form but singular in meaning.

The following are some common words that are plural in form but singular in meaning.

checkers	molasses
civics	mumps
economics	news
mathematics	physics
measles	statistics

> *Checkers* **is called** draughts in Great Britain.
> *Measles* **is** a contagious childhood disease.
> The *news* **is broadcast** around the clock on some radio stations.

The words *pants*, *trousers*, and *scissors* are considered plural and take a plural verb form. However, if they are preceded by the words *pair of*, the verb form is singular, since *pair* is the subject.

> The *scissors* **need** to be sharpened.
> The *pair* of scissors **needs** to be sharpened.

The *pants* **match** the jacket.
The *pair* of pants **matches** the jacket.

Indefinite pronoun subjects

The following indefinite pronouns are considered singular. Use a singular verb form with them.

anybody	either	neither	one
anyone	everybody	nobody	somebody
each	everyone	no one	someone

Neither **is** the best pizza parlor in town.
Everybody **is going to vote** on Tuesday.

Do not be confused by prepositional phrases that follow the indefinite pronoun. The verb must agree with its subject, not with the object of a preposition.

Each of the apartments in the north wing of the building **has** a fireplace.
Either of those methods **is** feasible.

The following indefinite pronouns are considered plural. Use a plural verb form with them.

both   few   many   several

Few **are** certain enough of their beliefs to take a stand.
Several **are** riding their bicycles to school.
Both of the paintings **were** sold at the auction.

The following indefinite pronouns may be singular or plural. If the noun to which the pronoun refers is singular, use a singular verb form. If the noun is plural, use a plural verb form.

all   any   enough   more   most   some

All of the *money* **was** recovered. (*singular*)
All **was** recovered. (*singular*)

All of these *records* **are** scratched. (*plural*)
All **are** scratched. (*plural)*

Most of the *cake* **was** eaten. (*singular*)
Most **was** eaten. (*singular*)

Most of the *guests* **were** hungry. (*plural*)
Most **were** hungry. (*plural*)

The indefinite pronoun *none* can be used with either a singular or a plural verb form when it refers to a plural noun. For example, both of the following sentences are acceptable.

None of the books **was** missing.
None of the books **were** missing.

Relative pronoun subjects

A verb whose subject is a relative pronoun should agree with the antecedent of the pronoun.

The man *who* **narrates** the film has a raspy voice. (*singular antecedent*)

The radios *that* **were made** in Japan are selling well. (*plural antecedent*)

The newspaper, *which* **was founded** in 1893, is closing. (*singular antecedent*)

The phrase *one of those* is worth mentioning. Usually, the relative pronoun that follows this phrase is plural because its antecedent is *those* or the plural noun following *those*. Therefore, the relative pronoun takes a plural verb form.

Dolores is one of those people *who* never **make** mistakes.

Ralph is one of those *who* **gain** weight.

However, when the words *the only* come before this phrase, the relative pronoun is singular because its antecedent is *one*. Therefore, it takes a singular verb form.

This is the only one of those songs *that* **has been published.**

Mitch is the only one of those men *who* **is** athletic.

Titles

Use a singular verb form with a title, even if the title contains plural words.

Guys and Dolls **was** a popular Broadway musical.
Three Coins in the Fountain **is** on television tonight.
Wuthering Heights **tells** the story of a doomed love.

Units of measurement, time, and money

Use a singular verb form with a plural noun phrase that names a unit of measurement, a period of time, or an amount of money.

Five miles **is** too far to walk to school.
One hundred years **is** the usual life span for the crocodile.
Twenty-five thousand dollars **is** a good salary for this job.

Inverted sentence order

Use a verb that agrees with its subject, even when the subject follows the verb.

Outside the building **were** *crowds* of spectators.
From the chimneys **rises** thick black *smoke*.
On the wall **are** *portraits* of her ancestors.

Do not be confused by sentences beginning with *there* and *here*. These words are never the subject.

> There **is** a *chicken* roasting in the oven.
> Here **are** the *groceries* you asked me to pick up.

Agreement with subject, not predicate nominative

Use a verb that agrees with the subject, not with the predicative nominative.

> A firm *moral sense* and a *belief* in the goodness of human beings **were** his inheritance.
> His *inheritance* **was** a firm moral sense and a belief in the goodness of human beings.

Exercise. Revise any of the following sentences in which a verb does not agree with its subject. Some of the sentences are correct as written.

1. Neither the rocking chair nor the trunk are for sale.

2. *The Grapes of Wrath* are considered one of John Steinbeck's finest novels.

3. The grandparents of the children in this neighborhood has formed a social club.

4. One hundred dollars are too much to pay for a child's toy.

5. When he opened the oven, he found that the cake and the cookies was burnt.

6. The congregation is proud of its choir.

7. Ham and cheese are a popular sandwich combination.

8. Neither the mayor nor the members of his council are available today.

9. Mumps is not as common today as it was twenty years ago.

10. Standing on a raft in the river was the three boys.

11. Each of these jobs requires a college degree.

12. None of the students in this class lives off campus.

13. Phyllis is one of those people who are never late.

14. More and more people who live in the suburbs also work in the suburbs.

15. Mr. Lawrence will treat to dinner each of his students who volunteer to give blood.

16. It is the only one of the health clubs that meet her standards.

17. A hamburger, fries, and a milkshake is not my idea of a good dinner.

18. One hundred eighty-five pounds are my normal weight.

19. The records that Howie was listening to last night was given to him for his birthday.

20. Few from that town receives financial aid.

10 Pronouns: agreement, reference, and usage

By themselves, most pronouns have little meaning. For a pronoun's meaning to be clear, it usually must have a clear antecedent, and it must agree with its antecedent in number and gender.

> After the *pilot* checked **her** instruments, **she** prepared for takeoff.

> After the *pilots* checked **their** instruments, **they** prepared for takeoff.

10a Pronoun-antecedent agreement

Indefinite pronouns as antecedents

Use a pronoun that agrees in gender and number with an indefinite pronoun antecedent.

Use a masculine pronoun with an indefinite pronoun that refers to a masculine noun. Use a feminine pronoun with an indefinite pronoun that refers to a feminine noun. Use a neuter, or indeterminate, pronoun with an indefinite pronoun that refers to a neuter noun.

> There are twenty men in the training program. *Each* is a unique individual with **his** own goals and ideals.

Many times, however, a singular indefinite pronoun refers to a group consisting of both males and females, as in the following sentence:

> Everyone should cast _____ vote in the next election.

What should the pronoun in the blank be? Traditionally, a masculine pronoun (*his*) was used in such constructions to refer to an antecedent that included both men and women. Today, many people consider this usage sexist and prefer to use *his or her*. However, a paragraph or a paper can become tedious and hard to read if it is filled with too many pairs of *his or her*, *he or she*, *him or her*, and so on. Here are three suggestions for rewriting sentences like this to avoid the problem of pronoun choice.

1. Make the pronouns plural.

   All should cast **their** votes in the next election.

2. Use an article (*a*, *an*, or *the*) in place of the possessive pronoun.

   Everyone should cast **a** vote in the next election.

3. Rewrite the sentence more extensively.

   Everyone should vote in the next election.

Although *everyone* and *everybody* are considered grammatically singular, they obviously refer to more than one person. Therefore, a plural pronoun is often used with these antecedents when the pronoun is not in the same clause as the antecedent.

> Although *everyone* made enthusiastic noises about the project, **they** fell silent when asked to contribute money.
> *Everybody* in the audience felt that the speaker had insulted **their** intelligence.

Relative pronouns

Use the appropriate relative pronoun.

The pronouns *who*, *whom*, and *whose* refer to people. They also refer to animals thought of in human terms and called by name. The pronoun *that* usually refers to animals and things, but it is sometimes used to refer to people. The pronoun *which* refers to animals and things.

> The *ballplayer* **who** broke Babe Ruth's career home run record is Hank Aaron.

> The *movie* **that** Gene saw last night was *Terms of Endearment*.

> Orwell's *1984*, **which** was published in 1949, is still in print.

Do not use *what* as a relative pronoun.

> **Not:** The stereo **what** I want costs three hundred dollars.
> **But:** The stereo **that** I want costs three hundred dollars.

To avoid an awkward sentence, use the possessive pronoun *whose* to mean "of which."

> **Not:** The car the windshield wipers **of which** are not working failed to pass inspection.
> **But:** The car **whose** windshield wipers are not working failed to pass inspection.

A relative pronoun takes its number from its antecedent. The number of the relative pronoun determines the number of any other pronouns used with it.

> *Students* **who** show **their** identification cards will get a discount.

> A *man* **who** cannot make up **his** mind is of no use to this company.

Compound antecedent

Use a plural pronoun to refer to a compound antecedent joined by *and.*

Grant and Howard have finished **their** assignments.

The judge and the district attorney have completed **their** terms of office.

When the antecedent is a compound joined by *or* or *nor* or by *either . . . or, neither . . . nor,* or *not only . . . but also,* make the pronoun agree with the part of the compound that is closer to it.

Neither the district attorney nor the defense *lawyers* stated **their** cases clearly.

Not only the jurors but also the *judge* found **his** attention wandering.

Collective nouns as antecedents

Use a singular pronoun with a collective noun antecedent if the members of the group are thought of as one unit. Use a plural pronoun if the members are thought of as individuals.

After winning the race, the *crew* placed **its** trophy on the mantelpiece.

The leader asked the *group* to lower **their** voices.

10b Pronoun reference

Vague reference

Provide a clear antecedent for each pronoun that needs one.

In general, do not use a pronoun to refer to the entire idea in a previous sentence or clause or to an antecedent that has not been clearly stated.

> **Vague:** Harry usually taps his feet, rolls his eyes, and fidgets when he is nervous, **which** annoys his girlfriend.

The pronoun *which* refers vaguely to the entire idea of Harry's behavior when he is nervous.

> **Clear:** Harry's habit of tapping his feet, rolling his eyes, and fidgeting when he is nervous annoys his girlfriend.

> **Vague:** Lou is an excellent mechanic, and she uses **this** to earn money for college.

The pronoun *this* refers vaguely to the idea of Lou's skill as a mechanic.

> **Clear:** Lou is an excellent mechanic, and she uses her skill to earn money for college.

> **Vague:** The tourists stared in awe as the great Christmas tree in Rockefeller Center was lit. They listened in rapt attention to the speeches and sang along with the carolers. **It** was something they would tell their friends about back home.

> **Clear:** The tourists stared in awe as the great Christmas tree in Rockefeller Center was lit. They listened in rapt attention to the speeches and sang along with the carolers. The spectacle was something they would tell their friends about back home.

> **Vague:** Now that her children were away at school, she felt free to pursue her own interests for the first time in years.

Perhaps she would get a job. Perhaps she would go back to school. Suddenly she felt alive again. Until this moment, she hadn't realized how badly she had needed **this.**

Clear: Now that her children were away at school, she felt free to pursue her own interests for the first time in years. Perhaps she would get a job. Perhaps she would go back to school. Suddenly she felt alive again. Until this moment, she hadn't realized how badly she had needed a change in her life.

Vague: In the novel Christophine tries to discourage Antoinette from going to England. She says England is a cold place with bad weather and bad people, and she cautions Antoinette not to do **it.**

Clear: In the novel Christophine tries to discourage Antoinette from going to England. She says England is a cold place with bad weather and bad people, and she cautions Antoinette not to go there.

Ambiguous reference

Do not use a pronoun that could refer to either of two or more antecedents.

Ambiguous: Malcolm told Henry that **he** had won a trip to France.

The pronoun *he* could refer to either Malcolm or Henry. If it refers to Malcolm, rewrite the sentence to make this reference clear.

Clear: Malcolm told Henry, "I have won a trip to France."
Or: Malcolm, who had won a trip to France, told Henry the news.

If the pronoun refers to Henry, rewrite the sentence a different way.

Clear: Malcolm told Henry, "You have won a trip to France."
Or: Malcolm knew that Henry had won a trip to France and told him so.

Ambiguous: Darlene met Dr. McCluskey when **she** visited the lab last week.

The pronoun *she* could refer to either Darlene or Dr. McCluskey.

Clear: When Darlene visited the lab last week, she met Dr. McCluskey.

Clear: When Dr. McCluskey visited the lab last week, Darlene met her.

Ambiguous: In the saga Luke Skywalker and Han Solo are at first rivals. Both want to win the affection of the princess. As the saga progresses, however, the two young men gain respect for each other, until finally the rivalry ends when **he** discovers he is Leia's brother.

The pronoun *he* could refer to either Luke or Han.

Clear: In the saga Luke Skywalker and Han Solo are at first rivals. Both want to win the affection of the princess. As the saga progresses, however, the two young men gain respect for each other, until finally the rivalry ends when **Luke** discovers he is Leia's brother.

Ambiguous: Fourteenth-century Europe was scarred by war and plague. It is hard to tell which was worse. The figures given by the chroniclers differ, but according to some accounts, **it** reduced the population by a third.

Clear: Fourteenth-century Europe was scarred by war and plague. It is hard to tell which was worse. The figures given by the chroniclers differ, but according to some accounts, **plague alone** reduced the population by a third.

10c Pronoun usage

Do not use a personal pronoun immediately following its antecedent.

Pronouns are often used this way in conversation to emphasize the antecedent, but this construction is inappropriate in writing.

Not: The dictator **he** would not give up any of his power.
But: The dictator would not give up any of his power.

Not: Cuckoos **they** lay their eggs in other birds' nests.
But: Cuckoos lay their eggs in other birds' nests.

Use a pronoun ending in -*self* or -*selves* only when an antecedent for this pronoun appears in the sentence.

I bought the tickets for Doris and **myself.**

Not: Give the tickets to Doris and **myself.**
But: Give the tickets to Doris and **me.**

Not: The invitation was addressed to his wife and **himself.**
But: The invitation was addressed to his wife and **him.**

Exercise 1. Rephrase any of the following sentences in which a pronoun does not agree with its antecedent. Some of the sentences are correct as written.

1. Neither of the men brought their tennis racket.

2. Several of the employees are standing in line to cash their paychecks.

3. Some researchers are studying the cockroach, since their behavior may help us to predict earthquakes.

4. In this company each of the cab drivers owns their own cab.

5. The artist which painted *Stag at Sharkey's* is George Bellows.

6. Television shows that lose their sponsors are rapidly canceled.

7. Each of the men in this squad boxes in their spare time.

8. The Senator and the Congresswoman are preparing their speeches.

9. Neither my mother nor my aunts have her pilot's license yet.

10. The collection has been in my family for years; its value to a dealer is far less than its value to me.

Exercise 2. Rephrase each of the following sentences to eliminate the vague or ambiguous pronoun antecedent.

1. On the way to the restaurant, Marge told Kate that she had received a telegraph that morning.

2. The chef hired Ed as a cook because he appreciated good food.

3. The baby started to cry whenever company came, which embarrassed her parents.

4. Jenkins broke up with Mullagan when he got an offer from a club in Las Vegas to do a solo act.

5. The man on the bus was sneezing and coughing. It made the person sitting next to him uncomfortable.

6. Many people crowded around the woman and asked for her autograph. It was because she was a movie star.

7. Shortly after Don opened a restaurant at the shopping mall, it closed.

8. He has dinner and plays squash with his friends every Friday night, and this is excellent exercise.

9. When the stockholders met with the company's directors and the reporters, they started to ask questions.

10. Roy was playing pool with Larry, and he looked as if he was losing.

Exercise 3. Rephrase any of the following sentences that contain pronoun usage problems.

1. Make sure you mail the books to my sister and myself.

2. The governor she opposed the budget changes.

3. The donations were collected by Frank and himself.

4. Anita and she campaigned for Laffety.

5. The critics they all thought the play was boring.

11 Pronoun case

Personal pronouns are placed in the subjective, the possessive, or the objective case, depending on their use in the sentence.

The pronouns *who* and *whoever* also have different forms to indicate case.

Subjective: I, you, he, she, it, we, they, who, whoever
Possessive: my, mine, your, yours, his, her, hers, its, our, ours, their, theirs, whose
Objective: me, you, him, her, it, us, them, whom, whomever

He wrote *The Way to Rainy Mountain*. (*subjective*)
Scott Momaday has increased **our** awareness of the daily struggle of American Indians. (*possessive*)
Many awards have been given to **him**. (*objective*)

Most people have little trouble choosing the appropriate case when a personal pronoun is used by itself. Many do have trouble, though, when the pronoun is part of a compound structure. Almost everyone has trouble at times with *who* and *whom* and with *whoever* and *whomever*.

In compound subjects and objects

Place a pronoun that is part of a compound subject in the subjective case.

Not: Fanny and **me** have tickets for the football game.
But: Fanny and **I** have tickets for the football game.

Not: Neither Wally nor **him** is on the wrestling team.
But: Neither Wally nor **he** is on the wrestling team.

Place a pronoun that is part of a compound direct object or a compound indirect object in the objective case.

Not: The fly ball bounced off the fence and then hit Christine and **I**.
But: The fly ball bounced off the fence and then hit Christine and **me**. (hit . . . me)

Not: Give Mel and **she** the blueprints so that they can check the measurements.
But: Give Mel and **her** the blueprints so that they can check the measurements. (Give . . . her)

Place a pronoun that is part of a compound object of a preposition in the objective case.

Not: Although there are thirty people competing, everyone knows the race is really between you and **I**.

But: Although there are thirty people competing, everyone knows the race is really between you and **me**.

Not: The symposium is being conducted by Dr. Fell and **she**.

But: The symposium is being conducted by Dr. Fell and **her**. (by . . . her)

Not: Several of **we** amateurs were allowed to play in the pro tournament.

But: Several of **us** amateurs were allowed to play in the pro tournament. (of us, *not* of we)

In predicate nominatives

Place a pronoun that is part of a predicate nominative in the subjective case.

Not: The people to see for tickets are Blake and **him**.
But: The people to see for tickets are Blake and **he**.

Not: The winners are Sharon and **her**.
But: The winners are Sharon and **she**.

In speech, many people accept the informal use of the objective case of the pronoun following the verb *be*. In formal writing, however, the subjective case is still required in this construction.

Informal: It is **me**.
Formal: It is **I**.

Informal: Was it **him** who asked you to the dance?
Formal: Was it **he** who asked you to the dance?

After *than* or *as*

In an elliptical, or incomplete, clause, place the pronoun in the case it would be in if the clause were complete.

Not: Kenneth is stronger than **him.**
But: Kenneth is stronger than **he.** (than he is)

Not: No one could have worked more skillfully than **her.**
But: No one could have worked more skillfully than **she.** (than she did)

Not: Martha knew she could love no one as much as **he.**
But: Martha knew she could love no one as much as **him.** (as she loved him)

In appositives

Place a pronoun that is part of a compound appositive in the same case as the noun to which the appositive refers.

An **appositive** is a noun or noun substitute that renames or identifies the noun or noun substitute preceding it.

Not: The partners—Fran, Scott, and **me**—plan to open a bicycle repair shop in July.
But: The partners—Fran, Scott, and **I**—plan to open a bicycle repair shop in July.

Not: Only two people, the manager and **him,** knew the combination of the safe.
But: Only two people, the manager and **he,** knew the combination of the safe.

Before verbals or verbal phrases

Place a pronoun that precedes a gerund or gerund phrase in the possessive case.

Not: The audience applauded **them** dancing.
But: The audience applauded **their** dancing.

Not: I resented **him** criticizing me in front of my friends.
But: I resented **his** criticizing me in front of my friends.

Not: Pauline liked everything about Ron but **him** singing first thing in the morning.
But: Pauline liked everything about Ron but **his** singing first thing in the morning.

Place a pronoun that precedes a participle or participial phrase in the objective case.

> **Not:** When Penny recalled her grandfather, she pictured **his** smiling.
> **But:** When Penny recalled her grandfather, she pictured **him** smiling.

> **Not:** I heard **his** starting the car.
> **But:** I heard **him** starting the car.

> **Not:** Phil had seen **their** racing to class.
> **But:** Phil had seen **them** racing to class.

To decide which case of the pronoun to use, you have to decide whether the verbal following it is a gerund or a participle. Look at the next two sentences.

> I can hear your singing.
> I can hear you singing.

Both of these sentences are grammatically correct, but they have slightly different meanings. In the first sentence, *singing* is a gerund modified by the possessive pronoun *your*; in the second sentence, *singing* is a participle that modifies the objective pronoun *you*. The first sentence emphasizes an action, *singing*, while the second sentence emphasizes the performer of the action, *you*. Thus, in writing sentences like these, you can often convey different shades of meaning by using the possessive or the objective case of the pronoun.

Who and *whom; whoever* and *whomever*

In conversation, many people no longer use *whom* or *whomever* except directly after a preposition. In writing, however, you should always be careful to distinguish between *who* and *whom* and between *whoever* and *whomever*.

Use *who* and *whoever* as the subject of a sentence or clause.

> **Who** founded the American Red Cross? (*subject of sentence*)

The book is about Clara Barton, **who** founded the American Red Cross. (*subject of clause*)

Whoever lost the book will have to pay for it. (*subject of clause*)

Use *whom* and *whomever* as the direct object or the object of a preposition.

Whom shall I call? (*direct object*)

Whomever the *Union Leader* endorsed enjoyed a substantial advantage. (*direct object*)

The person to **whom** I gave the packages was Pete. (*object of preposition*)

How can you tell whether the pronoun should be *who* or *whom*? For sentences, mentally rephrase the question as a declarative statement. Then substitute *who* for *he, she,* or *they,* or *whom* for *him, her,* or *them.*

(Who/Whom) founded the American Red Cross?
She founded the American Red Cross.
Who founded the American Red Cross?

(Who/Whom) shall I call?
I shall call **him.**
Whom shall I call?

For clauses, follow the same process. Rephrase the clause as a statement and substitute *who* for *he, she,* or *they,* or *whom* for *him, her,* or *them.*

The person (who/whom) founded the American Red Cross was Clara Barton.
She founded the American Red Cross.
The person **who** founded the American Red Cross was Clara Barton.

The writer (who/whom) she enjoyed most was Dickens.
She enjoyed **him** most.
The writer **whom** she enjoyed most was Dickens.

(Whoever/Whomever) the *Union Leader* endorsed enjoyed a substantial advantage.
The *Union Leader* endorsed **him.**

Whomever the *Union Leader* endorsed enjoyed a substantial advantage.

If words intervene between the pronoun and the main verb of the sentence or clause, mentally delete them as you rephrase.

(Who/Whom) ~~did he think~~ he had offended?
He had offended **them.**
Whom did he think he had offended?

One person (who/whom) ~~the newspaper said~~ was killed was actually unhurt.
She was killed.
One person **who** the newspaper said was killed was actually unhurt.

The stores gave away the food to (whoever/whomever) ~~they knew~~ could use it.
They could use it.
The stores gave away the food to **whoever** they knew could use it.

Exercise 1. Select the appropriate form of the pronoun in each of the following sentences.

1. The members of the clergy and (we/us) are united in our efforts to prevent child abuse.

2. The movie was reviewed by Cynthia O'Connell and (I/me).

3. The cleanup committee—Sam, Moe, and (I/me)—worked until two in the morning.

4. It was (she/her) who alerted us to the danger of unsealed medicine bottles.

5. Although Carmen is brighter than (he/him), her brother does better in school because he works harder.

6. Professor Reiger objected to (his/him) coming into class late.

7. The profits were divided between David and (he/him).

8. Although both women have fine qualities, Leo admires Rose far more than (she/her).

9. It had to be (he/him).

10. I appreciated (you/your) writing a recommendation for me.

Exercise 2. Select the appropriate form of the pronoun in each of the following sentences.

1. (Who/whom) did you say you met at the rally?

2. The governor (who/whom) commuted the sentence was Williams.

3. (Whoever/Whomever) the local political boss favored was given the job.

4. The reporter (who/whom) spoke had been to Lebanon.

5. The waiter (who/whom) was serving us has left for the night.

6. The person to (who/whom) you should direct your questions is Sydney Weinberg.

7. The district attorney's office intends to prosecute (whoever/whomever) the investigation finds is involved.

8. (Who/Whom) did the newspaper say would be appointed?

9. The former president would not say (who/whom) he would vote for.

10. (Who/Whom) did Napoleon defeat at the Battle of Austerlitz?

12 Adjectives and adverbs

An adjective is a word that modifies a noun or a pronoun. An adverb is a word that modifies a verb, an adjective, or another adverb. Do not confuse the two parts of speech.

Although most adjectives and adverbs have different forms, a few words can function as both. Among them are the following:

deadly	fast	late	loud	slow	tight
deep	hard	little	low	soon	well
far	kindly	long	parallel	straight	wild

12a Misused adjective forms

Do not use an adjective to modify a verb, an adjective, or an adverb. Use an adverb instead.

Not: The lawyer answered very **quick**.

But: The lawyer *answered* very **quickly**.

Not: The director thought Marie's reading was **near** perfect.

But: The director thought Marie's reading was **nearly** *perfect*.

Not: The group performing at the club plays **real** well.

But: The group performing at the club plays **really** *well*.

Do not be confused by words separating the adverb from the word it modifies. For example:

The lawyer *answered* each of her client's questions very **quickly**.

Do not use an adjective ending in -ly in place of an adverb or an adverb phrase.

Although the suffix -*ly* usually signals an adverb, a few adjectives end in -*ly* too. For example:

earthly	ghostly	holy	lovely
friendly	heavenly	homely	manly

Do not mistake these adjectives for adverbs or try to use them as adverbs. Either use another word or express your idea as a phrase.

Not: A figure was moving **ghostly** through the darkened room.
But: A figure was moving **like a ghost** through the darkened room.
Or: A figure was moving **ghostlike** through the darkened room.

Not: They do not generally answer the questions of American tourists very **friendly**.
But: They do not generally answer the questions of American tourists **in a very friendly way**.
Or: They do not generally answer the questions of American tourists **very pleasantly**.

12b Misused adverb forms

Do not use an adverb to modify a direct object. Use an adjective instead.

Think about the difference in meaning between the following two sentences.

> The instructor considered the student's paper careful.
> The instructor considered the student's paper carefully.

In the first sentence, the adjective *careful* modifies the direct object *paper*. It tells what opinion the professor held of the paper. In the second sentence, the adverb *carefully* modifies the verb *considered*. It tells in what manner the professor considered the paper.

> **Not:** He keeps his work station **tidily.**
>
> **But:** He keeps his *work station* **tidy.**

> **Not:** She considers her grades **excellently.**
>
> **But:** She considers her *grades* **excellent.**

> **Not:** The jury found the defendant **guiltily.**
>
> **But:** The jury found the *defendant* **guilty.**

Do not use an adverb after a linking verb. Use the corresponding adjective instead.

> **Not:** After the operation, the patient felt **badly.**
>
> **But:** After the operation, the *patient* felt **bad.**

> **Not:** This proposal sounds **sensibly** enough.
>
> **But:** This *proposal* sounds **sensible** enough.

Not: After he took that cooking course, his meals tasted **differently**.

But: After he took that cooking course, his *meals* tasted **different**.

Two words that are especially confusing are *good* and *well*. *Good* is always used as an adjective. *Well* is usually used as an adverb, but it can also be used as an adjective that means "healthy" or "satisfactory."

The preliminary *findings* look **good**. (*adjective*)

Janet *dances* **well**. (*adverb*)

The town crier shouted, "*All* is **well**!" (*adjective*)

Notice the difference between the following two sentences:

He feels good.
He feels well.

The adjective *good* describes the person's mood. The adjective *well* describes his health.

Some verbs can be used as both action verbs and linking verbs. These verbs include the following:

die	grow	feel	turn
go	look	smell	taste

Action: The customs officer *looked* **carefully** through our luggage. (*adverb*)

Linking: This *book* looks **interesting**. (*adjective*)

Action: The cute little puppy *grew* **quickly** into a 150-pound dog. (*adverb*)

Linking: After drinking the potion, the old *man* grew **young** before our very eyes. (*adjective*)

Action: He *died* **peacefully** in his sleep. (*adverb*)

Linking: The *poet* died **young.** (*adjective*)

12c Comparative and superlative forms of adjectives and adverbs

Form the comparative of most one-syllable adjectives and adverbs by adding the suffix *-er* (or *-r*) to the base, or positive, form of the word. Form the superlative of most one-syllable adjectives and adverbs by adding the suffix *-est* (or *-st*) to the base form.

Positive	Comparative	Superlative
slow	slower	slowest
late	later	latest
deep	deeper	deepest

Form the comparative of most longer adjectives and adverbs by placing the word *more* before the base word. Form the superlative of most longer adjectives and adverbs by placing the word *most* before the base word.

Positive	Comparative	Superlative
graceful	more graceful	most graceful
gracefully	more gracefully	most gracefully
sensible	more sensible	most sensible
sensibly	more sensibly	most sensibly

Some adjectives and adverbs have irregular comparative and superlative forms.

Positive	Comparative	Superlative
good well	better	best
bad ill badly	worse	worst

Positive	Comparative	Superlative
many ⎱ much ⎰	more	most
little (quantity)	less	least

A dictionary usually lists the *-er* and *-est* comparative and superlative forms for adjectives and adverbs that have these forms.

Use the comparative form to compare two things. Use the superlative form to compare three or more things.

> This dish is **spicier** than that one.
> This dish is the **spiciest** one on the menu.
>
> Harry is a **more skillful** carpenter than his partner.
> Harry is the **most skillful** carpenter in town.
>
> Lois works **harder** than Carol.
> Lois works the **hardest** of the three students.
>
> Sharon speaks **more distinctly** than her sister.
> Sharon speaks the **most distinctly** of anyone in her family.

Do not use the superlative form when only two things are being compared.

> **Not:** Of the two sexes, women live **the longest.**
> **But:** Of the two sexes, women live **longer.**
>
> **Not:** Both of the proposals were reasonable, but Johnson's was **the most complex.**
> **But:** Both of the proposals were reasonable, but Johnson's was **more complex.**
>
> **Not:** Henry James and Edith Wharton both wrote of a certain type of society—the society of the very rich and the very secure—and of the effects of this society on the idealistic woman. It is hard to say whose vision was the **clearest.**
> **But:** Henry James and Edith Wharton both wrote of a certain type of society—the society of the very rich and the very secure—and of the effects of this society on the idealistic woman. It is hard to say whose vision was the **clearer.**

Do not make double comparisons (comparisons using both -*er* or -*est* and *more* or *most*).

> **Not:** He was **more wealthier** than John D. Rockefeller.
> **But:** He was **wealthier** than John D. Rockefeller.
>
> **Not:** It is the **most sleekest** craft on the lake.
> **But:** It is the **sleekest** craft on the lake.

Do not compare words like *complete, dead, perfect, round, square,* and *unique.*

These words, called absolutes, name conditions that cannot be compared. For example, people are either dead or not dead; one person cannot be *more dead* than another person. If something is perfect, something else cannot be *more perfect.* Except for *dead,* however, you can compare the steps in reaching these conditions. For example, something may be *more nearly perfect* than something else, or one thing may be *the most nearly complete* of three.

> **Not:** His solution was **more perfect** than John's.
> **But:** His solution was **more nearly perfect** than John's.

12d Double negatives

Use only one negative word to express a negative meaning.

A **double negative** occurs when two negative words are used to make a negative statement. Although this device was often used in earlier centuries to emphasize the idea of negation, it is not acceptable in standard modern English.

> **Not:** Felicity **didn't** bring **nothing** to the party.
> **But:** Felicity **didn't** bring **anything** to the party.
> **Or:** Felicity brought **nothing** to the party.
>
> **Not:** I **don't** know **no one** by that name.
> **But:** I **don't** know **anyone** by that name.
> **Or:** I know **no one** by that name.

Not: She **can't hardly** see in this light.
But: She **can hardly** see in this light.

Exercise. Identify the incorrect adjective and adverb forms in the following sentences. One sentence is correct as written.

1. In the late eighteenth and early nineteenth centuries, some social critics looked close at the plight of the child laborer.

2. Among these critics were two of the most famousest writers of their time, William Blake and Charles Dickens.

3. One job usually held by children was that of the chimney sweep, since most adults couldn't hardly fit through the real tortuous passageways connecting chimneys and fireplaces.

4. Blake and Dickens could not help considering a chimney sweep's job dangerously, since many sweeps died young from consumption and black lung disease.

5. In his poem "The Chimney-Sweeper," William Blake tells of a pitiful sweep who mournfully cries the words "Weep! Weep!"

6. In *Oliver Twist*, Charles Dickens writes very moving of the real dreadful conditions of a sweep's daily life.

7. A sweep who felt badly was not given the day off to rest.

8. In spite of their health, sweeps had to get up early to be ready to work prompt at 5:00 A.M.

9. They had to crawl through passageways that were often unbearable hot and uncomfortable narrow, while scraping the soot meticulously.

10. Often, when the young sweeps seemed wearily, they had to endure harsh treatment by their masters, who tried to keep their youngsters moving rapid and working hard.

13 Comparisons

In addition to using the appropriate comparative or superlative form of an adjective or adverb, if necessary, a writer who is making a comparison has to keep a number of other points in mind. Be sure that your comparisons are sensible, complete, and unambiguous; do not leave out anything necessary to make your meaning clear.

13a False comparisons

Be careful that your comparative statements compare what you intended to compare. Do not compare things that are essentially unlike.

> **False:** Mark's smile was broader than Dora.

In the sentence above, the writer is trying to compare Mark's smile with Dora's smile. But the sentence as written compares Mark's smile with Dora herself.

> **Valid:** Mark's smile was broader than Dora's.

> **False:** Her style of dressing is like the 1960's.

The sentence above compares a style of dressing with a period of time. Obviously, it should compare this style of dressing with the style of dressing popular in that period.

> **Valid:** Her style of dressing is like **that of** the 1960's.

> **False:** Tuition at private colleges has become much more expensive than state colleges.
> **Valid:** Tuition has become much more expensive at private colleges than **at** state colleges.

13b Incomplete comparisons

Do not introduce the idea of a comparison without specifying one of the things being compared.

> **Incomplete:** This cake tastes better.

Tastes better than what?

> **Complete:** This cake tastes better than any of the others.

> **Incomplete:** Growing up in a small town is different.

Different from what?

Complete: Growing up in a small town is different from growing up in a large city or a suburb.

13c Ambiguous comparisons

Do not make a comparative statement that has two possible meanings.

Ambiguous: I know Eliot better than Pound.

The sentence above is unclear. You can interpret it in two ways.

Clear: I know Eliot better than I know Pound.
Clear: I know Eliot better than Pound knows him.

Ambiguous: I can recall the family vacation we took when I was five better than my sister.
Clear: I can recall the family vacation we took when I was five better than my sister can recall it.
Clear: I can recall the family vacation we took when I was five better than I can recall my sister.

13d Omitted comparative words

Do not omit the words *as* or *than* when they are necessary in a comparative construction.

Not: The candidate was better prepared although not as well spoken as her opponent.
But: The candidate was better prepared **than,** although not as well spoken as, her opponent.

Not: His grades were as good, if not better than, his brother's.
But: His grades were as good **as,** if not better than, his brother's.

Not: All of their friends were as poor or even poorer than they.
But: All of their friends were as poor **as** they or even poorer. (than they *is understood*)

Use the word *other* or *else* when you compare one thing with other members of the group to which it belongs.

> **Not:** The flutist plays more beautifully than any member of the orchestra.
> **But:** The flutist plays more beautifully than any **other** member of the orchestra.

> **Not:** Hal can throw farther than anyone on his team.
> **But:** Hal can throw farther than anyone **else** on his team.

> **Not:** The clipper cut through the water more gracefully than any of the ships.
> **But:** The clipper cut through the water more gracefully than any of the **other** ships.

Exercise. Rephrase the following sentences to eliminate any false, ambiguous, or incomplete comparisons. Where necessary, supply any comparative words that have been omitted.

1. The game was as long, if not longer than, usual.
2. The quarterback is taller than anyone on the team.
3. Her manner of speaking is like my grandmother.
4. His decision was as firm as Kenneth.
5. These tires last longer.
6. I understand calculus better than Harry.
7. The vice-presidential candidate campaigned as hard, if not harder than, her running mate.
8. Agatha Christie is more famous than any mystery writer.
9. Housing in cities is more expensive than rural areas.
10. Mark wanted to date Christine as much as Lee.

14 Shifts

While you should always strive for variety in your writing, some kinds of variety are not desirable. Shifting for no good reason from the active to the passive voice or from the past to the present tense is confusing and irritating to the reader. Be consistent in your use of number, person, tense, voice, mood, and point of view.

In number

Do not shift awkwardly and inconsistently between the singular and the plural.

Many shifts of this kind are actually problems with pronoun-antecedent agreement (see pages 75–78).

Inconsistent:	Just before **a person** speaks in public, **they** should do several relaxation exercises.
Consistent:	Just before **a person** speaks in public, **he or she** should do several relaxation exercises.
Or:	Just before speaking in public, a person should do several relaxation exercises.

Inconsistent:	**A warthog** may appear ungainly, but **these animals** can run at a speed of 30 miles an hour.
Consistent:	**A warthog** may appear ungainly, but **this animal** can run at a speed of 30 miles an hour.
Or:	**Warthogs** may appear ungainly, but **these animals** can run at a speed of 30 miles an hour.

Inconsistent:	**Anyone** who travels to Greece will see many sites about which **they** have read.
Consistent:	**People** who travel to Greece will see many sites about which **they** have read.
Or:	**Travelers** to Greece will see many sites about which **they** have read.

In person

Do not shift awkwardly between the second person and the third person.

All nouns and all indefinite pronouns are in the third person. However, personal pronouns may be in the first person, the second person, or the third person.

	Singular	Plural
1st person:	I, me, my, mine	we, us, our, ours
2nd person:	you, your, yours	you, your, yours
3rd person:	he, him, his	they, them, their, theirs
	she, her, hers	
	it, its	

Inconsistent: It has been said that unless **you** have a knowledge of history, a **person** is condemned to repeat the mistakes of history.

Consistent: It has been said that unless **you** have a knowledge of history, **you** are condemned to repeat the mistakes of history.

Or: It has been said that without a knowledge of history, a person is condemned to repeat the mistakes of history.

Inconsistent: When a **person** reads Jefferson's *Notes on Virginia*, **you** are amazed by his wide range of interests.

Consistent: When **people** read Jefferson's *Notes on Virginia*, **they** are amazed by his wide range of interests.

Or: People who read Jefferson's *Notes on Virginia* are amazed by his wide range of interests.

Inconsistent: As **you** read about the slaughtering of the rhinoceros for its horn and the elephant for its tusks, **one** becomes appalled by the selfishness of humankind.

Consistent: As **you** read about the slaughtering of the rhinoceros for its horn and the elephant for its tusks, **you** become appalled by the selfishness of humankind.

Or: Reading about the slaughtering of the rhinoceros for its horn and the elephant for its tusks, one becomes appalled by the selfishness of humankind.

In tense

Do not shift awkwardly between the present tense and the past tense.

When writing about literature or history, you can often use

either the present tense or the past tense. However, if you start writing in the present tense, continue writing in this tense. If you start writing in the past tense, continue writing in this tense.

Inconsistent: At the end of the war, Ezra Pound **is accused** of treason. He **was confined** at St. Elizabeth's Hospital, where he **spends** the next twelve years.

Consistent: At the end of the war, Ezra Pound **is accused** of treason. He **is confined** at St. Elizabeth's Hospital, where he **spends** the next twelve years.

Inconsistent: *The Day of the Scorpion* **is** the second book in Paul Scott's *The Raj Quartet*. It **tells** the story of an English family living in India in the last years of British rule. The book **opened** on August 9, 1942. On this day Gandhi and other prominent Indians who had voted for independence from Britain **were sent** to prison.

Consistent: *The Day of the Scorpion* **is** the second book in Paul Scott's *The Raj Quartet*. It **tells** the story of an English family living in India in the last years of British rule. The book **opens** on August 9, 1942. On this day Gandhi and other prominent Indians who had voted for independence from Britain **are sent** to prison.

Inconsistent: Lincoln **came** to national attention as a result of a series of debates with Stephen A. Douglas. Although he **loses** the senatorial election to Douglas, two years later he **gains** the Republican nomination for president.

Consistent: Lincoln **came** to national attention as a result of a series of debates with Stephen A. Douglas. Although he **lost** the senatorial election to Douglas, two years later he **gained** the Republican nomination for president.

In voice

Do not shift awkwardly between the active voice and the passive voice.

Inconsistent:	John F. Kennedy **won** the presidency with only 49.7 percent of the popular vote because a majority of the electoral vote **was captured** by him.
Consistent:	John F. Kennedy **won** the presidency with only 49.7 percent of the popular vote because he **captured** a majority of the electoral vote.
Inconsistent:	André-Jacques Garnerin **made** the first parachute jump, and the first aerial photographs **were taken** by Samuel Archer King and William Black.
Consistent:	André-Jacques Garnerin **made** the first parachute jump, and Samuel Archer King and William Black **took** the first aerial photographs.
Inconsistent:	A group of ants **is called** a colony, but you **refer** to a group of bees as a swarm.
Consistent:	A group of ants **is called** a colony, but a group of bees **is referred** to as a swarm.

In mood

Do not shift awkwardly between the indicative, imperative, and subjunctive moods.

Inconsistent:	First **brown** the onions in butter. Then you **should add** them to the beef stock.
Consistent:	First **brown** the onions in butter. Then **add** them to the beef stock.
Inconsistent:	If I **were** president of this club and he **was** my second in command, things would be very different.
Consistent:	If I **were** president of this club and he **were** my second in command, things would be very different.
Inconsistent:	First **proofread** your paper and **make** any necessary changes. Next you **ought to retype** it.
Consistent:	First **proofread** your paper and **make** any necessary changes. Next **retype** it.

In point of view

Do not shift awkwardly from one point of view to another.

Point of view is the perspective from which something is told. In writing, be sure to distinguish between your own point of view and that of a person you are writing about.

Inconsistent: During the late 1960's and early 1970's, many Americans felt that the war in Vietnam could not be won. However, President Nixon believed the opposite. The South Vietnamese could be trained to take over the fighting, a process called "Vietnamization."

Is the last sentence the view of Nixon or that of the writer?

Consistent: During the late 1960's and early 1970's, many Americans felt that the war in Vietnam could not be won. However, **President Nixon believed** the opposite. **He felt** that the South Vietnamese could be trained to take over the fighting, a process **he called** "Vietnamization."

Inconsistent: The critic says that people should avoid this movie. It is filled with despicable people performing senseless acts of violence.

Consistent: **The critic says** that people should avoid this movie, **which he claims** is filled with despicable people performing senseless acts of violence.

Inconsistent: According to the newspaper article, many people living in the United States are not well enough informed to participate effectively in a democracy. They do not read newspapers, let alone magazines and books. They do not listen to political debates or presidential news conferences. In fact, some people do not even know the name of the Vice President.

Consistent: **According to the newspaper article,** many people living in the United States are not well enough informed to participate effectively in a democracy. **The article asserts** that many people do not read newspapers, let alone magazines and books, and that they do not listen to political debates or presidential news conferences. In fact, **it maintains** that some people do not even know the name of the Vice President.

Exercise. Rephrase each of the following items to eliminate awkward shifts in number, person, tense, voice, mood, and point of view.

1. When you apply for a passport, a person should bring a copy of his or her birth certificate.

2. In this play a group of strangers are stranded in a mission during what may be a nuclear disaster. The priest helped each of them examine his or her life.

3. A person should follow certain rules when mountain climbing. First, they should never go climbing alone.

4. The article claims that if you work but want to keep a cat as a pet, you should keep two, not one. Two cats will play with each other and keep each other company.

5. Start with a clean coffeepot. Then you should grind the coffee beans. Measure the ground coffee carefully.

6. Many people like the mysteries of Agatha Christie, but those of Dorothy Sayers and Amanda Cross are preferred by me.

7. Before a person begins a program of running, you should see your doctor for a complete medical checkup.

8. When his aunt makes him whitewash the fence, Tom pretended the task was fun. He then persuaded another boy to pay for the privilege of whitewashing.

9. If I were rich and he was poor, I would give him all my money.

10. If one were to travel to Egypt, you could see the Sphinx and the Pyramids.

15 Sequence of tenses

Maintain a logical sequence of tenses to indicate when events happen in relation to one another.

The English tense system is extremely complicated, but most of the time, native speakers of the language have few problems using it correctly. One problem that some people do have is shifting unnecessarily from one tense to another (see pages

102–103). Some writers, on the other hand, have the opposite problem: they do not change tenses when they need to in order to show that one event happened before or after another. The following rules cover some of the most common problems with sequence of tenses.

With clauses

If you begin a sentence in the present tense, shift to the past tense when you begin to write about past action.

Not: To a large extent, we **remember** Alice B. Toklas because she **is** Gertrude Stein's friend.

But: To a large extent, we **remember** Alice B. Toklas because she **was** Gertrude Stein's friend.

Not: Today he **supports** moving the embassy, while just three weeks ago he **opposes** this action.

But: Today he **supports** moving the embassy, while just three weeks ago he **opposed** this action.

Not: She always **goes** to the mountains on vacation because she **spends** her childhood there.

But: She always **goes** to the mountains on vacation because she **spent** her vacation there.

Use the past perfect tense to indicate that one past action occurred before another.

Not: Hitler **purged** the Nazi Party before he **gained** complete control of the state.

But: Hitler **had purged** the Nazi Party before he **gained** complete control of the state.

Not: After they **double-checked** the results of their experiment, they **announced** their findings to the press.

But: After they **had double-checked** the results of their experiment, they **announced** their findings to the press.

Not: Since spring **came** early, they **were hoping** for a long growing season.

But: Since spring **had come** early, they **were hoping** for a long growing season.

With infinitives

Use the present infinitive to express action that occurs at the same time as or later than the action of the main verb. Use the present perfect infinitive to express action that occurs before the action of the main verb.

> **Not:** They **need to purchase** their tickets by now.
> **But:** They **need to have purchased** their tickets by now. (*The need is in the present; the purchase, if it happened, was in the past.*)

> **Not:** The artist **wanted to have captured** the variations in the light.
> **But:** The artist **wanted to capture** the variations in the light. (*The wanting occurred before the capturing.*)

> **Not:** The designer **had hoped to have gotten** the job.
> **But:** The designer **had hoped to get** the job.

Compare the following three sentences.

> He **would like to review** the book favorably. (would like *in the present* to review *in the present*)
> He **would have liked to review** the book favorably. (would have liked *in the past* to review *in the past*)
> He **would like to have reviewed** the book favorably. (would like *in the present* to have reviewed *in the past*)

With participles

Use the present participle to express action that occurs at the same time as the action of the main verb. Use the present perfect participle or the past participle to express action that occurs before the action of the main verb.

The present perfect participle of a verb consists of the word *having* followed by the past participle of the verb: *having done, having been, having seen,* etc.

> **Not:** **Winning** the battle, the general planned the next day's campaign.

But: **Having won** the battle, the general *planned* the next day's campaign. (*action of participle occurred before action of main verb*)

Not: **Having hoped** for good news, he rushed for the telephone.

But: **Hoping** for good news, he *rushed* for the telephone. (*action of participle occurred at the same time as action of main verb*)

Not: **Being encouraged** by her friends, she eagerly filled out the form for entrance in the marathon.

But: **Having been encouraged** by her friends, she eagerly *filled out* the form for entrance in the marathon. (*action of participle occurred before action of main verb*)

Or: **Encouraged** by her friends, she eagerly *filled out* the form for entrance in the marathon.

Exercise. Correct any error in sequence of tenses in the following sentences. Identify any correct sentences.

1. Because they deciphered the enemy's message, they were ready for the attack.

2. They raised the money by the time the mortgage was due.

3. Edmund Wilson felt that there are better things to read than mysteries.

4. Since she has won an Oscar last year, she wasn't counting on winning one this year.

5. Stuart Palmer based his fictional detective, Hildegarde Withers, on a teacher he had in high school.

6. They pledged to have dedicated their lives to the poor.

7. Having disliked the novel, she had been surprised to like the film made from it.

8. Having found no one for the role of Scarlett, the studio started shooting the film without a leading lady.

9. Being discouraged by his lack of public recognition, the artist abandoned painting.

10. *Da* played off-Broadway before it moved to Broadway.

16 Sentence structure

The parts of a sentence, like those of a building or a jigsaw puzzle, must be put together in a certain way in order to fit with one another. For example, verbs must agree with their subjects, and pronouns with their antecedents. In constructing sentences, you must also be sure to maintain a consistent structure throughout a sentence, to make subjects and predicates fit together logically, to express parallel grammatical elements in parallel form, and to place modifiers correctly.

16a Mixed structure

Maintain a consistent sentence structure. Do not start a sentence with one type of structure and end it with another type.

Inconsistent: First rub olive oil over the outside of the chicken; then salt the chicken lightly, but no pepper.

The writer of the sentence above begins with an independent clause, continues with another independent clause, and then begins the third part of the sentence with the conjunction *but*, indicating that another independent clause will follow. However, the writer then ends the sentence with a phrase rather than a clause. The problem can be eliminated by turning the phrase into a clause.

Consistent: First rub olive oil over the outside of the chicken; then salt the chicken lightly, but do not pepper it.

Another kind of mixed sentence structure is created by clauses that are not clearly related to one another.

Inconsistent: When your parents were poorly educated and you youself have attended substandard schools, what kind of odds for success are those?

In this sentence, the writer begins with an adverb clause that should modify a word in an independent clause. However, the independent clause that follows does not contain any word for the adverb clause to modify. To correct the problem, simply provide such a word.

Consistent: What kind of odds for success do you have when your parents were poorly educated and you yourself have attended substandard schools?

Inconsistent: Those black pilots who fought so valiantly during World War II, many people do not even know of their existence.

Here the writer begins with a noun modified by an adjective clause but does not provide a predicate for the noun. Instead, the sentence ends with an independent clause that is not grammatically related to what precedes it.

Consistent: Many people do not even know of the existence of those black pilots who fought so valiantly during World War II.

The following sentence is from a television program about training business executives to answer (or evade) reporters' questions.

Inconsistent: How you could be a newsperson and work with people you might one day have to interview, I could not do it.

Consistent: As a newsperson, I could not work with people I might one day have to interview.

Or: I do not understand how you could be a newsperson and work with people you might one day have to interview.

111

16b Faulty predication

Make the subject and predicate of a sentence fit together both grammatically and logically.

A sentence with a poorly matched subject and predicate is said to have **faulty predication.**

> **Not:** More versatile and more manageable account for the popularity of the latest breed of home computers.

In the sentence above, the writer used two adjectives as the subject of the predicate *account for . . . computers.* A subject, however, must always be a noun or a noun equivalent.

> **But:** Their greater **versatility** and increased **manageability** account for the popularity of the latest breed of home computers.

Other sentences with faulty predication are grammatically acceptable but make no sense or do not say what the writer intended.

> **Not:** Flattery and snobbery are people who will not be effective as political advisers.

The nouns *flattery* and *snobbery* do not sensibly fit the predicate *are people.*

> **But:** The flatterer and the snob will not be effective as political advisers.

> **Not:** My opinion of his latest movie is poorly directed and ineptly filmed.

According to the sentence above, it is the writer's opinion that is poorly directed and ineptly filmed. Obviously, the writer meant to say this of the movie, not of the opinion.

> **But:** In my opinion, his latest movie is poorly directed and ineptly filmed.
>
> **Or:** My opinion of his latest movie is that it is poorly directed and ineptly filmed.

Not: Our criminal-justice system, which allows the victims of crime to suffer more than the perpetrators of crime, should be punished more severely.

The subject *our criminal-justice system* does not fit the predicate *should be punished more severely.*

But: Our criminal-justice system, which allows the victims of crime to suffer more than the perpetrators of crime, should be changed.

Or: Our criminal-justice system should be changed so that perpetrators of crime suffer more than their victims.

Do not use an adverb clause as a predicate nominative.

Not: The reason the Liberty Bell was moved to Allentown during the Revolutionary War is because the British were occupying Philadelphia.

The word *because* introduces an adverb clause. Change this to a noun clause.

But: The reason the Liberty Bell was moved to Allentown during the Revolutionary War is **that** the British were occupying Philadelphia.

Not: The year 1778 is when the Liberty Bell was returned to Independence Hall.

But: The Liberty Bell was returned to Independence Hall in 1778.

Not: Ironically, England is where the Liberty Bell was cast.

But: Ironically, the Liberty Bell was cast in England.

16c Faulty parallelism

Use the same grammatical form for elements that are part of a series or a compound construction.

The speech was **concise, witty,** and **effective.**
Today's "supermom" is both **a mother** and **an executive.**
He tried to be honest **with himself** as well as **with others.**

Sentence elements that have the same grammatical structure are said to be *parallel*. When elements that are part of a series or a compound construction do not have the same form, a sentence is said to have **faulty parallelism**.

Repeat articles, prepositions, and the sign of the infinitive to make the meaning of a sentence clear.

The audience applauded the composer and lyricist.

The sentence above is clear if the composer and the lyricist are the same person. It is misleading if they are not the same person. Repeat the article *the* to indicate two people.

The audience applauded **the** composer and **the** lyricist.

Unclear: She was a prominent critic and patron of young poets.
Clear: She was **a** prominent critic and **a** patron of young poets.

Unclear: She quickly learned to supervise the maid and cook.
Clear: She quickly learned to supervise **the** maid and **the** cook.
Clear: She quickly learned **to** supervise the maid and **to** cook.

Unclear: His father had taught him to shoot and ride a horse.
Clear: His father had taught him **to** shoot and **to** ride a horse.

Unclear: Among other things, members of the sect did not believe in drinking alcohol or kneeling during Communion.
Clear: Among other things, members of the sect did not believe **in** drinking alcohol or **in** kneeling during Communion.

Place elements joined by a coordinating conjunction in the same grammatical form. Balance a noun with a noun, an adjective with an adjective, a prepositional phrase with a prepositional phrase, and so on.

Not Parallel: The scientific community in general regarded him

               adjective   adjective   noun
as **outspoken, eccentric,** and a **rebel.**

Parallel: The scientific community in general regarded him

         adjective   adjective   adjective

as **outspoken, eccentric,** and **rebellious.**

                                           noun

Not Parallel: In *Searching for Caleb*, the protagonist is a **wife,**

           noun   clause

a **mother,** and **she tells fortunes.**

                                           noun

Parallel: In *Searching for Caleb*, the protagonist is a **wife,**

           noun   noun

a **mother,** and a **fortune-teller.**

                                           adjective

Not Parallel: Reviewers praised the play for its **realistic**

           noun

portrayal of a sensitive young woman and **because**

                 adverb clause

it gave a penetrating depiction of a family.

                                           adjective

Parallel: Reviewers praised the play for its **realistic**

           noun

portrayal of a sensitive young woman and its

           adjective   noun

penetrating depiction of family life.

                                       prepositional phrase

Not Parallel: A hobbit is a creature **with a hearty appetite** and

           adjective clause

who loves home.

                                          verb

Parallel: A hobbit is a creature who **has** a hearty appetite

            verb

and **loves** home.

Place elements joined by correlative conjunctions in parallel form.

    Not Parallel: He was not only **her husband** but also **she considered him her friend.**

Parallel:	He was not only **her husband** but also **her friend.**
Not Parallel:	Knute Rockne would be either **a science teacher** or **someone who coached football.**
Parallel:	Knute Rockne would be either **a science teacher** or **a football coach.**
Not Parallel:	After his vision, Scrooge becomes not only **a generous man** but also **happy.**
Parallel:	After his vision, Scrooge becomes not only **a generous man** but also **a happy one.**

Take care with the placement of correlative conjunctions.

Not Parallel:	Solar energy is **both** used to heat houses **and** to run small appliances.

In the sentence above, the first part of the correlative conjunction (*both*) is followed by a verb, but the second part (*and*) is followed by an infinitive. The problem can be corrected by moving the *both* to a later position in the sentence so that it, too, is followed by an infinitive.

Parallel:	Solar energy is used **both** to heat houses **and** to run small appliances.
Not Parallel:	She would **either** run as the presidential candidate **or** the vice presidential candidate.
Parallel:	She would run as **either** the presidential candidate **or** the vice presidential candidate.
Not Parallel:	He **not only** wanted money **but also** fame.
Parallel:	He wanted **not only** money **but also** fame.

16d Dangling modifiers

An introductory phrase must clearly and sensibly modify the noun or pronoun that follows it.

A phrase that does not do this is called a **dangling modifier,** because it is not clearly attached to the rest of the sentence.

Unclear: **Frightened by the huge, gnarled tree outside his window,** his head dived under the covers.

In the sentence above, the introductory participial phrase seems to modify *his head*, but it was obviously not the boy's head, but the boy himself, who was frightened. A simple way to revise this sentence is to rewrite the independent clause so that it begins with the noun that the introductory phrase actually refers to.

Clear: **Frightened by the huge, gnarled tree outside his window,** the boy hid his head under the covers.

Unclear: **Unable to make a living in Detroit,** relocating to Houston seemed a good idea.

The introductory phrase does not sensibly modify *relocating*, the gerund that follows it. This sentence can also be revised by rewriting the independent clause so that it begins with the noun or pronoun that the introductory phrase actually refers to.

Clear: **Unable to make a living in Detroit,** she thought relocating to Houston was a good idea.

Or: **Unable to make a living in Detroit,** she thought she might move to Houston.

Another way to revise the sentence is to turn the phrase into a clause.

Clear: **Since she was unable to make a living in Detroit,** relocating to Houston seemed a good idea.

Here are some more examples of dangling modifiers.

Unclear: **While trying to control my temper,** the sergeant forced me to do a hundred push-ups.

Clear: **While trying to control my temper,** I was forced to do a hundred push-ups by the sergeant.

Or: **As I tried to control my temper,** the sergeant forced me to do a hundred push-ups.

Unclear: **As a young girl,** my grandfather told me stories of his life in Sweden.

Clear: **When I was a young girl,** my grandfather told me stories of his life in Sweden.

A few introductory phrases are idiomatic. They modify the entire sentence, not a particular word.

To tell the truth, no one knows where he is.
Relatively speaking, my grades are not that bad.
As a matter of fact, the sea is not wine-red but blue.

16e Misplaced modifiers

Place a modifying word or phrase as close as possible to the word it modifies. Be careful not to place it so that it seems to refer to a word other than the one you intended.

The placement of a modifier in a sentence is very important. Notice the difference in meaning between the following two sentences.

He **almost** spent two hundred dollars.
He spent **almost** two hundred dollars.

In the first sentence, *almost* modifies the verb *spent*. It tells us that he did not complete his action. In the second sentence, *almost* modifies *two hundred*. It tells us that the amount he spent came close to, but did not total, two hundred dollars.

Misplaced modifiers make a sentence confusing or even ridiculous, as shown in the following examples.

Unclear: He almost spoke for two hours.
Clear: He spoke for **almost** two hours.

Unclear: She only quoted from three sources.
Clear: She quoted from **only** three sources.

Unclear: He sang a ditty about filling a bottomless hole with his sister.
Clear: **With his sister,** he sang a ditty about filling a bottomless hole.
Or: He sang a ditty **with his sister** about filling a bottomless hole.

Unclear: He described his years spent alone on the island after the rescue.

Clear: **After the rescue** he described his years spent alone on the island.

16f Squinting modifiers

Do not place a modifier in such a way that it could refer to either the preceding or the following element in the sentence.

Such a modifier is called a **squinting modifier.**

Unclear: The mayor announced **in March** he would run for reelection.

Was it the announcement or the election that was in March?

Clear: The mayor announced he would run for reelection in March.

Clear: In March, the mayor announced he would run for reelection.

Unclear: Carlson said **today** he is leaving for California.
Clear: Carlson said he is leaving for California today.
Clear: Today Carlson said he is leaving for California.

Unclear: Professor Quinn asked us **before we left** to turn in our papers.
Clear: Before we left, Professor Quinn asked us to turn in our papers.
Clear: Professor Quinn asked us to turn in our papers before we left.

Exercise. Revise each of the following sentences to eliminate the problem in sentence structure.

1. The committee debated for hours, but no decision.

2. In his spare time he liked to read and write poetry.

3. A generous person is a quality to be admired.

4. Believing he had won the election, the celebration was already under way.

5. He often lies, but I only tell the truth.

6. Why anyone would prefer communism to democracy, he could not accept the idea.

7. During his twenties, he not only wrote three books but also five plays.

8. Depth of perception and simplicity of style are why I like Hemingway.

9. Shining in the church tower, the townspeople saw the beacon.

10. Overcoming his "morbid propensity toward sloth," the dictionary was completed by Johnson.

PUNCTUATION
AND
MECHANICS

PUNCTUATION AND MECHANICS

Punctuation marks are signals designed to help people understand what they are reading. They tell readers when to pause, when to stop, and when to read something with emphasis.

Mechanics deals with the technical aspects of writing. These aspects include when to underline, when to use numerals, and how to form contractions.

17 End punctuation

End punctuation separates sentences and marks the end of other elements, such as abbreviations. The three end punctuation marks are the period, the question mark, and the exclamation mark.

17a The period

Use a period to end a sentence that makes a statement.

In 1979 the United States ceded control of the Panama Canal Zone to the Panamanian government.

The Japanese painter Hokusai changed his style many times.

Adlai E. Stevenson ran for the presidency against Dwight D. Eisenhower.

Use a period to end a sentence that makes a request, expresses a mild command, or gives directions.

Please help the needy.

Open your books to page 178.

Turn left at the next corner.

If you wish the command or request to be given a great deal of emphasis or force, use an exclamation point instead of a period.

Help!

Sign up now!

Quit smoking!

Use a period at the end of a sentence that asks an indirect question.

The editorial questions whether NATO is effective.

The reporter asked how the fire had started.

The doctor wondered why the patient's temperature had risen.

Use a period at the end of a request politely expressed as a question.

Will you please type this letter for me.

Will you kindly keep your voices down.

(See pages 150–151 for the use of the period with parentheses. See page 157 for the use of the period with quotation marks.)

Use a period after most abbreviations and initials.

If a sentence ends with an abbreviation requiring a period, use only one period.

> The first admiral in the U•S• Navy was David G• Farragut.
> The Marine Corps traces its beginnings to Nov• 10, 1775.
> Thomas Jefferson's home, Monticello, is near Charlottesville, Va•

The current trend in abbreviations is away from the use of periods. The following two rules are now considered standard. However, if you are in doubt about whether to use a period after an abbreviation, consult your dictionary.

Do not use a period with abbreviations of metric units of measure.

> 86 m   275 kg   2.4 cm   20 cc

Do not use a period with acronyms or other abbreviations of businesses, organizations, and government and international agencies.

> The **NAACP** has not endorsed a presidential candidate.
> My mother served in the **WAC**s for eight years.
> The impartiality of **UNESCO** is being questioned.

17b The question mark

Use a question mark at the end of a sentence that asks a direct question.

> Who invented the safety pin**?**
> Have you registered to vote**?**
> Why did Nixon go to China**?**

Use a question mark at the end of an interrogative element that is part of another sentence.

How can I keep my job? was the question on every worker's
  mind.
Will he actively support women's rights? she wondered.
The telegram said that Malcolm is alive—can it be true?—and
  will be returned to the United States on Friday.

**In general, when a question follows an introductory element,
use a capital letter to begin the question and a question
mark to end it.**

The question to be decided is, How can we improve our public
  transportation system?
Before buying on credit, ask yourself, Do I really need this?
A good detective inquires, What was the motive for the crime?

Usage varies somewhat on capitalization of questions following
introductory elements. The more formal the question, the
greater the tendency to use a capital letter. The less formal,
the greater the tendency to use a lower-case letter.

Formal: The book raises the question, What role should the
          United States play in the Middle East?
Informal: I wondered, should I bring my umbrella?

**Use a question mark, usually in parentheses, to express
doubt or uncertainty about a date, a name, or a word.**

The *Vedas* (written around 1000 B.C.?) are the sacred books of
  Hinduism.
A dialect of Germanic, called Angleish (?), is the basis of modern-
  day English.
Sir Thomas Malory (?–1471) wrote *Morte d'Arthur*, an account
  of the exploits of King Arthur and his knights.

17c The exclamation point

**Use an exclamation point at the end of a sentence, word,
or phrase that you wish to be read with emphasis, with
surprise, or with strong emotion.**

> Don't give up**!**
> We shall resist this onslaught**!**
> Impossible**!**
> What a terrible time**!**

Do not overuse the exclamation point. Too many exclamation points are distracting and ineffective. The more you use, the less effective each one will be.

Exercise. Identify the end punctuation missing from the following sentences. Some of the sentences need more than one punctuation mark.

1. Have you ever wondered why people go trick-or-treating on Halloween

2. The Christian church created Christian holidays to take the place of pagan holidays

3. All Saints' Day—did you know this—was established to replace the Celtic holiday Samhain, the festival of the dead

4. St Patrick (AD 389–461) helped convert the Celts to Christianity

5. Will you please check these dates

6. How can we use the customs of the Celts to convert these people was the question the Church considered

7. You might wonder, Is *hallow* another word for *saint*

8. An excellent question

9. All Saints' Day, or All Hallows' Day, is celebrated on Nov 1; therefore, All Saints' Eve, or All Hallows' Eve, or Halloween, is Oct 31

10. The custom of dressing like ghouls and goblins and trick-or-treating mimics the Celtic belief that the dead walk the earth during Samhain, doesn't it

18 The comma

The comma groups elements within a sentence. It also sets off modifiers and parenthetical expressions.

Between two independent clauses

Use a comma between two independent clauses joined by a coordinating conjunction: *and, but, for, nor, or, so, yet*.

> Many Caribbean people emigrate to other countries, and 700,000 of these emigrants settled in the United States between 1971 and 1979.
>
> Halloween has its origins in the Celtic religious festival of the dead, but today Halloween is largely a children's holiday of tricks and treats.
>
> Travel to the countryside to buy fresh apples, for there at roadside stands you can find many varieties not available in supermarkets.

The comma may be omitted between two short independent clauses.

> She handed him the note and he read it immediately.
> Take notes in class and study them.

If in doubt, use the comma.

Between items in a series

Use commas to separate three or more items in a series.

Words in a series

> A zoo veterinarian is called upon to treat such diverse animals as elephants, gorillas, and antelopes.
> Murillo, Velázquez, and El Greco were three major seventeenth-century Spanish painters.
> The sporting goods store carries equipment for skiing, track, hockey, and weight lifting.

Phrases in a series

> The subway carried children going to school, adults going to work, and derelicts going to nowhere at all.
> The children playing hide-and-seek hid behind boulders, under bushes, or in trees.
> Running in the halls, smoking in the bathrooms, and shouting in the classrooms are not allowed.

127

Clauses in a series

Edward Steichen photographed the Brooklyn Bridge, Georgia O'Keeffe painted it, and Hart Crane wrote about it.

Foster stole the ball, he passed it to Kennedy, and Kennedy made a basket.

The yellow press proclaimed boldly that the man's character was hateful, that he was guilty as sin, and that he should be punished severely.

Usually the comma before the conjunction is considered optional with items in a series. It is often omitted in newspapers and magazines. Follow your instructor's preference, and be consistent in using or not using the comma throughout a single piece of writing.

Unacceptable:	Britain France and Russia formed the Triple Entente.
Often acceptable:	Britain, France and Russia formed the Triple Entente.
Always acceptable:	Britain, France, and Russia formed the Triple Entente.

Always use the comma if it is necessary to avoid misreading, as in the following cases.

Use a comma before the conjunction with a series of personal names.

Harry, Anita, and Jayne have left already.

Without a comma before the conjunction, it is possible to read such sentences as directly addressing the first person named.

Harry, Anita and Jayne have left already. (*Someone is addressing Harry and giving him information about Anita and Jayne.*)

Use a comma before the conjunction with a series when the last two items in the series could be read as one item.

The menu listed the following sandwiches: bologna, chicken salad, pastrami, ham and cheese. (*four sandwiches*)

The menu listed the following sandwiches: bologna, chicken salad, pastrami, ham, and cheese. (*five sandwiches*)

The florist made up several bouquets: lilies, gladiolas, roses, snapdragons and chrysanthemums. (*four bouquets*)

The florist made up several bouquets: lilies, gladiolas, roses, snapdragons, and chrysanthemums. (*five bouquets*)

Between coordinate adjectives

Use a comma between coordinate adjectives that are not joined by *and*.

Coordinate adjectives each modify the noun independently.

The comic was censored for his *audacious, vulgar* routine.

The traveler paused before walking into the *deep, dark, mysterious* woods.

The advertisement requested a *cheerful, sensitive, intelligent* woman to serve as governess.

Do not use a comma between cumulative adjectives.

Cumulative adjectives each modify the whole group of words that follow them.

He gave her a *crystal perfume* bottle.

On top of the stove was a set of *large shiny copper* pots.

She carried an *expensive black leather* briefcase.

How can you distinguish coordinate adjectives from cumulative adjectives? In general, coordinate adjectives would sound natural with the word *and* between them, since each modifies the noun independently.

The comic was censored for his audacious and vulgar routine.

The traveler paused before walking into the deep and dark and mysterious woods.

The advertisement requested a cheerful and sensitive and intelligent woman to serve as governess.

In addition, coordinate adjectives would sound natural with their order changed or reversed.

The comic was censored for his vulgar, audacious routine.

The traveler paused before walking into the mysterious, dark, deep woods.

The advertisement requested an intelligent, sensitive, cheerful woman to serve as governess.

The order of cumulative adjectives cannot be changed. For example, no native English speaker would write sentences like the following:

He gave her a perfume crystal bottle.

On top of the stove was a set of copper shiny large pots.

She carried an expensive leather black briefcase.

After introductory words and phrases

Use a comma after an introductory word or expression that does not modify the subject of the sentence.

Why, we didn't realize the telegram was merely a hoax.

Yes, Washington did sleep here.

Well, that restaurant is certainly expensive.

On the other hand, its prices are justified.

By the way, what were you doing last night?

Use a comma after an introductory verbal phrase.

While sleeping, Coleridge conceived the idea for "Kubla Khan."

To sketch a tree accurately, you must first study it closely.

Hoping to find happiness at last, Poe married his cousin.

Use a comma after an introductory series of prepositional phrases.

Under cover of night, the secret agent slipped across the border.

In this album of music from the 1960's, you will find several traditional folk songs.

In Jack London's famous story of a fight for survival in the Arctic, the man fails to light a fire.

Use a comma after any introductory phrase if there is a possibility that the sentence will be misread without it.

The day before, he had written her a letter.
After the tournament, winners received trophies and certificates.
Without hunting, the deer would soon become too numerous for the available food supply.

With contrasted elements

Use a comma to set off an element that is being contrasted with what precedes it.

Robert Graves claims he writes novels for profit, not for pleasure.
Birds, unlike reptiles, are warm-blooded.
The concept of true religious toleration, as opposed to the mere absence of persecution, was slow to develop in Western thought.

With interrogative elements

Use a comma before a short interrogative element at the end of a sentence.

I don't know anyone who hasn't seen at least one of Hitchcock's films, do you?
Tom Stoppard's new play is wonderful, isn't it?
The Vietnam War was never officially a war, was it?

With parenthetical expressions

Use commas to set off a parenthetical expression within a sentence.

Expressions that comment on or give additional information about the main part of the sentence are considered parenthetical.

Jazz, many critics feel, is America's greatest contribution to the arts.
You, like most people, probably do not know that the person responsible for the completion of the Brooklyn Bridge was a woman.
George Washington, according to the old-style calendar used by the colonists, was born on February 11.

Use commas to set off conjunctive adverbs (*however, accordingly, moreover, nevertheless,* etc.) and transitional phrases (*in addition, to sum up, on the other hand, for example*) used parenthetically.

> Many acclaimed writers, however, have written mysteries.
> A popular mystery set in a fourteenth-century monastery, moreover, was written by a professor of semiotics.
> Edmund Wilson, on the other hand, considered mysteries simply a waste of time.

Use commas to set off words that identify the source of a quotation within a sentence.

> "The advance for the book," said Calvin Trillin, "should be at least as much as the cost of the lunch at which it was discussed."
> "You can be a little ungrammatical," Robert Frost claimed, "if you come from the right part of the country."
> "Just get it down on paper," advised Maxwell Perkins, "and we'll see what to do with it."

With adverb clauses

Use a comma after an introductory adverb clause.

> Because John F. Kennedy was assassinated on the same day Aldous Huxley died, Huxley's death was given little attention by the press.
> Although the alligator once faced extinction, its numbers are now increasing dramatically.
> If the earth were to undergo another ice age, certain animals would flourish.

The comma after a very short introductory adverb clause is considered optional, unless its placement prevents misreading.

In general, use commas to set off an internal adverb clause that is parenthetical or that separates the subject of the main clause from its predicate.

> Harry Truman, although a newspaper headline prematurely

declared otherwise, won the 1948 election over Thomas E. Dewey.

Columbus, as we have seen, died without his true accomplishments recognized or honored.

In general, do not use a comma before an adverb clause that follows the main clause.

Many people wept *when they saw the monument honoring the veterans of the war in Vietnam.*

A national holiday has been established *so that Americans can honor Martin Luther King, Jr.*

Who ruled England *before the Normans invaded it?*

However, there are several exceptions to the above rule.

Use a comma before a terminal adverb clause that begins with *although* or *even though*.

Columbus found a rich world for the Spanish, although it was not the world he set out to reach.

Use a comma before a terminal adverb clause that begins with *as, since,* or *while* when these words express cause or condition. Do not use a comma when these words express time.

Cause: We decided not to go out on the lake, *as the Coast Guard had posted small craft warnings.*

Time: He wrote the assignment on the board *as he waited for his first class to come in.*

Cause: He advocated prison reform, *since he knew firsthand the dehumanizing effects of prison life.*

Time: Mighty empires have come and gone *since the world began.*

Condition: Many critics praised her new play, *while others felt it was the worst she had ever written.*

Time: She wrote her first play *while she was vacationing in Venice.*

Use a comma before a terminal adverb clause beginning with *because* if the clause does not modify the verb nearest it.

Notice the difference in meaning between the two sentences below.

I knew he *was absent* from work *because his supervisor was looking for him.*

I *knew* he was absent from work, *because his supervisor was looking for him.*

In the first sentence above, the adverb clause modifies *was absent*. It tells why he was absent—because his supervisor was looking for him. In the second sentence, the comma tells us that the adverb clause does not modify the verb closest to it. Instead, it modifies the verb *knew*. It tells how I knew he was absent—because his supervisor was looking for him.

Use a comma before a terminal adverb clause that begins with *so that* when *so that* indicates result. Do not use a comma when *so that* indicates purpose.

Result: *Huckleberry Finn* combines strong plot and characterization with a profound insight into the human condition, *so that it can be read by children and adults alike.*

Purpose: Oliver Twist set out for London *so that he could escape punishment by the beadle.*

With nonessential appositives and adjective clauses

Use commas to set off a nonessential appositive. Do not use commas to set off an essential appositive.

A nonessential, or nonrestrictive, appositive gives additional information about the noun it refers to but is not essential to the meaning of the noun or the sentence. In the following sentences, the nonessential appositives appear in *italics*.

> Neil Armstrong, *winner of the 1970 Silver Buffalo award for distinguished service to youth,* was the first man to walk on the moon.
>
> Duke Ellington, *a famous composer and bandleader,* helped gain acceptance for jazz as a serious musical form.
>
> St. Augustine, *the oldest city in the United States,* was founded by the Spanish.

An essential, or restrictive, appositive identifies the noun it refers to. As its name suggests, it is essential to the meaning of the sentence. In the following sentences, the essential appositives appear in *italics*.

> My friend *George* works in a bookstore.
>
> The word *nice* has undergone many changes in meaning.
>
> Truman Capote's book *In Cold Blood* established a new literary form.

Use commas to set off a nonessential adjective clause. Do not use commas to set off an essential adjective clause.

A nonessential, or nonrestrictive, adjective clause provides extra information about the noun it modifies but is not essential to the meaning of the noun or the sentence. In the following sentences, the nonessential adjective clauses appear in *italics*.

> Dinah Washington, *whom many consider the queen of the blues,* sang with Lionel Hampton's band.
>
> Elvis Presley, *whose records still sell well,* is regarded as the king of rock 'n' roll.
>
> Modern dance, *which was originated by Martha Graham,* has had a profound influence on the dance world.

An essential, or restrictive, adjective clause limits or identifies the noun it refers to. It is essential to the meaning of the sentence. In the following sentences, the essential adjective clauses appear in *italics*.

> The person *who buys the first ticket* will win a trip to Mexico.

135

The scientist *whose research is judged the most important* will be given a grant.

The performance *that they gave last night* was not up to their usual standard.

Note: The pronoun *that* is used only with essential clauses. The pronoun *which* may be used with either essential or nonessential clauses.

Whether or not an adjective clause is set off with commas can make a major difference to the meaning of a sentence. For example, compare the following two sentences:

Essential: The first president who was born in Virginia was George Washington.

Nonessential: The first president, who was born in Virginia, was George Washington.

The first sentence tells you that George Washington was the first Virginia-born president. The second sentence tells you that George Washington was the first president. As additional information, it mentions that he was born in Virginia.

Now compare the next two sentences.

Essential: The first president who was born in New York was Martin Van Buren.

Nonessential: The first president, who was born in New York, was Martin Van Buren.

The first sentence tells you that Martin Van Buren was the first New York-born president. This statement is true. However, the second sentence says that Martin Van Buren was the first president. This statement is obviously not true.

Finally, compare these two sentences.

Essential: The tenants who did not pay their rent were evicted.

Nonessential: The tenants, who did not pay their rent, were evicted.

The first sentence tells you that only the tenants who did not pay their rent were evicted. The second sentence tells you that all the tenants were evicted. As additional information, it tells the reason they were evicted: they did not pay their rent.

With dates and addresses

With dates, use commas to separate the day of the week from the month, the day of the month from the year, and the year from the rest of the sentence.

> Please reply by Tuesday, January 7.
> The *Titanic* hit an iceberg and sank on April 15, 1912.
> The Allies landed at Normandy on Tuesday, June 6, 1944, and began the offensive that would lead to the downfall of the Third Reich.

Note: Do not use a comma when only the month and the day or only the month and the year are given.

With addresses, use a comma to separate the name from the street address, the street address from the city, and the city from the state. Use a comma after the zip code (or after the state if no zip code is given) to separate the entire address from the rest of the sentence. Do not use a comma between the state and the zip code.

> The book is available from the Macmillan Publishing Company, 866 Third Avenue, New York, New York 10022.
> He lived at 579 Montenegro Avenue, Frisco, Colorado, until 1982.

Misused commas

Do not use a comma to separate a subject from its predicate.

> **Not:** The album that he cut last year, sold over a million copies.
> **But:** The album that he sold last year sold over a million copies.
>
> **Not:** The painting hanging on the wall, was of the last duchess.
> **But:** The painting hanging on the wall was of the last duchess.
>
> **Not:** How a bill becomes a law, was the subject discussed in class today.
> **But:** How a bill becomes a law was the subject discussed in class today.

Do not use a comma to separate a verb from its complement.

Not: Did you know, that chimpanzees can communicate through sign language?

But: Did you know that chimpanzees can communicate through sign language?

Not: After discussing the issue for several hours, we realized that our decision must be, to place safety concerns before cost considerations.

But: After discussing the issue for several hours, we realized that our decision must be to place safety concerns before cost considerations.

Not: The speaker declared that the government must let us know, why we are involved in this conflict.

But: The speaker declared that the government must let us know why we are involved in this conflict.

Do not use a comma between cumulative adjectives.

Not: She declared him to be a handsome, young man.
But: She declared him to be a handsome young man.

Not: He was sentenced to a nine-year, prison term.
But: He was sentenced to a nine-year prison term.

Not: She wore a knee-length, red, suede skirt.
But: She wore a knee-length red suede skirt.

Do not use a comma to separate the two parts of a compound subject, a compound verb, or a compound complement.

Not: High ceilings, and cathedral windows are two features I look for in a house.

But: High ceilings and cathedral windows are two features I look for in a house.

Not: The skier cleaned his boots, and then sprayed them with a water repellent.

But: The skier cleaned his boots and then sprayed them with a water repellent.

THE COMMA **18**

Not: For breakfast he ordered a ham omelet **,** and a side dish of home fries.

But: For breakfast he ordered a ham omelet and a side dish of home fries.

Do not use a comma to separate two dependent clauses joined by *and*.

Not: They promised that they would obey the laws of their new country **,** and that they would uphold its principles.

But: They promised that they would obey the laws of their new country and that they would uphold its principles.

Not: Anyone who attends this school **,** and who lives off-campus must sign this list.

But: Anyone who attends this school and who lives off-campus must sign this list.

Not: He wrote that he would stop loving her when dogs could fly **,** and when fish could sing.

But: He wrote that he would stop loving her when dogs could fly and when fish could sing.

Do not use a comma to separate the parts of a comparison.

Not: During the five months she spent alone in the woods, she was more productive **,** than she had ever been before.

But: During the five months she spent alone in the woods, she was more productive than she had ever been before.

Not: The situation is not as bad **,** as we had expected.

But: The situation is not as bad as we had expected.

Not: It is difficult to imagine another museum containing such a magnificent collection of medieval art **,** as the Cloisters in New York City.

But: It is difficult to imagine another museum containing such a magnificent collection of medieval art as the Cloisters in New York City.

Do not use a comma before an opening parenthesis. However, a comma may follow a closing parenthesis.

Not: David McCullough, who wrote *The Path Between the Seas*, (winner of a National Book Award) visited the Panama Canal.

But: David McCullough, who wrote *The Path Between the Seas* (winner of a National Book Award), visited the Panama Canal.

Exercise 1. Identify where commas are needed in the following sentences. Some of the sentences are correct as written.

1. In the 1970's the music industry experienced falling sales but in the 1980's video cassettes gave new life to the industry.

2. Bring the soup to a boil and then let it simmer.

3. Read Jane Austen's *Persuasion* and George Eliot's *Middlemarch* if you want to better understand the nineteenth-century woman.

4. He said he would announce his decision in the morning for he wanted time to speak to his advisers.

5. After the performance the actor removed his makeup and took off his costume.

6. In the back of this book you will find a glossary, a brief atlas, and an index.

7. At this clinic the hearing-impaired learn to use hearing aids to read lips and to understand sign language.

8. The picture in the hall and the one in the library are by the same artist.

9. Mac, Sal and Harry are the three candidates for class president.

10. She vowed to stop throwing away her money and wasting her time.

Exercise 2. Identify where commas are needed in the following sentences. Some of the sentences are correct as written.

1. The chairperson opened the meeting with a long boring recital of his goals.

2. Did you read their list of the twenty best modern novels?

3. The senator was praised for her long distinguished career.

4. On top of the bureau sat a big yellow cat.

5. By the way have you seen the new exhibit at the museum?

6. Why he was in town just last week.

7. In the middle of the night we heard the screeching of sirens.

8. I can't solve this equation can you?

9. The lecture will be held in Maxwell Hall not in Jefferson.

10. Dag Hammarskjöld, secretary general of the United Nations was killed in a plane crash.

Exercise 3. Identify where commas are needed in the following sentences. Some of the sentences are correct as written.

1. Hammurabi, you probably know was a Babylonian king.

2. The Carthaginian general Hannibal led his army across the Alps.

3. Benito Juárez, a Mexican hero took part in the overthrow of Santa Anna.

4. This new sweetener however is not completely safe.

5. Little is known about the life of Confucius whose teachings are the basis of Confucianism.

6. Zaire which was formerly called the Belgian Congo is located in south-central Africa.

7. He competed in the race although he had no hope of winning.

8. The article that I read last night is about primitive art.

9. "Few people can be happy" claimed Bertrand Russell "unless they hate some other person, nation, or creed."

10. "Anybody who hates children and dogs," said W. C. Fields "can't be all bad."

Exercise 4. Identify where commas are needed in the following sentences. Some of the sentences are correct as written.

1. As a result of *Brand* and *Peer Gynt* Ibsen became known around the world.

2. The author of what is considered one of the great novels of modern times Marcel Proust had to subsidize the publishing of *Swann's Way* himself.

3. Because most of us have read *The Scarlet Letter* we are familiar with Hawthorne's views on the nature of sin.

4. Hawthorne gained notice after the publication of *The Scarlet Letter*.

5. Samuel Johnson who wrote *Lives of the Poets* which consists of fifty-two brief biographies is perhaps best remembered for his dictionary.

6. James Boswell on the other hand is best remembered for his biography of his friend Dr. Johnson.

7. He obviously had not read the work since he failed to answer the question about it.

8. The library will be open even though the rest of the school will be closed.

9. While at times he is brooding and introspective at other times he is fun-loving and outgoing.

10. According to the police psychologist the murderer left his lighter at the scene of the crime so that he would be discovered.

19 The semicolon

The semicolon links independent clauses or separates items in a series. The semicolon indicates a pause longer than that taken for a comma but not so long as that taken for a period.

Between independent clauses

Use a semicolon between two closely related independent clauses not joined by a coordinating conjunction or by another connecting word.

> Years ago caviar was an inexpensive food often given away free at taverns; today it is one of the most expensive foods in the world.
> Truffles are the food of the rich; turnips are the food of the poor.
> Truffles are the food of the rich; turnips, of the poor.

The comma in the third sentence indicates that a part of the second clause has been left out.

Use a semicolon between two independent clauses joined by a conjunctive adverb or by a transitional phrase.

Columbus sent cacao beans back to Spain; however, the Spanish were not particularly impressed.

Cortez brought back more cacao beans; moreover, he brought back the knowledge of how to prepare them.

In some cultures insects are considered delicacies; for example, the ancient Romans thought the cicada a delightful morsel.

Use a semicolon between two independent clauses joined with a coordinating conjunction if one or both of these clauses contain internal commas or if the clauses are particularly complex.

With fairly short clauses, either a comma or a semicolon is acceptable.

Persephone was the daughter of Demeter, the goddess of agriculture, and she was represented by the pomegranate, the symbol of fertility.

Persephone was the daughter of Demeter, the goddess of agriculture; and she was represented by the pomegranate, the symbol of fertility.

With longer and more complex clauses, the semicolon is preferred.

In Greek mythology Persephone was the daughter of Demeter, the goddess of agriculture; and she was represented by the pomegranate, the symbol of fertility, of which she ate the seeds after Hades carried her down into the underworld.

In Italy during the Renaissance, the inside of the opened pomegranate, which is divided into compartments containing colorful seeds, was used as the basis for a popular fabric design; and in the Middle East during ancient times, this beautiful fruit figured prominently in the decorative arts.

Because of its abundance of seeds, some Westerners find the pomegranate, which originated in the Middle East, unpalatable as a food, although pleasing as a decoration; but supporters of the pomegranate, of whom there are many, find the seeds no drawback, since they like to chew these crunchy tidbits.

Between items in a series

Use semicolons to separate items in a series if the individual items are long or contain commas.

> In the language of flowers, each flower represents a particular attribute: belladonna, which is a deadly poison, silence; citron, which produces a sour, inedible fruit, ill-natured beauty; blue periwinkle, which is small and delicate, early friendship.
>
> The guide grouped wildflowers into many families, four of which were the cattail family, Typhaceae; the arrowhead family, Alismataceae; the yellow-eyed grass family, Xyridaceae; and the lizard-tail family, Saururaceae.

Misused semicolons

Do not use a semicolon between noncoordinate elements.

> **Not:** In Shakespeare's *Hamlet*, after Ophelia is rebuffed; she communicates her despair through the language of flowers.
>
> **But:** In Shakespeare's *Hamlet*, after Ophelia is rebuffed, she communicates her despair through the language of flowers.

> **Not:** She became famous for her photographs of wildflowers; especially for those of mountain laurel.
>
> **But:** She became famous for her photographs of wildflowers, especially for those of mountain laurel.

Exercise. Identify where the punctuation mark should be replaced by a semicolon in each of the following sentences. Two of the sentences are correct as written.

1. Some people collect rocks and minerals, others, seashells.

2. The color of turquoise ranges from sky blue to apple green, however, gem-quality turquoise is blue.

3. Turquoise can be found in the American Southwest; however, the finest turquoise comes from Iran.

4. Quartz is abundant in North America, for example, it can be found in Ontario, New Jersey, Arkansas, Colorado, and California.

5. Amethyst, which is a violet to red-purple quartz, is particularly beautiful, as a result, it is often used for jewelry.

6. Tigereye, a quartz with a changeable luster, is often used for cameos, which are stones cut in such a way that the raised design is of one hue and the background of another, and, like adventurine and rose quartz, it is fashioned into cabochons, which are highly polished, unfaceted gems.

7. Like rocks and minerals, seashells can be used for decoration, in fact, they can be found on Greek and Roman vases as well as in modern jewelry.

8. Some members of the cowry family are particularly interesting: the measled cowry, *Cypraea zebra*, which has circular white spots on its back, the chestnut cowry, *Cypraea spadicea*, which has an irregular spot of light chestnut or grayish brown on the middle of its back, and the Atlantic gray cowry, *Cypraea cinerea*, which has small blackish spots or streaks on its sides.

9. One living mollusk that is particularly beautiful is the ringed top shell, another is the four-toothed nerite.

10. Many of the shells called jewel boxes are also brightly colored, but most jingle shells are translucent.

20 The colon

The colon introduces elements that explain, illustrate, or expand the preceding part of the sentence. It calls attention to the word, phrase, clause, or quotation that follows it.

Before elements introduced formally

Use a colon when formally introducing a statement or a quotation.

Capitalize the first word of a formal statement or a quotation following a colon.

> One of the guiding principles of our government may be stated as follows: All people are created equal.
> In reference to Charles Laughton's refusal to play Falstaff, James Agate quotes Laughton as saying: "I had to throw too many of his kind out of our hotel when I was sixteen."

Use a colon when formally introducing a series of items.

> The picture gallery at the Vatican contains magnificent treasures: Raphael's *Madonna of Foligno*, Titian's *Madonna of San Niccolô dei Frari*, Leonardo's *St. Jerome*, Caravaggio's *Deposition*, Rouault's *Autumn*, and Utrillo's *The Church of St.-Auxonne*.
>
> From 1933 through 1981, unsuccessful assassination attempts were made on the lives of the following presidents: Franklin Roosevelt, Harry Truman, Gerald Ford, and Ronald Reagan.
>
> Nine planets circle the sun: Mercury, Venus, Earth, Mars, Jupiter, Saturn, Uranus, Neptune, and Pluto.

Before formal appositives

Use a colon before a formal appositive, including one beginning with a phrase such as *namely, that is, specifically,* or *in other words.*

In many cases a dash would also be appropriate in this situation.

> The scholar wrote mysteries for one reason and one reason only: to make money.
>
> Domemicos Theotocopoulos, whom many consider one of the greatest painters of all times, is better known by his pseudonym: El Greco.
>
> In 1961 Kennedy made one of the toughest decisions of his presidency: namely, to back the invasion at the Bay of Pigs.

Notice that the colon in the third example appears *before* the word *namely*.

Between two independent clauses

Use a colon between two independent clauses when the second clause explains or expands the first.

> Cubism was more than a new movement: it was a revolution.
>
> After reading the letter, he did something that surprised me: he laughed.

The clause following the colon may begin with a capital or a lower-case letter. However, a lower-case letter is preferred.

In salutations and bibliographical entries

Use a colon after a salutation in a formal letter or speech.

> Dear Dr. Jacoby:
> Ladies and Gentlemen:
> Members of the Board:

Use a colon between the city and the publisher in a bibliographical entry.

> New York: Macmillan
> London: John Murray
> Chicago: The University of Chicago Press

Use a colon between a title and its subtitle.

> *Tutankhamun: The Untold Story*
> *Nooks and Crannies: An Unusual Walking Tour Guide to New York City*
> *The Seeing Hand: A Treasury of Great Master Drawings*

Misused colons

Do not use a colon after a form of the verb *be*, after a preposition, or between a verb and its object.

> **Not:** Three devices the ancient Romans used to tell time were: sundials, water clocks, and sand-filled glasses.
> **But:** Three devices the ancient Romans used to tell time were sundials, water clocks, and sand-filled glasses.
> **Or:** The Romans used three devices to tell time: sundials, water clocks, and sand-filled glasses.

> **Not:** In 1966 France effectively withdrew from NATO, which thereafter consisted of: Belgium, Canada, Denmark, Great Britain, Greece, Iceland, Italy, Luxembourg, the Netherlands, Norway, Portugal, Turkey, the United States, and West Germany.
> **But:** In 1966 France effectively withdrew from NATO, which thereafter consisted of Belgium, Canada, Denmark, Great Britain, Greece, Iceland, Italy, Luxembourg, the Nether-

lands, Norway, Portugal, Turkey, the United States, and West Germany.

Not: The store manager ordered**:** six microwave ovens, four dishwashers, seven coffee makers, and eleven toasters.

But: The store manager ordered six microwave ovens, four dishwashers, seven coffee makers, and eleven toasters.

Exercise. Identify where a colon is necessary in each of the following sentences. Some of the sentences are correct as written.

1. Poets would do well to listen to Ezra Pound "Music rots when it gets *too far* from the dance. Poetry atrophies when it gets *too far* from music."

2. The United Kingdom includes England, Scotland, Wales, and Northern Ireland.

3. Although titled *Trout Fishing in America*, Brautigan's book is not about trout fishing it is about life.

4. She subscribes to the following magazines *Smithsonian, Newsweek, Time,* and *The Atlantic.*

5. The reference books he has at home are an atlas, an almanac, two dictionaries, and an encyclopedia.

21 The dash

The dash is less formal than the colon. It is used to give emphasis or clarity to extra information in a sentence. When typing, indicate a dash by two hyphens without a space before, after, or between them.

With an introductory series

Use a dash to separate an introductory series from its summarizing clause.

His own party, the opposition, and the public——all were astounded by his resignation.

Chaucer, Shakespeare, Malory——these were his favorite writers.

With parenthetical elements

Use dashes to set off a parenthetical element you wish to emphasize.

> The castle was surrounded by a moat and contained——I found this astounding——an actual dungeon.
> On his first day as a volunteer, he fought a fire in——of all places——the firehouse.

Use dashes to clarify a parenthetical element that contains commas.

> Of our first five presidents, four——George Washington, Thomas Jefferson, James Madison, and James Monroe——came from Virginia.
> The first recorded Olympic Games——which, you will be surprised to know, this reporter did not see——were held in 776 B.C.

With terminal elements

Use a dash to introduce informally a terminal element that explains or illustrates the information in the main part of the sentence.

> They pledged to prevent what seemed inevitable——war.
> He battled his worst enemy——himself.
> He little appreciated her greatest attribute——her sense of humor.

Use a dash to introduce informally a terminal element that is a break in thought or a shift in tone.

> He confessed that he was desperately in love——with me.
> No one loves a gossip——except another gossip.
> "But she said she had——I can't believe it," Patrick exclaimed.

Exercise. Indicate where dashes belong in each of the following sentences.

1. Wordsworth, Keats, Shelley, Byron these are the most popular of the Romantic poets.

2. People who live in glass houses shouldn't throw stones and neither should you!

3. Three of the most beautiful bridges in the world the Brooklyn Bridge, the George Washington Bridge, and the Verrazano-Narrows Bridge are in New York City.

4. We found Dr. Jekyll in his library no one will believe this changing into Mr. Hyde.

5. The speaker hesitated, then sputtered, "I just want to let me start again."

22 Parentheses

Parentheses enclose information or comments that break the continuity of the sentence or paragraph. Unlike the dash, which tends to emphasize, parentheses minimize the importance of the material they enclose. The information within parentheses should be of such a nature that it may be omitted without changing the essential meaning of the sentence.

With parenthetical comments and additional information

Use parentheses to enclose comments or additional information that you do not wish to emphasize.

On August 11, 1960, Chad (see map) became independent.
Charles Darwin (1809–1882) was a contemporary of Abraham Lincoln.
Ibsen's *A Doll's House* (which was quite revolutionary for its time) ends with Nora walking out on her husband.

Do not use a capital letter or a period for a parenthetical sentence within another sentence. Use a capital letter and a period for a parenthetical sentence that stands by itself.

Sentence within another sentence

After the Civil War, carpetbaggers (their name came from their habit of carrying their belongings in a bag made of carpet material**)** took advantage of Southern blacks who had just been given the vote.

Demosthenes warned the Athenians against King Philip of Macedon **(**he felt King Philip was a threat to their liberty**)**.

The Democratic Party **(**this is the party founded by that lover of liberty, Thomas Jefferson**)** was divided on the question of slavery.

Notice that in the second example the period ending the main sentence goes *outside* the closing parenthesis.

Sentence standing by itself

In the fifteenth century Christian I founded the Oldenburg dynasty. **(**In modern Denmark the ruling family traces its roots to him●**)** Christian II, however, was removed from the throne in 1523.

Elizabeth Barrett Browning is remembered in part for her beautiful love poems. **(**She was married to Robert Browning●**)**

In the original *King Kong*, the huge creature climbed what was then the tallest building in the world, the Empire State Building. **(**In the second version of the movie, he climbed the World Trade Center●**)** There he was attacked by airplanes.

Notice that the period ending the parenthetical sentence goes *inside* the closing parenthesis.

With items in a series

Use parentheses to enclose numerals and letters designating items in a series.

When accepting a credit card from a customer, you should **(**a**)** check the customer's signature against the card, **(**b**)** call the credit-card company for approval, and **(**c**)** write the approval code on the credit slip.

In the nineteenth century the United States was involved in four wars: **(**1**)** the War of 1812, **(**2**)** the Mexican War, **(**3**)** the Civil War, and **(**4**)** the Spanish-American War.

With other punctuation marks

Place a comma, semicolon, or colon *outside* a closing parenthesis.

Although most Americans have heard of the Battle of Lexington and Concord (which occurred on April 19, 1775**),** many do not know that it is commemorated as Patriots' Day in Massachusetts.

Maine has successfully preserved its northern moose population (the moose is Maine's official state animal**);** however, the state's deer population is now endangered by the growing moose herd.

Carter carried only six states (plus the District of Columbia**):** Georgia, Hawaii, Maryland, Minnesota, Rhode Island, and West Virginia.

Place a question mark or exclamation point inside a closing parenthesis if the parenthetical expression itself is a question or an exclamation.

Sean was astonished when he opened the door to his room and found a letter (who could have put it there**?)** lying on the floor.

The Founding Fathers considered many different animals (Benjamin Franklin suggested the turkey**!)** before they decided to make the bald eagle the national symbol of the United States.

Place a question mark or exclamation point outside a closing parenthesis if the sentence is a question or exclamation but the parenthetical expression is not.

Did you know that Lewis Carroll wrote *Alice in Wonderland* for a real girl named Alice (Alice Liddell**)?**

Never was I more surprised than when I found wild berries growing in a New York City park (there were both raspberries and blackberries**)!**

23 Brackets

Brackets enclose information inserted into quotations, and they take the place of parentheses within parentheses. Brackets are used mainly in formal writing.

With inserted information

Use brackets to enclose information inserted into direct quotations for clarification.

> "The fellow [Rubens] mixes blood with his colors," claimed Guido Reni.
> Groucho Marx quipped, "From the moment I picked your [S. J. Perelman's] book up until I laid it down, I was convulsed with laughter. Someday I intend reading it."
> "Government [in a democracy] cannot be stronger or more tough-minded than its people," said Adlai Stevenson.

Use brackets to enclose editorial comments inserted into quoted material.

> According to Clarence Darrow, "The first half of our lives is ruined by our parents [how many people under twenty agree with this!] and the second half by our children."

Notice that the exclamation point is placed inside the closing bracket because it is part of the editorial comment.

The word *sic* or *thus* enclosed in brackets is used to indicate that an incorrect or seemingly incorrect or inappropriate word is not a mistake on the part of the present writer but appears in the original quotation.

> Jane Austen parodied the popular melodramatic fiction of her day in "Love and Freindship [*sic*]," which she completed at the age of fourteen.

Notice that the comma is placed outside the closing bracket.

With parentheses

Use brackets to replace parentheses within parentheses.

> Some humpback whales reach a length of over fifty feet. (See p. 89 [chart] for a comparison of the size of whales.)
> Several books are available on the life and times of "Boss" Tweed. (For a revisionist picture of Tweed, we suggest Leo Hershkowitz's *Tweed's New York* [Garden City, N.Y.: Anchor Press/Doubleday, 1977].)

Notice that the period is placed inside the closing parenthesis because the entire sentence is enclosed by parentheses.

> The reading list contains several books dealing with the issue of freedom of the press (for example, Fred W. Friendly's *Minnesota Rag: The Dramatic Story of the Landmark Supreme Court Case That Gave New Meaning to Freedom of the Press* [New York: Random House, 1981]).

Notice that the period is placed outside the closing parenthesis because only part of the sentence is enclosed by parentheses.

Exercise. Add parentheses and/or brackets where necessary to enclose information in each of the following sentences.

1. According to George Bernard Shaw, "The road to ignorance is paved with good editions *sic*."

2. Until recently, Picasso's *Guernica* see p. 458 could be seen at the Museum of Modern Art.

3. A month after the assassination of Archduke Franz Ferdinand on June 28, 1914, Emperor Franz Josef Austria declared war on Serbia.

4. Unlike many paintings of the time, the portraits of Modigliani show a world of tranquility how far away this world is from the reality of Modigliani's life!.

5. Dance plays an important role in the art of the early part of the twentieth century. (In 1909 Matisse completed his mural *The Dance* [see plate 7.

24 Quotation marks

Quotation marks enclose quoted material and certain kinds of titles. They are always used in pairs.

For direct quotations

Use quotation marks to enclose a direct quotation—the exact words of a speaker or writer.

When one character says to Mae West, **"**My goodness, those diamonds are beautiful,**"** West replies, **"**Goodness had nothing whatever to do with it.**"**

In *The Code of the Woosters*, Bertie vividly describes the aunt he fears: **"**Aunt Agatha, who eats broken bottles and wears barbed wire next to the skin.**"**

The opening lines set the tone of the poem: **"**I will be the gladdest thing/Under the sun!**"** (*The slash indicates the end of a line.*)

When writing dialogue, begin a new paragraph each time the speaker changes.

> **"**This coat costs $25.00,**"** said the seller at the flea market.
> **"**That's too much,**"** said the customer.
> **"**Did I say $25.00?**"** responded the seller. **"**I meant $15.00.**"**

When quoting four or more lines of prose, single-space the material and indent it five spaces from the left margin. (If the first line begins a new paragraph, indent this line an additional five spaces.) Do not use quotation marks.

In <u>Slang in America</u>, Walt Whitman wrote:

> Language is not an abstract construction of the learned, or of dictionary-makers, but is something arising out of the work, needs, ties, joys, affections, tastes, of long generations of humanity, and has its bases broad and low, close to the ground.

In a speech he made in New York in 1912, Woodrow Wilson underscored the importance of business:

> Business underlies everything in our national life, including our spiritual life. Witness the fact that in the Lord's Prayer the first petition is for daily bread. No one can worship God or love his neighbor on an empty stomach.

In <u>Psychological Types</u>, Jung stated:

> The dynamic principle of fantasy is play, which belongs also to the child, and as such it

> appears to be inconsistent with the principle of
> serious work. But without this playing with fan-
> tasy no creative work has ever yet come to birth.
> The debt we owe to the play of imagination is in-
> calculable.

When quoting four or more lines of poetry, single-space the lines and indent each line five spaces. Type the poem line for line. Do not use quotation marks.

> In Hinton's The Outsiders, the protagonist, a
>
> street-smart kid you might not expect to respond to
>
> poetry, is moved by Robert Frost's poem "Nothing Gold
>
> Can Stay."
>
>> Nature's first green is gold,
>> Her hardest hue to hold.
>> Her early leaf's a flower;
>> But only so an hour.
>> Then leaf subsides to leaf.
>> So Eden sank to grief,
>> So dawn goes down to day.
>> Nothing gold can stay.
>
> In the first four lines of "Oysters," Anne Sexton
>
> makes the oysters seem human.
>
>> Oysters we ate,
>> sweet blue babies,
>> twelve eyes looked up at me,
>> running with lemon and Tabasco.

For quotations within quotations

Use single quotation marks to enclose quoted material contained in a quotation.

> In "Silence," Marianne Moore wrote: "My father used to say,/ 'Superior people never make long visits.'"
> The British humorist Robert Morley once joked, "Beware of the conversationalist who adds 'in other words.' He is merely starting afresh."

Jensen looked up from his research and declared, "I've found the answer. It was Henry Clay who said, 'I would rather be right than President.'"

For titles of short works

Use quotation marks to enclose the quoted titles of short stories, short poems, one-act plays, essays, articles, subdivisions of books, episodes of a television series, songs, short musical compositions, and dissertations.

In his poem "Son of Frankenstein," Edward Field reveals the loneliness of the Frankenstein monster.

In the second half of *Brideshead Revisited*, which is entitled "A Twitch upon the Thread," Charles returns from South America, and Lord Marchmain returns to Brideshead to die.

Joan Didion details the pattern of shopping malls in "On the Mall."

Use underlining for the titles of longer works. (See pages 160–161.)

With other punctuation marks

Place a period or a comma *inside* a closing quotation mark.

In "Perseid," John Barth writes, "Stories last longer than men, stones than stories, stars than stones."

"I don't want to talk grammar," Eliza Doolittle says in *Pygmalion*. "I want to talk like a lady."

"After all," says Scarlett, "tomorrow is another day."

Place a semicolon or a colon *outside* a closing quotation mark.

The critic wrote that the play demonstrated the playwright's "dissatisfaction with satisfaction"; this comment, I felt, was more preposterous than the play itself.

In the American detective story, few women are private eyes. One of the best known of these women appears in Stuart Palmer's "The Riddle of the Twelve Amethysts": Hildegarde Withers.

Place a question mark or an exclamation point inside a closing quotation mark if the quotation itself is a question or exclamation.

> The song I was trying to recall is "Will You Love Me in December?"
>
> Upon reaching the summit of Mount Everest, Sherpa Tensing declared, "We've done the bugger!"

Place a question mark or an exclamation point outside the closing quotation mark if the sentence is a question or exclamation but the quotation itself is not.

> Who first said, "Big Brother is watching you"?
>
> What a scene she caused by saying, "I don't want to"!

If both the sentence and the quotation are questions or exclamations, use only one question mark or exclamation point, and place it *inside* the closing quotation mark.

Of course, the rules for using other punctuation marks with quotation marks apply to single quotation marks as well.

> Harold asked, "Do you know who coined the term 'the brain trust'?" (*Question mark ends Harold's quotation.*)
>
> Gordon said, "I can hear the crowd shouting, 'Long live the king!'" (*Exclamation point ends quotation within quotation.*)

Misused quotation marks

Do not use quotation marks to enclose indirect quotations.

> **Not:** The seer declared that "they would win the war against the Macedonians."
>
> **But:** The seer declared that they would win the war against the Macedonians.
>
> **Not:** The editorial proclaimed that "the President would win the next election."
>
> **But:** The editorial proclaimed that the President would win the next election.

Do not use quotation marks to enclose a title used as the heading of a paper, theme, or essay.

> Suicide and the Modern Poet
> Science Fiction in the 1930's
> Communication Among Chimpanzees

Exercise. Identify where quotation marks are needed in the following sentences. Some of the sentences do not need quotation marks.

1. Aristotle said, There is no great genius without a mixture of madness.

2. Who claimed that genius is only great patience?

3. Drew asked, Do you know who called a best-seller a gilded tomb of mediocre talent?

4. Have you read Jayne Anne Phillips' short story The Heavenly Animal?

5. Charlotte advised, Try to remember Cicero's statement on grief: There is no grief which time does not lessen and soften.

6. Balzac said, If we could but paint with the hand as we see with the eye!

7. The best is the cheapest, announced Ben Franklin.

8. Nature, like man, declared Disraeli, sometimes weeps for gladness.

9. Robert Frost concludes his poem Birches with the line, One could do worse than be a swinger of birches.

10. One review described the book as a waste of time and paper; however, another called it a soufflé of words and experiences.

25 Ellipsis points

Ellipsis points are equally spaced dots, or periods. They indicate that part of a quotation has been omitted.

Use three ellipsis points within a quotation to indicate that part of the quotation has been left out, or omitted.

When typing, leave a space before the first ellipsis point, a space between each of the points, and a space after the last point.

> In *The Other America: Poverty in the United States*, Michael Harrington writes: "They [the poor] are not simply neglected ● ● ● they are not seen."
>
> In *The Quiet Crisis*, Stewart Udall writes: "The most common trait ● ● ● is a reverence for the life-giving earth, and the native American shared this elemental ethic: the land was alive to his touch, and he, its son, was brother to all creatures."
>
> The Atlantic Charter states: "Eighth, they believe that all of the nations of the world ● ● ● must come to the abandonment of the use of force."

Use a period and three ellipsis points to indicate that the end of a sentence has been left out of a quotation.

> Huck said, "It most frose me to hear such talk● ● ● ● Thinks I, this is what comes of my not thinking."
>
> The review said, "The book promises a cornucopia of unusual characters● ● ● ● That promise is fully realized."
>
> In Susan Fromberg Schaeffer's *The Madness of a Seduced Woman*, Margaret says, "I don't read books much anymore because I don't much care about how things turn out● ● ● ● What interests me, I suppose, is how people get to where they find themselves in the end."

26 Underlining

Underlining in a typed or handwritten paper serves the same purpose as italics in a printed work. It highlights, or sets apart, certain titles, words, or phrases.

Underline the titles of books, full-length musical compositions, plays, and long poems and the names of newspapers, magazines, ships, boats, and aircraft.

> The Light in the Forest (*book*)

Madame Butterfly (*opera*)
The Rape of the Lock (*long poem*)
the Mayflower (*ship*)

Be careful to underline only the exact title or name. Do not underline words added to complete the meaning of the title.

The Atlantic magazine (*The word* magazine *is not part of the name.*)
the London Times or The Times of London (London *is not part of the name.*)

Be careful to underline all the words that make up the title.

The Decline and Fall of the Roman Empire (The *is part of the title.*)
A Childhood (A *is part of the title.*)
Standard & Poor's New Issue Investor (Standard & Poor's *is part of the title.*)

(Do not underline the heading of your own paper.)

Underline foreign words or phrases that are not commonly used in English.

In general, a word or phrase need not be underlined if it is listed in a standard English dictionary. For example, the Spanish word *siesta*, the French phrase *coup de grace*, and the Latin phrase *ad infinitum* are now considered part of English and are not underlined.

German women were traditionally expected to confine themselves to Kinder, Kirche, Küche.
Chacun à son goût proved a difficult principle to apply in this case.
The great English public schools attempted to follow the ideal of mens sana in corpore sano.

Underline letters, words, or phrases being named.

How many i's are in Mississippi?

His life demonstrates the meaning of the word <u>waste</u>.

What is the derivation of the phrase <u>on the ball</u>?

In most cases, it is also appropriate to use quotation marks instead of underlining for this purpose.

Underline words and phrases for emphasis.

I did <u>not</u> say I would do that.

You <u>must</u> stop overeating!

You plan to do <u>what</u>?

Do not overuse this device. Too much underlining weakens the effect. Emphasize only what deserves emphasis.

Exercise. Identify which items should be underlined in each of the following sentences.

1. Satirical portraits were a regular feature in the Tatler and the Spectator, two periodicals of the eighteenth century.

2. What does the word satire mean?

3. One of Swift's satires is called A Tale of a Tub; another is called The Battle of the Books.

4. However, Swift is best remembered for Gulliver's Travels, which brought the words yahoo and lilliputian into our language.

5. Of Voltaire's satiric novels, Candide is best remembered; this novel stands in opposition to Pope's optimistic Essay on Man.

27 Abbreviations

In general, avoid abbreviations in formal writing. However, abbreviations are acceptable in certain situations.

Use an abbreviation for the following designations preceding names.

Mr.   Messrs.   St. or Ste. (Saint)

Mrs.	Mmes.	Mt. (Mount)
Ms.	Dr.	Rev. (unless preceded by *the*)

Is **Mrs.** Dalloway a fully realized character?
For what musicals are **Messrs.** Rogers and Hart responsible?
Rev. James Spenser read the service.

Note: Spell out *Reverend* when it is preceded by *the*.

The **Reverend** James Spenser read the service.

Do not use an abbreviation for any other designation preceding a name.

Not: No one was surprised when **Pres.** Reagan said that he would run again.
But: No one was surprised when **President** Reagan said that he would run again.

Not: Are you campaigning for **Sen.** Jones?
But: Are you campaigning for **Senator** Jones?

Not: In his new book, **Prof.** Rosenthal discusses the use of imagery in the poetry of Ted Hughes.
But: In his new book, **Professor** Rosenthal discusses the use of imagery in the poetry of Ted Hughes.

Use an abbreviation preceded by a comma for a designation or an academic degree following a name.

Jr.	Ph.D. (Doctor of Philosophy)
Sr.	Ed.D. (Doctor of Education)
Esq.	D.D.S. (Doctor of Dental Science)
B.A. (Bachelor of Arts)	D.D. (Doctor of Divinity)
B.S. (Bachelor of Science)	J.D. (Doctor of Jurisprudence)
M.A. (Master of Arts)	D.V.M. (Doctor of Veterinary Medicine)
M.S. (Master of Science)	
M.D. (Doctor of Medicine)	

The speaker will be Thomas Dean, **Jr.**
The academy announced the appointment of Marion Unger, **Ph.D.**

Do not use the abbreviation *Dr.* before a name that is followed by an abbreviation denoting a doctoral degree.

Use abbreviations without periods for many well-known agencies, organizations, and businesses.

The newspaper accused the **CIA** of covert activities in that country.

The **YMHA** is presenting a revival of Arthur Miller's *All My Sons*.

The candidate sought the support of the **AFL–CIO**.

With numerals, use the abbreviations *B.C.* (before Christ) and *A.D.* (*anno Domini,* "in the year of the Lord") for dates. Use the abbreviations *A.M.* or *a.m.* (before noon) and *P.M.* or *p.m.* (after noon) for time.

Confucius, China's most important teacher and philosopher, was born in 551 **B.C.**

In **A.D.** 37, Caligula was made emperor of Rome.

The child was born at 6:37 **A.M.**

The abbreviation *B.C.* should be put after the date, and the abbreviation *A.D.* is usually put before the date. However, the practice of putting *A.D.* after the date is now also considered acceptable. *B.C.* and *A.D.* are sometimes replaced with the abbreviations *B.C.E.* (Before the Common Era) and *C.E.* (Common Era), respectively.

A.M. and *P.M.* may be written with either capital or lower-case letters, but be consistent within a single piece of writing.

Use the following abbreviations for common Latin words and expressions.

c. or *ca.* (about)	*etc.* (and others)
cf. (compare)	*i.e.* (that is)
e.g. (for example)	*viz.* (namely)

Moses (**c.** 1350–1250 B.C.) led his people out of slavery.

Taoism is based on the teachings of Lao-zu (**cf.** Confucianism).

Monotheistic religions (**e.g.,** Christianity and Islam) worship only one god.

Do not overuse these Latin abbreviations. Where possible, try substituting the English equivalent.

Spell out the names of days and months.

> **Not:** The first game of the World Series will be played on **Oct. 11.**
> **But:** The first game of the World Series will be played on **October 11.**
>
> **Not:** The committee met on **Wed.,** not **Thurs.**
> **But:** The committee met on **Wednesday,** not **Thursday.**
>
> **Not:** It snowed heavily on the first **Sat.** in **Dec.**
> **But:** It snowed heavily on the first **Saturday** in **December.**

Spell out the names of cities, states, and countries, except in addresses.

> **Not:** He came to **N.Y.C.** to study music.
> **But:** He came to **New York City** to study music.
>
> **Not:** Emily Dickinson was born in Amherst, **Mass.**
> **But:** Emily Dickinson was born in Amherst, **Massachusetts.**
>
> **Not:** The Mediterranean fruit fly was accidentally introduced into the **U.S.**
> **But:** The Mediterranean fruit fly was accidentally introduced into the **United States.**

Spell out first names.

> **Not:** The editor of this collection is **Thom.** Webster.
> **But:** The editor of this collection is **Thomas** Webster.
>
> **Not:** **Benj.** Disraeli worked for passage of the Reform Bill of 1867.
> **But:** **Benjamin** Disraeli worked for passage of the Reform Bill of 1867.
>
> **Not:** **Chas.** Lindbergh was the first person to fly nonstop across the Atlantic Ocean.
> **But:** **Charles** Lindbergh was the first person to fly nonstop across the Atlantic Ocean.

In names of businesses, spell out the words *Brothers, Corporation,* and *Company,* except in addresses or in bibliographic information.

> **Not:** She was employed by the firm of Magnum **Bros.**
> **But:** She was employed by the firm of Magnum **Brothers.**

> **Not:** The employees at Thomas Smythe and **Co.** are on strike.
> **But:** The employees at Thomas Smythe and **Company** are on strike.

In formal, nontechnical writing, spell out units of measure.

> **Not:** The pamphlet claims that anyone who is more than ten **lbs.** overweight is a candidate for a heart attack.
> **But:** The pamphlet claims that anyone who is more than ten **pounds** overweight is a candidate for a heart attack.

> **Not:** The father rebuked his lazy children with tales of how he had had to walk fifteen **mi.** to school each day.
> **But:** The father rebuked his lazy children with tales of how he had had to walk fifteen **miles** to school each day.

> **Not:** How many **qts.** of milk did you sell?
> **But:** How many **quarts** of milk did you sell?

In technical writing, abbreviations are acceptable and often preferred.

28 Contractions

A contraction is a shortened form of a word or words. In a contraction, an apostrophe takes the place of the missing letter or letters. Contractions are widely used in speech and in informal writing.

In general, avoid contractions in formal writing.

> **Informal:** During his lifetime, Mark Twain **didn't** receive the serious critical attention he deserved.

Formal: During his lifetime, Mark Twain **did not** receive the serious critical attention he deserved.

Informal: He asserted that it **isn't** necessary to separate Samuel Clemens from Mark Twain.

Formal: He asserted that it **is not** necessary to separate Samuel Clemens from Mark Twain.

Informal: She, on the other hand, claimed that **it's** important to know where the autobiography stops and the fiction begins.

Formal: She, on the other hand, claimed that **it is** important to know where the autobiography stops and the fiction begins.

29 Numerals

A numeral is a symbol that denotes a number. In formal, nontechnical writing, use numerals only in specific instances.

Use numerals for numbers that cannot be written as one or two words.

During its first year, the book sold only **678** copies.
There are **365** days in the normal year, and **366** days in the leap year.
Last Saturday this shop sold **1,059** doughnuts.

However, never begin a sentence with a numeral.

Nine hundred seventy-six people bought tickets for the concert, but only 341 attended.
Two hundred twenty-six poems are anthologized in this volume.
Three hundred sixteen photographs of San Francisco are on exhibit.

Spell out all numbers that can be written as one or two words and that modify a noun.

She sang a medley of **sixteen** Sondheim songs.
The gestation period for a rabbit is about **thirty-one** days.
We need **one hundred** squares to make this quilt.

Use numerals for decimals or fractions.

We had 2½ inches of rainfall last month.
What do they mean when they claim that the average family has 2.3 children?

Use numerals for addresses.

702 West 74th Street   **1616** South Street

However, it is acceptable to spell out the name of a numbered street in an address.

417 **Eleventh** Avenue   201 East **Seventh** Street

Use numerals for page numbers, percentages, degrees, and amounts of money with the symbol $ or ¢.

Turn to **page 82** for an analysis of the works of Van Gogh.
The survey found that **70.2%** of registered voters favor Brosnan.
The account yields **9.5 percent** interest annually.
An acute angle is an angle under **90°**.
The computer costs **$1,667.99.**

Use numerals for dates and for hours expressed with *A.M.* or *P.M.*

At **6:07 A.M.** the snow began to fall.
The First International Peace Conference, held at The Hague, began on May **18, 1899.**

Use numerals with units of measurement.

The course is **127** kilometers.
The room is **11′7″** × **13′4″.**
The tree is **6′5″** from the garage door.

However, simple numbers may be spelled out: *six feet.*

Use numerals with numbers in a series.

A grizzly bear can run at a speed of **30** miles per hour; an elephant, **25**; a chicken, **9**; but a tortoise, only **0.17**.

The commercial traveler logged his sales for his first five days on the job: **7, 18, 23, 4, 19**.

Use numerals for identification numbers.

His social security number is **142–45–1983**.

For service call the following number: **(800) 415–3333**.

Flight **465** has been canceled.

When one number immediately follows another, spell out the first number and use a numeral for the second number.

He ran in **two** 50-meter races.

We have **three** 6-foot ladders in the garage.

There are **five** 7-foot players in the conference.

Exercise. Identify the errors in the use of abbreviations and numbers in the following sentences. Two of the sentences contain no error.

1. The kindly Dr. Jekyll turned into the terrible Mr. Hyde.

2. Has the Rev. Joseph Parker been assigned to this church?

3. Some people feel that Pres. Nixon's greatest accomplishment was reestablishing relations between the U.S. and China.

4. The speaker at yesterday's meeting was James Colby, Junior.

5. J. Edgar Hoover headed the F.B.I.

6. The comet fell at 6:57 A.M.

7. The program cannot be shown until Wed., Dec. nineteenth.

8. 32 African nations formed the O.A.U. in May 1963.

9. An excellent source for information about N.A.T.O. is Jas. Huntley's *The NATO Story*, which was published in nineteen sixty-nine.

10. Honduras has a Caribbean coastline of six hundred forty-four kilometers.

30 Manuscript form

The following are general guidelines for preparing handwritten and typewritten papers. If your college or your instructor specify different or additional guidelines, however, follow their directions.

For handwritten papers

1. Use blue or black ink. Do not use pencil.
2. Use 8½" × 11" ruled white paper. If you tear the paper from a notebook, cut off the ragged edge. Do not use paper with narrowly spaced lines.
3. Skip every other line, unless your instructor tells you otherwise. (Do not skip lines between the lines of a quotation.)
4. Write on only one side of the paper.
5. Center your title. Leave an extra line of space between the title and the first line of text. Do not underline or put quotation marks around the title. (Of course, if a part of your title is a quotation or the title of another work, use the appropriate punctuation for this part.)
6. Capitalize all words in the title except articles, short (under five letters) conjunctions, and short prepositions. Do not put a period at the end of the title.
7. Leave about an inch and a half of space at the top of each page. (The first rule on ruled paper is usually about an inch and a half from the top.) Leave about an inch of space at the bottom of each page.
8. Leave about an inch-and-a-half margin at the left-hand side of each page. (Ruled paper usually has a vertical line on the left-hand side to indicate this margin.) Leave about a one-inch margin at the right-hand side.
9. Indent the first line of each new paragraph about one inch from the left margin.
10. Use hyphens to divide words at the end of lines. (See pages 201–202 for information on word division at the end of a line.)

11. Do not end a line with an opening bracket, parenthesis, or quotation mark. Do not begin a line with a comma, a colon, a semicolon, or an end punctuation mark. Do not separate ellipsis points over two lines.

12. When underlining, underline the complete item, including the space between words.

13. Correct an error by drawing a line through it and writing the correction above it. (Rewrite any page that contains more than one error.)

14. Number each page with arabic numerals. On the first page, center the number at the bottom of the page. (You may omit the number from the first page.) On all other pages, write the number in the upper right-hand corner of the page.

15. Follow carefully your instructor's directions for writing your name and any other necessary identifying information on your paper.

16. Fold your paper only if your instructor says you may do so.

17. Write legibly.

18. Proofread your paper carefully before turning it in.

For typewritten papers

1. Use a black typewriter ribbon.

2. Use $8\frac{1}{2}'' \times 11''$ unruled white bond paper. Do not use onionskin.

3. Double-space each line. (Single-space quotations.)

4. Type on only one side of the paper.

5. Center your title. Leave an extra line of space between the title and the first line of text. Do not underline or put quotation marks around the title. (Of course, if a part of your title is a quotation or the title of another work, use the appropriate punctuation for this part.)

6. Capitalize all words in the title except articles, short (under five letters) conjunctions, and short prepositions. Do not put a period at the end of the title.

7. Leave about an inch and a half of space at the top of each

page. Leave about an inch of space at the bottom of each page.

8. Leave about an inch-and-a-half margin at the left-hand side of each page. Leave about a one-inch margin at the right-hand side.

9. Indent the first line of each new paragraph five spaces from the left margin.

10. Use hyphens to divide words at the end of lines. (See pages 201–202 for information on word division at the end of a line.)

11. Do not end a line with an opening bracket, parenthesis, or quotation mark. Do not begin a line with a comma, a colon, a semicolon, or an end punctuation mark. Do not separate ellipsis points over two lines.

12. Leave two spaces after end punctuation marks and colons. Leave one space after all other punctuation marks.

13. Indicate a dash with two hyphens (--). Do not leave space before, after, or between the hyphens.

14. When underlining, underline the complete item, including the space between words.

15. If your typewriter does not have the numeral 1 on its keyboard, use a lowercase "el" for this numeral.

16. Number each page with arabic numerals. Do not number the first page. On all other pages, type the number in the upper right-hand corner of the page.

17. Follow carefully your instructor's directions for typing your name and any other necessary identifying information on your paper.

18. Fold your paper only if your instructor says you may do so.

19. Make corrections neatly. Use correction fluid where possible. Retype any page that appears messy.

20. Proofread your paper carefully before turning it in.

SPELLING

SPELLING

Mastery of English spelling is a difficult task, though perhaps not as difficult as poor spellers believe. Simply remember to follow a few simple guidelines and—most important—to use your dictionary when you are not sure of a spelling.

31 Spelling rules

Although spelling rules are not infallible, mastery of the few below will help you. They cover some of the most common spelling problems: adding suffixes to words, forming noun plurals, and choosing between *ei* and *ie*.

31a Doubling the final consonant

In a word ending with a consonant-vowel-consonant (c-v-c) combination, the vowel usually has a short vowel sound.

bat	dot	shun
pen	begin	occur

When a suffix is added to such a word, sometimes the final consonant is doubled to maintain the short vowel sound.

With suffixes beginning with a consonant

Do not double the final consonant of a c-v-c word when adding a suffix beginning with a consonant.

ship + ment = shipment   mob + ster = mobster
wet + ness = wetness   pen + man + ship = penmanship

With suffixes beginning with a vowel

Double the final consonant of a one-syllable c-v-c word when adding a suffix beginning with a vowel.

pen + ed = penned   brag + art = braggart
skip + er = skipper   grip + ing = gripping

Exception: bus + ing = busing

When adding a suffix beginning with a vowel to a c-v-c word of more than one syllable, double the final consonant if the word is accented on the last syllable. Do not double the consonant, however, if the accent shifts to the first syllable when the suffix is added.

begín + er = beginner   regrét + ed = regretted
recúr + ence = recurrence   defér + ence = déference
emít + ing = emitting   prefér + ence = préference

When adding a suffix beginning with a vowel to a c-v-c word of more than one syllable, do not double the final consonant if the word is not accented on the last syllable.

pénal + ize = penalize   bánter + ing = bantering
lábor + er = laborer   abándon + ed = abandoned

Do not double the final consonant when adding any suffix to any word that does not end in a consonant-vowel-consonant.

cheap + er = cheaper   ordain + ed = ordained
chant + ing = chanting   pretend + er = pretender

31b Dropping the silent *e*

Many English words end with a silent *e*. At times this *e* indicates that the vowel before the consonant should have a long sound. For example, notice the difference in the vowel sound in each of the following word pairs.

hat—hate   rot—rote   pan—pane
din—dine   run—rune   spit—spite

At times the silent *e* indicates that the *c* or *g* preceding it should have a soft, rather than a hard, sound.

notice   trace   courage
peace   engage   outrage

Drop a final silent e when adding most suffixes beginning with a vowel.

fade + ing = fading   grimace + ed = grimaced
write + er = writer   cohere + ence = coherence
pleasure + able = pleasurable escape + ist = escapist

Exceptions

acre + age = acreage   line + age = lineage
dye + ing = dyeing   mile + age = mileage
hoe + ing = hoeing   singe + ing = singeing

Retain a final silent e when adding the suffix *able* or *ous* to a word in which the silent e is preceded by a c or a g.

notice + able = noticeable   advantage + ous = advantageous
peace + able = peaceable   change + able = changeable
outrage + ous = outrageous   courage + ous = courageous

Retain a final silent e when adding a suffix beginning with a consonant.

delicate + ness = delicateness   move + ment = movement
loose + ly = loosely   decisive + ness = decisiveness

Exceptions

acknowledge + ment = acknowledgment
argue + ment = argument
judge + ment = judgment
nine + th = ninth
true + ly = truly
whole + ly = wholly

31c Changing *y* to *i*

When a final *y* is preceded by a consonant, change the *y* to *i* when you add most suffixes.

lovely + er = lovelier   happy + ly = happily
likely + hood = likelihood   lazy + ness = laziness
risky + est = riskiest   tally + ed = tallied

Exceptions

dry + er = dryer (machine)   sly + ly = slyly
dry + ly = dryly   sly + ness = slyness
dry + ness = dryness   wry + ly = wryly
shy + ly = shyly   wry + ness = wryness
shy + ness = shyness

However, do not change a final *y* to *i* when you add the suffix *ing* or *ist*.

spy + ing = spying   hurry + ing = hurrying
copy + ist = copyist   pacify + ing = pacifying

If a final *y* is preceded by a vowel, do not change the *y* to *i* when you add a suffix.

employ + ee = employee   destroy + er = destroyer
essay + ist = essayist   convey + ance = conveyance
survey + ing = surveying   overstay + ed = overstayed

177

Exceptions

day + ly = daily	pay + ed = paid
gay + ly = gaily	say + ed = said
lay + ed = laid	

31d Forming noun plurals

For most nouns, form the plural by adding s to the singular.

pot—pots	table—tables	magazine—magazines
lamp—lamps	picture—pictures	recorder—recorders

For nouns ending in *y* preceded by a vowel, form the plural by adding s to the singular.

monkey—monkeys	holiday—holidays
display—displays	jersey—jerseys
journey—journeys	odyssey—odysseys

For nouns (except proper nouns) ending in *y* preceded by a consonant, form the plural by changing the *y* to *i* and adding es.

jelly—jellies	theory—theories
quality—qualities	frequency—frequencies
heresy—heresies	fraternity—fraternities

For nouns ending in *s*, *ch*, *sh*, *x*, or *z*, form the plural by adding es to the singular.

genius—geniuses	miss—misses
ditch—ditches	brush—brushes
hoax—hoaxes	waltz—waltzes

For nouns ending in *o* preceded by a vowel, form the plural by adding s to the singular.

cameo—cameos	trio—trios

duo—duos	folio—folios
radio—radios	scenario—scenarios

For nouns ending in *o* preceded by a consonant, form the plural by adding either *s* or *es* to the singular.

Add *s*

piano—pianos	memo—memos
burro—burros	dynamo—dynamos
alto—altos	magneto—magnetos

Add *es*

hero—heroes	echo—echoes
mosquito—mosquitoes	tomato—tomatoes
potato—potatoes	mulatto—mulattoes

Add *s* or *es*

flamingo—flamingos *or* flamingoes
salvo—salvos *or* salvoes
banjo—banjos *or* banjoes
lasso—lassos *or* lassoes
domino—dominos *or* dominoes
cargo—cargos *or* cargoes

For most nouns ending in *f* or *fe* and for all nouns ending in *ff*, form the plural by adding *s* to the singular.

belief—beliefs	muff—muffs
waif—waifs	staff—staffs
safe—safes	rebuff—rebuffs

For some nouns ending in *f* or *fe*, form the plural by changing the *f* or *fe* to *ve* and adding *s*.

calf—calves	knife—knives
leaf—leaves	wife—wives
self—selves	life—lives

The following nouns ending in *arf* have alternative plural forms.

dwarf—**dwarfs** *or* dwarves
scarf—**scarfs** *or* scarves
wharf—**wharfs** *or* wharves

For compound nouns written as one word, form the plural by applying the preceding rules to the last part of the compound.

cupful—cupfuls	tablespoon—tablespoons
handful—handfuls	hemstitch—hemstitches
housewife—housewives	toolbox—toolboxes
takeoff—takeoffs	horsefly—horseflies

Exception: passerby—passersby

For compound nouns in which the words are joined by a hyphen or written separately, make the chief word plural.

mother-in-law	mothers-in-law
sergeant at arms	sergeants at arms
runner-up	runners-up
attorney general	attorneys general
father-to-be	fathers-to-be

but

tape recorder	tape recorders
sound track	sound tracks
high school	high schools
hope chest	hope chests

Exceptions

drive-in	drive-ins
five-year-old	five-year-olds
jack-in-the-box	jack-in-the-boxes
frame-up	frame-ups
sit-in	sit-ins
stand-in	stand-ins

For numbers, letters, symbols, and words being named, form the plural by adding 's to the singular.

9's	*'s	*a*'s
and's	abc's	+ 's

Learn the irregular plural forms.

Some nouns have an irregular plural or form the plural according to the rules of their language of origin.

woman—women	louse—lice	foot—feet
man—men	mouse—mice	tooth—teeth
ox—oxen	alumnus—alumni	analysis—analyses
child—children	radius—radii	crisis—crises

Learn the nouns that have the same form for both singular and plural.

deer	trout	species	moose
salmon	sheep	series	

Form the plural of proper nouns by adding *s* or *es*.

Tuesdays	the Joneses	the Kennedys

In the example on the right, note that no apostrophe is used and that the final *y* is not changed to *i*.

31e Choosing between *ei* and *ie*

In most cases, place *i* before *e* except after *c*. Place *e* before *i* when these letters are pronounced as ā.

I before *e*

pierce	niece	mien
believe	interview	shield

After *c*

receive	deceit	deceive
conceive	perceive	ceiling

Pronounced as ā

neighbor	weight	feign
freight	vein	reign

Exceptions

either	height	neither
feisty	heir	seize
heifer	leisure	weird

Note: The rule does not apply to words in which the *i* and the *e* or the *e* and the *i* are pronounced as parts of separate syllables: *piety, deity, hierarchy, science.*

Exercise. Identify the misspelled word in each of the following groups.

1. shipped, remitted, driped, excelled, distilled
2. quitting, outwitting, outfitting, benefitting, permitting
3. committee, committment, committed, committing, committable
4. recurence, deference, inference, reference, preference
5. describing, singeing, placing, juiceing, liking
6. acknowledgement, ninety, noticeable, outrageous, peaceably
7. rectifing, slyly, wryly, satisfying, hurriedly
8. travesties, journeys, salaries, delays, frequencys
9. hitches, quizzes, folioes, mosquitoes, heroes
10. deign, deceive, hienous, relieve, frontier

32 Troublesome words

A large number of spelling errors are caused by omitting one or two letters from a word or by adding letters where they do not belong. The most common errors of this kind are caused by not doubling a consonant or by doubling one incorrectly. The following is a list of words that are often misspelled by adding or omitting letters. The part or parts of the word that commonly cause spelling problems are in **boldface**.

abandoned
academic
academically
accelerator
acceptable
accessible
accidentally
accommodate
accompanied
accompanying
accomplish
accumulate
accuracy
accustomed
achievement
acknowledge
acknowledgment (no *e* after *g*)
acquaintance
acquire
acquit
acreage
across
actually
address
admission
admittance
adolescent
advantageous
advertisement
aerial
aggravate
aggressive
aisle
allotting
almost
already
altogether
always
amateur
among (no *u* after *o*)
amount

analysis
analyze
ancestry (no *a* after *t*)
annihilate
announcement
annual
another
apartment
apologetically
apology
apparatus
apparent
appearance
applies
appoint
appreciate
appropriate
appropriately
approximate
approximately
arctic
arguing (no *e* after *u*)
argument (no *e* after *u*)
aspirin
assassination
association
atheist
athlete (no *e* after *h*)
athletic (no *e* after *h*)
attitude
awful (no *e* after *w*)
bankruptcy
bargain
basically
battalion
beautiful
becoming
before
beginning
benefited
biggest

biscuit
biting
boundary
bracelet
bulletin
business
calendar
camouflage
candidate
career
carrying
challenge
changeable
channel
characteristics
chocolate
chosen (no *o* after *o*)
clothes
column
coming
commercial
commission
commitment
committee
communism
communists
compel
compelled
competition
completely
conceivable (no *e* after *v*)
condemn
conferred
confused
connoisseur
conscience
conscientious
consists
continuous
controlled
controlling

controversial
convenient
coolly
criticism
crowded
cruelty (no *i* after *l*)
curriculum
dealt
decision
decorate
deferred
define
definitely
definition
descend
desirable (no *e* after *r*)
desperate
develop (no *e* after *p*)
diarrhea
different
dilemma
dilettante
dining
disagree
disappear
disappoint
disapprove
disaster
disastrous (no *e* after *t*)
discipline
discussion
dispel
dissatisfied
disservice
dissipate
distinct
drunkenness
during
ecstasy
efficiency
efficient

eliminate
embarrass
eminent
empty
endeavor
enemy
enthusiastically
entirely
entrance (no *e* after *t*)
environment
equipment (no *t* after *p*)
equipped
especially
essential
everything
exaggerate
excellent
excess
exercise (no *c* after *x*)
exhaustion
exhibition
exhilarate
existence (no *h* after *x*)
experience
explanation (no *i* after *l*)
extremely
fallacy
familiar
family
fascinate
fascism
favorite
February
fiery
final (no *i* after *n*)
financially
fission
fluorine
foreign
foresee
forfeit (no *e* after *r*)

forty (no *e* after *r*)
forward (no *e* after *r*)
fourth
frantically
fulfill
gaiety
generally
genius (no *o* after *i*)
government
grammatically
grievous (no *i* after *v*)
gruesome
guarantee
guerrilla
handicapped
handkerchief
harass
height (no *h* after *t*)
hemorrhage
heroes
hindrance (no *e* after *d*)
holiday
hopeless
hurriedly
hygiene
hypocrite
ideally
illogical
imagine
imitate
immediately
immense
impossible
incidentally
indispensable (no *e* after *s*)
individually
ingenious
initially
initiative
innocent
innocuous

inoculate
intellectual
intelligence
intelligent
interest
interfered
interference
interrupt
iridescent
irrelevant
irresistible
irritable
jewelry (no *e* after *l*)
judgment (no *e* after *g*)
knowledge
laboratory
larynx
later
laundry (no *e* after *d*)
lenient
liable
liaison
library
lightning (no *e* after *t*)
likely
listening
literature
loneliness
lonely
magazine
maintenance
manageable
maneuver
manner
manual
marriage
marriageable
mathematics
meanness
meant
medicine

medieval
mileage
millennium
miniature
miscellaneous
mischievous (no *i* after *v*)
missile
misspelled
mortgage
muscle
narrative
naturally
necessary
necessity
nineteen
ninety
ninth (no *e* after *in*)
noticeable
nowadays
nuisance
numerous
occasion
occasionally
occurred
occurrence
official
omission
omit
omitted
operate
opinion
opponent
opportunity
opposite
oppression
outrageous
pageant
pamphlet (no *e* after *h*)
panicked
paraffin
parallel

parliament
particular
pastime
peaceable
peculiar
permissible
picnicked
planned
playwright
pneumonia
pollute
Portuguese
possess
possession
possible
practically
preference
preferred
prejudiced
primitive
privilege (no *d* after *le*)
probably (no *a* after *ab*)
procedure (no *e* after *ce*)
profession
professor
pronunciation (no *o* after *on*)
psalm
psychology
ptomaine
publicly (no *al* after *c*)
pumpkin
quantity
quarrel
questionnaire
realize
rebellion
recession
recommend
reference
referring
relative

remember
remembrance (no *e* after *b*)
reminisce
remittance
restaurant
rhythm
roommate
saccharine
safety
satellite
scientists
scintillate
sergeant
shepherd
sheriff
shining
shrubbery
similar (no *i* after *l*)
sincerely
skiing
sophomore
souvenir
specifically
statistics (no *s* after *a*)
strenuous
stretch
stubbornness
studying
subtle
succeed
success
succession
sufficient
summary
summation
summed
supposed
suppress
surely
surrounding
swimming

syllable	used
symmetric	useful
tariff	usually
temperament	vacuum
temperature	valuable
therefore	various
thorough	vaudeville
tobacco	vegetable
tomorrow	vehicle
transferred	vengeance
trespass	villain
truly (no *e* after *u*)	violence
tyranny	warring
unconscious	where
uncontrollable	whether
undoubtedly	whistle
unmistakably (no *e* after *k*)	wholly
unnatural	whose
unnecessary	writing
until	written

The following is a list of other words that are often misspelled.

abundant	burial	despicable
acre	buried	detrimental
against	carburetor	dictionary
a lot	caricature	diphtheria
anonymous	catalogue	doesn't
arithmetic	catastrophe	eighth
article	category	eligible
attendance	cellar	emphasize
ballet	cemetery	espionage
beggar	children	exuberant
behavior	circumstantial	financier
believe	colossal	galaxy
beneficial	comparative	guidance
bibliography	complexion	hers
blasphemy	counselor	hospital
boulevard	courtesy	hundred
buffet	criticize	hypocrisy
bureaucrat	debacle	idiomatic

imagery	paralysis	siege
incredible	penicillin	significance
independent	performance	source
inevitable	permanent	specimen
insurance	perseverance	speech
interpretation	perspiration	supersede
involve	phenomenon	surprise
January	physician	susceptible
leisurely	pigeon	technical
license	poison	technique
liquor	predominate	tendency
luxurious	prescription	theirs
magnificent	prestige	themselves
malicious	prevalent	tolerance
martyrdom	proceed	tortoise
mediocre	propaganda	tragedy
melancholy	propagate	tried
minuscule	pursue	Tuesday
minute	pursuit	unscrupulous
naive	repetition	versatile
neurotic	ridiculous	vigilance
nickel	sacrifice	vinegar
nuclear	salary	Wednesday
nucleus	schedule	woman
ogre	secretary	yacht
optimism	seize	yours
ours	seizure	zinc
paid	separate	

Exercise. Identify the misspelled word in each of the following groups.

1. assassination, acquit, salery, permanent, galaxy

2. intepretation, ogre, paralysis, communism, appearance

3. challenge, artic, ancestry, forfeit, vigilance

4. technique, colossal, lightning, curriculum, nineth

5. pronounciation, interrupt, diarrhea, compel, inoculate

6. iridescent, necessary, harrass, acquire, aerial

7. embarass, disaster, nuisance, parallel, annihilate

8. condemn, biscuit, souvenir, rememberance, bureaucrat

9. carburetor, mischievous, irritable, sacharine, occasion

10. millennium, hemorrhage, questionaire, benefited, ecstasy

33 Capitalization rules

Capitalize the first word of a sentence, the pronoun *I*, and the interjection *O*.

> Many writers have created imaginary universes.
> Do I think that life exists on other planets?
> These creatures, O mighty Gork, come from the other side of the universe.

Capitalize the first word of a direct quotation that is a complete sentence.

> At the climax of the movie, Rhett says, "Frankly, my dear, I don't give a damn."
> The book begins with the present Mrs. de Winter recounting a dream: "Last night I dreamt I went to Manderley again."
> When Cuyloga prepares to leave his son, he tells him, "Give me no more shame."

Capitalize the first word of every line of verse unless the poet has written the line with a lower-case letter.

> The first two lines of Reed Whittemore's poem "Still Life" immediately capture your interest: "I must explain why it is that at night, in my own house,/Even when no one's asleep, I feel I must whisper."
> Keats's poem ends with the lines, "Though the sedge is withered from the lake/And no birds sing."
> The Eliot poem that I am trying to remember begins with the following two lines: "Macavity's a Mystery Cat: He's called the hidden paw—/For he's the master criminal who can defy the Law."

Note: In quotations, always capitalize whichever words the writer has capitalized.

Capitalize proper nouns.

Sharon	Keats
Andrew Jackson	Lake Michigan
Portuguese	Hawaii
Greta Garbo	the Empire State Building
the Middle Ages	the Revolutionary War

Do not capitalize compass points unless they are part of a proper noun: *northwest of Chicago* but *the Pacific Northwest.*

Capitalize an official title when it precedes a name.

The guest speaker will be Congresswoman Katherine Murphy.
The nation mourned the death of President Lincoln.
The changes were supported by Governor Celeste.

Capitalize the title of a high official when it is used in place of the person's name.

The guest speaker will be the Congresswoman.
The nation mourned the death of the President.
The changes were supported by the Governor.

Note: Do not capitalize a title that does not name a specific individual.

Capitalize abbreviations and designations that follow a name. Do not capitalize titles used as appositives.

Eugene Anderson, Jr.
Anne Poletti, Ph.D.
Louise Tate, Attorney at Law
Seymour Rosen, a chemistry professor, submitted an article to the magazine.
Lois Kean, a first-year law student, won the award.
Malcolm Kennedy, an intern at the hospital, was interviewed on television.

Capitalize the title of a relative when it precedes a name or is used in place of a name. Do not capitalize the title if it is used with a possessive pronoun.

> Aunt Joan   Cousin Mary
> Uncle Carlos   Grandfather Tseng

> Is Grandmother coming to visit?
> You look well, Grandpa.
> My uncle Bill could not come to the performance.

Capitalize proper adjectives.

> Shakespearean sonnet   Machiavellian goals
> Parisian style   Grecian urn
> Islamic teacher   Christian faith

Do not capitalize most proper adjectives that are part of a compound noun.

> french fries   danish pastry
> roman numeral   venetian blind

Note: Usage in this area varies. Consult your dictionary for capitalization of compound nouns formed from proper adjectives.

Capitalize the names of specific academic courses. Do not capitalize general subject areas unless the subject area is a proper noun, such as a language.

> History 121   *but* a world history course
> The Modern American Novel   *but* an American literature course
> Advanced Biology   *but* a biology course

Capitalize words naming the Deity, sacred books, and other religious documents and names of religions, religious denominations, and their adherents.

Jehovah	Allah	the Lord
the Bible	the Koran	the Upanishads
Catholicism	Moslem	Lutheran

Note: Pronouns referring to the Deity are usually capitalized.

Capitalize names of months, days of the week, and holidays.

April	December	January
Tuesday	Saturday	Wednesday
Halloween	New Year's Eve	the Fourth of July

Note: Do not capitalize the names of the seasons.

Capitalize the abbreviations *A.D.* and *B.C.*

| A.D. 172 | 500 B.C. |
| A.D. 356 | 275 B.C. |

For titles of literary works, capitalize the first and the last word and all other important words, including prepositions of five or more letters.

Do not capitalize articles, short prepositions, or coordinating conjunctions that do not begin or end a title.

> *The Decline and Fall of the Roman Empire*
> "The Case of the Irate Witness"
> *Much Ado About Nothing*
> "On the Morning After the Sixties"

Capitalize both parts of a hyphenated word in a title.

> "Home-Thoughts from Abroad"
> "Good-Bye, My Fancy!"
> *The Sot-Weed Factor*
> *Giles Goat-Boy*

Exercise. In each of the following items, change a lower-case letter to a capital letter wherever necessary. Some of the sentences are correct as written.

1. E. B. White once said, "writing is an act of faith, nothing else."

2. In "Morning song," Sylvia Plath describes the birth of her child: "Love set you going like a fat gold watch./the midwife slapped your footsoles and your bald cry/took its place among the elements."

3. Using silence as a symbol for a source of inspiration and power, Yeats ends each line of his poem "Long-legged Fly" with the lines, "Like a long-legged fly upon the stream/his mind moves upon silence."

4. In "When Lilacs last in the Dooryard bloom'd," Walt Whitman mourns the death of president Abraham Lincoln: "O powerful western fallen star!/O shades of night—o moody, tearful night!"

5. The word *sideburns* comes from general Ambrose Burnside, a union commander during the civil war who sported this style of whiskers.

6. The editor of this collection is Gregory Hastings, Jr.

7. Syngman Rhee, who was the first president of South Korea, sought Korean independence from Japan.

8. At the Yalta conference held near the end of world war II in the crimean peninsula, the allies planned the postwar reorganization of Europe.

9. When I agreed to take your Elizabethan literature course, professor, I didn't realize I would be required to read shakespearean sonnets.

10. The eighteenth-century followers of methodism, which is based on the teachings of John Wesley, were barred from the church of England.

34 The apostrophe

In possessive forms

The possessive case forms of all nouns and of many pronouns are spelled with an apostrophe. The following rules explain when to use an apostrophe for possessive forms and where to place the apostrophe.

Singular nouns

To form the possessive of a singular noun, add an apostrophe and *s.*

> **Kirsoff's** review emphasized the **dramatist's** outstanding contribution to the arts.
> A **woman's** effort to free herself from the past is the concern of Alice **Walker's** novel *Meridian.*
> The Greeks tried to appease **Zeus's** anger, just as the Romans tried to avoid **Jupiter's** wrath.

Exception: Use only an apostrophe when a singular noun ending in *s* is followed by a word beginning with *s.*

> The **boss'** salary is three times that of her assistant.
> We discussed **Keats'** sonnets in class today.
> In Langston **Hughes'** story "Thank You, M'am," a young boy finds kindness where he expected punishment.

Plural nouns

To form the possessive of a plural noun not ending in *s,* **add an apostrophe and** *s.*

> The **women's** proposal called for a day-care center to be set up at their place of employment.
> Dr. Seuss is a well-known name in the field of **children's** literature.
> The store has introduced a new line of **men's** fragrances.

To form the possessive of a plural noun ending in *s,* **add an apostrophe alone.**

> The **doctors'** commitment to their patients was questioned at the forum.
> This course highlights two **composers'** works—Haydn and Mozart.
> The **soldiers'** tales of atrocities enraged the public.

Compound nouns

To form the possessive of a compound noun, make the last word possessive.

Does anyone welcome a **mother-in-law's** advice?

As a result of the **Vice President's** remarks, the party asked for his removal from the ticket.

The editorial defended the **police officers'** conduct in the case.

Noun pairs or nouns in a series

To show joint possession, add an apostrophe and *s* to the last noun in a pair or a series.

Sociologists were concerned that **Charles and Diana's** announcement would set off a new baby boom in Britain.

Carter and Pollard's book examines certain nineteenth-century forgeries.

Lennon and McCartney's music had a dramatic effect on their contemporaries.

To show individual possession, add an apostrophe and *s* to each noun in a pair or series.

Anne Tyler's and **Sam Shepard's** styles have many similarities.

In *48 Hrs.*, **Nolte's** and **Murphy's** characters come from opposite sides of the law.

The **President's** and the **Vice President's** duties are clearly defined.

Nouns naming periods of time and sums of money

To form the possessive of a noun naming a period of time or a sum of money, add an apostrophe and *s*.

The value of **today's** dollar is less than the value of last **year's** dollar.

A good rule of thumb is that a **week's** salary should cover a **month's** rent.

The **dollar's** standing in the world market is affected by political conditions at home and abroad.

Indefinite pronouns

To form the possessive of an indefinite pronoun, add an apostrophe and *s*.

We can learn from **each other's** mistakes.

How we can improve our care of the elderly is a subject on almost **everyone's** mind.

It can be argued that **no one's** life has been so poignant as that of David, the boy who lived almost his entire short life in an isolation bubble.

Personal pronouns

Do not use an apostrophe with the possessive forms of personal pronouns.

Her analysis of the problem was more complete than **yours**.

The druids' methods of telling time were quite different from **ours**.

Our troops are better prepared than **theirs**.

In plural forms

Add an apostrophe and s to form the plural of words being named, letters of the alphabet, abbreviations, numerals, and symbols.

One drawback of this typeface is that the capital *i*'s and the lower-case *l*'s look exactly alike.

Avoid weakening your argument by including too many *but*'s and *however*'s.

Although the **1960's** saw the first man on the moon, it wasn't until the **1980's** that the United States sent a black or a woman into space.

In contractions

Use an apostrophe to indicate a missing letter or letters in a contraction.

In general, use contractions only in informal writing.

The Sherlock Holmes stories **weren't** Arthur Conan Doyle's only success.

She claimed that enough attention **isn't** being paid to the threat of nuclear war.

Note: *It's* is a contraction that means "it is" or "it has." *Its* is a possessive pronoun that means "belonging to it." Do not confuse the two.

For omissions

Use an apostrophe to indicate that part of a word or number has been omitted.

> In **'64** the Beatles invaded the United States with a new style of rock **'n'** roll.
> The manager told the singer to "go out and knock **'em** dead."

Exercise. In each of the following groups, identify the items that show the correct use of the apostrophe.

1. Shakespeare's sonnets, Dumas's stories, Brontë's novels
2. childrens' clothes, women's rights, mens' clothing
3. three employee's complaints, two student's papers, five athletes' visas
4. a year's salary, a season's growth, a day's labor
5. it's buzzer, his' youth, one of ours
6. anyone's knowledge, everybody's home, no ones' speech
7. the swinging '60's, the roaring '20's, the fabulous 50's
8. the 1820s, the 1930s, the 1980's
9. Hal and Marie's apartment, Annette and Tom's house, Sid's and Fran's car (*joint ownership*)
10. Nancy's and Jack's papers, Chris' and Paul's checks, Sal's and Harry's remarks (*individual ownership*)

35 The hyphen

In compound nouns

Use a dictionary to determine whether to spell a compound noun with a hyphen.

Relatively few compound nouns are hyphenated; most are written either solid (as one word) or open (as two or more separate words). The only kinds of compound nouns that are usually hyphenated are those made up of two equally important nouns and those made up of three or more words.

philosopher-king	city-state	man-hour
mother-in-law	free-for-all	jack-of-all-trades

In compound adjectives

Hyphenate two or more words that serve as a single adjective preceding a noun.

well-known painter   **law-school** degree
soft-spoken man   **sure-to-win** candidate
too-good-to-be-true behavior

Do you know the difference between **mass-market** paperbacks and trade paperbacks?
Cheever's stories provide insight into **middle-class** suburban life.
The company is investigating both the **short-term** and the **long-term** benefits of scattered work hours.

In general, do not hyphenate such words when they follow a noun.

painter who is **well known**
degree from a **law school**
man who is **soft spoken**
candidate who is **sure to win**
behavior that is **too good to be true**

Do you know the difference between novels that are considered **mass market** and novels that are considered trade?
Cheever's stories provide insight into the lives of suburban people who are **middle class**.
The benefits of scattered work hours are both **short term** and **long term**.

Do not hyphenate two or more words that precede a noun when the first of these words is an adverb ending in **-ly**.

Critics attacked the President's **rapidly expanding** budget.

When Menudo first came to this city, the police were called in to restrain the crowd of **wildly screaming** teenagers.

The government's **widely criticized** policies are the subject of the debate on television today.

Use a "hanging" hyphen after the first part of a hyphenated compound adjective used in a series, where the second part of the compound adjective is implied but omitted.

both **paid-** and complimentary-ticket holders
both **short-** and long-term disability
all **first-, second-,** and third-year students

In compound numbers and fractions

Hyphenate spelled-out numbers from *twenty-one* through *ninety-nine* and spelled-out fractions used as adjectives.

In spelled-out numbers larger than *ninety-nine*, do not use a hyphen before or after *hundred, thousand,* and so forth.

The Protestant Bible has **thirty-nine** books in the Old Testament and **twenty-seven** in the New Testament.

Two hundred fifty-seven people were killed in the fire.

The installation of computers has effected a **one-third** increase in productivity and an expected **three-quarter** growth in profits.

Do not hyphenate spelled-out fractions used as nouns.

About **one half** of Yugoslavia is covered with mountains.

Only **three eighths** of the adults in this community voted in the last election.

With prefixes and suffixes

In general, do not use a hyphen between a prefix and its root or a suffix and its root. However, there are several exceptions.

Use a hyphen between a prefix and its root to avoid ambiguity.

the **re-creation** of the world	*but*	tennis as **recreation**
to **re-count** money	*but*	to **recount** an event
a **co-op** apartment	*but*	a chicken **coop**

Use a hyphen between a prefix and its root when the last letter of the prefix and the first letter of the root are the same vowel or when the first letter of the root is capitalized.

semi-**i**ndustrial	anti-**i**ntellectual
supra-**a**uditory	re-**e**cho
un-**A**merican	pro-**W**estern

Use a hyphen between the prefixes *all-*, *ex-* ("former"), and *self-* and their roots and between the suffix *-elect* and its root.

all-star	all-time
ex-senator	ex-husband
self-control	self-sufficient
mayor-elect	president-elect

For word division at the end of a line

A hyphen is used to indicate that a word has been divided at the end of a line. However, some words may not be divided, and no word should be divided except between syllables. The following are some general rules for word division; consult a dictionary for words not covered by these rules.

Do not divide a one-syllable word.

truth	strayed	twelve
fifth	strength	gauche

Do not divide a word so that a one-letter syllable appears on a separate line.

Not:	a-mount	e-rase	sand-y
But:	amount	erase	sandy

Do not divide proper names.

Not:	Eliza-beth	Mal-ory	Pas-cal
But:	Elizabeth	Malory	Pascal

In general, divide words between double consonants.

sad-dle	com-mit-ted	cor-ruption	refer-ral
daz-zle	as-sistant	im-mortal	dif-ferent

In general, divide words between the prefix and the root or between the suffix and the root.

non-violent	in-sincere	re-dedicate
appease-ment	fellow-ship	mother-hood

Note: Do not carry over a two-letter suffix—*loaded* not *load-ed.*

Try to divide a hyphenated word at the hyphen.

Not:	self-de-nial	quick-tem-pered	cold-blood-edness
But:	self-denial	quick-tempered	cold-bloodedness

Exercise 1. Identify the correct form of each word in parentheses in the following sentences.

1. According to (well informed/well-informed) sources, Smith believes that (three eighths/three-eighths) of the voters now favor him, while (one quarter/one-quarter) are still undecided.

2. The (beatup/beat-up) car in the (parking-lot/parking lot) had a (for-sale/for sale) sign in its window.

3. His (winner-take-all/winner take all) attitude prevented him from turning his (newly-defeated/newly defeated) opponents into allies.

4. The (in house/in-house) (newsletter/news letter) contained an article that was (well-researched/well researched).

5. This (thought-provoking/thought provoking) article contained comments by (twenty one/twenty-one) lawyers on the emotional entanglements that can arise from a (lawyer client/lawyer-client) relation.

Exercise 2. Identify any correctly hyphenated words in each of the following groups.

1. self-control, in-discreet, dis-interested

2. anti-intellectual, semi-formal, de-escalate

3. bi-annual, mid-September, pro-West

4. all-time, all-star, all-American

5. senator-elect, non-aligned, un-democratic

Exercise 3. Imagine the following words appear at the end of lines. Identify any correctly divided words in each group.

1. non-committal, gam-y, brid-ge

2. self-con-fident, distrust-ful, impossibil-ity

3. impres-sion, pos-sess, specula-tion

4. avoid-ed, special-ty, adapt-able

5. Bo-wen, Eu-ler, Py-thagoras

DICTION

DICTION

Diction is the choice and arrangement of words in writing. Good diction helps you reach your audience, achieve your purpose, maintain an appropriate tone, and write with style.

36 Appropriate word choice

Whenever you write, the most basic decision you have to make about diction is whether to use formal or informal English. Formal English, as its name suggests, adheres strictly to the conventions of standard English. Most of the writing you do in college or in a profession—term papers, formal essays, theses, reports—should be in formal English. Informal English takes a more relaxed attitude to the conventions of standard English and may include contractions, colloquialisms, jargon, and sometimes even slang. It is appropriate for informal writing situations—journal and diary entries, informal essays, and creative writing in which you try to capture the sound of everyday speech.

Informal: The delegates **were savvy of the fact** that the document they were signing **wasn't** perfect.

Formal: The delegates **understood** that the document they were signing **was not** perfect.

Informal: The candidate **knocked** her opponent for often **changing his tune** on the issues.

Formal: The candidate **criticized** her opponent for often **changing his views** on the issues.

Informal: Stickley furniture may not be **real cushy**, but **it's pricey** and **in.**

Formal: Stickley furniture may not be **very comfortable**, but **it is expensive** and **fashionable.**

A good dictionary will help you determine whether a word or expression is formal or informal. The following is a list of three good desk dictionaries:

1. *The American Heritage Dictionary.* 2nd coll. ed. Boston: Houghton Mifflin, 1982.
2. *Webster's New World Dictionary of the American Language.* 2nd coll. ed. New York: Simon & Schuster, 1982.
3. *The Random House College Dictionary.* New York: Random House, 1973.

36a Slang

Slang is extremely informal language. It consists of colorful words, phrases, and expressions added to the language, usually by youthful or high-spirited people, to give it an exciting or ebullient flavor. Carl Sandburg described slang as "language that rolls up its sleeves, spits on its hands, and goes to work."

Slang is usually figurative and highly exaggerated. Each generation has its own slang; for example, in the 1960's someone who was approved of was *cool*, in the 1970's such a person was *with it*, and in the early 1980's, *awesome*. Although slang often begins as street language, some of it becomes so popular that with time it is accepted as part of formal language. Until a slang term becomes accepted, however, it is usually inappropriate in college writing.

Slang:	Some parents **came unglued** when they were **clued in to** how some children's programs on the **boob tube** were really just extended commercials.
Formal:	Some parents **became upset** when they were **made aware of** how some children's **television** programs were really just extended commercials.

Slang:	**It's a real downer to rap about** the number of employees who **got the boot** during the late 1970's and early 1980's.
Formal:	**It is sad to discuss** the number of employees who **were laid off** during the late 1970's and early 1980's.

Slang:	Elizabeth Blackwell was **bummed out** by the nineteenth century's view of the ideal woman, but she managed to find a doctor who was **in groove with** her goal of studying medicine.
Formal:	Elizabeth Blackwell was **disheartened** by the nineteenth century's view of the ideal woman, but she managed to find a doctor who was **sympathetic to** her goal of studying medicine.

Slang can be used judiciously for effect in formal writing. When you use slang this way, do not enclose it in quotation marks or underline it.

> The educated were turning in their diplomas for guitars, the rich were trading in their furs for jeans and love beads, and the middle-aged were pretending they were fifteen, not fifty; in fact, during this topsy-turvy time, everyone seemed to be **going bananas.**

> She was thoughtful, politically aware, well spoken, and well educated, but the movie directors of the 1950's preferred **bubblebrains.**

> As he grew older, he realized that his **old man** had been smarter than he thought.

36b Colloquialisms

Colloquial language is the conversational and everyday language of educated people. **Colloquialisms** are the words and expressions that characterize this language. While not as informal as slang, colloquial language is generally still too casual to be considered appropriate for formal writing.

Colloquial: The meeting will begin at 7:00 P.M. **on the dot.**
Formal: The meeting will begin **promptly** at 7:00 P.M.

Colloquial: In *Bodily Harm*, Rennie realizes she is **in a jam** when she opens the box and finds illegal guns.
Formal: In *Bodily Harm*, Rennie realizes she is **in trouble** when she opens the box and finds illegal guns.

Colloquial: When Colonel Pickering expresses doubt as to Higgins's ability to make a lady of Eliza, Higgins **tells him to put up or shut up.**
Formal: When Colonel Pickering expresses doubt as to Higgins's ability to make a lady of Eliza, Higgins **invites him to make a bet.**

Notice how the following sentences are improved when the colloquial qualifiers are replaced by more formal adverbs.

Colloquial: Harriet Tubman was a **terribly** brave woman, for she made several trips back into slave territory to lead fugitives into freedom.
Formal: Harriet Tubman was a **truly** brave woman, for she made several trips back into slave territory to lead fugitives into freedom.

Colloquial: General Harrison considered Tecumseh's plan to force the United States to relinquish its claims to Indian lands **awfully** clever, but not workable.
Formal: General Harrison considered Tecumseh's plan to force the United States to relinquish its claims to Indian lands **extremely** clever, but not workable.

Colloquial: Television viewers were **pretty** moved by the program about nuclear war.
Formal: Television viewers were **greatly** moved by the program about nuclear war.

36c Jargon

Jargon is the special language used by people in a particular field or group to communicate with others in this field or group. The problem with jargon, or "shop talk," is that people outside the group have trouble understanding it. Language aimed at people with a specific technical or professional knowledge may be appropriate for some classes, but it is not appropriate for most general college writing. If you must use a technical term in general college writing, make sure you define it.

Consider the following paragraph aimed at people with a specialized knowledge of word processing.

> All your files will be stored on diskettes, including text files and any data files you may require. For that matter, WordStar's program files are also stored on a diskette. A disk file can hold either text, data, or a computer program. You can have WordStar's files on one diskette and your typing files on another. Make sure you ask someone how the files are stored for your system. One typical set-up would be for you to have one WordStar disk, one working disk, and several backup disks kept on a shelf for emergencies. (The more you work with computers, the more you will learn to value backup disks.)

Someone who is familiar with word-processing programs will easily understand this paragraph. However, the general audience at which you aim most of your college writing will not understand the jargon; they will not know the meaning of the terms *diskette, text file, data file, program file, disk file, typing file, stored, system, working disk,* and *backup disk.*

Now consider the following paragraphs in which William Zinsser tells how he began to overcome his frustration with learning word processing.

> . . . A diskette, for example, was just a disk. But which kind of diskette was which? What exactly was the difference between the "program diskette" and the "work diskette"? Surely some kind of "work" got done on the program diskette. And where was the "work station" that the menu kept inviting me to use? I didn't remember unpacking it.
>
> As it turned out, the work station is the printer and the table that it sits on. As for the work diskette, it's the diskette that I'm supposed to put into the "diskette unit" (the toaster) to store my own work on. It's a blank disk that I can buy at the store, like a blank tape for a tape recorder. The program diskette is the disk that IBM does *its* work on; it's patented, and I can't buy it at any store. In short, the work diskette is my disk and the program diskette is their disk.

These paragraphs also contain jargon. Notice, though, that they are directed at a general audience of people who want to learn about word processing but right now do not have knowledge of it. Therefore, the author uses technical terms, but he defines these terms for his readers. In fact, to make his audience feel comfortable with so many technical terms, the author creates a persona for himself—that of someone who is technically inept and quite confused by all the jargon. If I can learn word processing, he implies, so can you.

36d Gobbledygook

Gobbledygook is stuffy, pretentious, inflated language that often contains an abundance of jargon. It is found in much government, legal, and academic writing, as well as in many other places, and it is sometimes called governmentese or legalese. Avoid gobbledygook, since it obscures meaning and lends both a timid and a pompous quality to your writing.

A major advocate of eliminating gobbledygook, especially from government writing, is Rudolf Flesch. In his book *How to Write Plain English*, he shows how Oregon's 1976 income tax instructions were rewritten in 1977 to eliminate gobbledygook.

1976

> *Deceased persons.* A return must be made by the executor or administrator of the decedent's estate or by the surviving spouse or other person charged with the care of the property of the deceased. If the surviving spouse or next of kin desires to claim the refund, an affidavit should be submitted with the return. This affidavit (Form 243) is available at all Oregon Department of Revenue district offices, or it can be obtained by writing the Oregon Department of Revenue, State Office Building, Salem, Oregon 97310.

1977

> *My husband died last year. Can I file for him?* Yes. The husband or wife of someone who dies, or the legal representative, must file the return. Use the form the person would have used if

living. If you claim a refund, attach Form 243 to show you have the right to the deceased person's refund. Write for Form 243 to: Oregon Department of Revenue, Salem, Oregon 97310, or pick it up at any of our district offices.

Exercise. Rephrase each of the following sentences in formal English.

1. When we turn our gray matter to the fate of the Cherokees, we can see that it was a real down day in our history when these folks were kicked out of their lands by Uncle Sam.

2. Hamlet knows that his old man didn't kick the bucket natural like but was knocked off by his brother, Hamlet's unk.

3. The Model T was the super-duper idea of Henry Ford, the whiz of the auto biz.

4. The nurse recorded the deceased's expiration date on his chart.

5. Kennedy didn't punk out when he came up against the Reds during the Cuban missile crisis; instead he stood pat and kept cool until Khrushchev chickened out and agreed to pull the missiles out of Cuba.

6. After he was caught with the goods, even his legal beagle couldn't keep him out of the monkey cage.

7. During the 1950's, idiot boxes sold like hotcakes, and whole families spent their evenings glued to the tube.

8. We hung out and chewed the fat about the latest glad rags from Paris.

9. For eight years the actress was an also-ran, but now she's numero uno.

10. The colonists merely kicked about the Sugar Act, but the Stamp Act got them real ticked off.

37 Exact word choice

Choose words that express your thoughts precisely. Do not settle for a near-synonym or an almost-right word, but pay attention to shades of meaning and nuances.

37a Specific and general words

Specific words are precise, focused, and restricted in scope. General words are not focused; they refer to a large group or a wide range of things. For example, compare the following general and specific words.

General:	painter	make	hungry	some
Specific:	Mary Cassatt	coerce	voracious	thirty-five

The word *painter* refers to a whole group of people. *Mary Cassatt* refers to just one. The word *make* refers to a wide range of actions; *coerce* limits this range, meaning "to make someone do something or to make something happen through the use of force or pressure." The word *hungry* indicates a desire for food or for something else, but *voracious* indicates that this desire is overwhelming and insatiable. The word *some* indicates a number larger than a few, but *thirty-five* indicates a specific number.

Consider how the following sentences are improved through the use of a specific word.

General: The **official** was accused of **working** for a **foreign government.**

Specific: **Alger Hiss** was accused of **spying** for **the Soviet Union.**

General: This **woman,** who is best known for **longer things,** also wrote **several good** ghost stories, which are collected in a **book.**

Specific: **Edith Wharton,** who is best known for her **novels,** also wrote **eleven riveting** ghost stories, which are collected in *The Ghost Stories of Edith Wharton.*

General: **Some writers** are **liked** for their **sense of humor.**

Specific: **Dorothy Parker and Robert Benchley** are **appreciated** for their **wry, and sometimes biting, wit.**

Of course, general words do have a place in your writing. They introduce topics that you can later elaborate on or narrow. When you use a general word, however, consider narrowing the scope of this word later in your writing, if not immediately. Always search for an alternative before using adjectives and adverbs such as *good, nice, bad, very, great, fine, awfully, well done,* or *interesting*. Words like these are so general, that is, have so many meanings, that paradoxically they convey almost no meaning at all.

37b Concrete and abstract words

Concrete words create vivid impressions. They name things that can be seen, touched, heard, smelled, or tasted—in other words, things that can be perceived by the senses. The words *skyscraper, microfilm, buzzer, gourmet, pizza,* and *porcupine* are concrete words. Abstract words name concepts, ideas, beliefs, and qualities—in other words, things that cannot be perceived by the senses. For example, the words *democracy, honesty, childhood,* and *infinity* are abstract words. Use abstract words with care, since, in general, they create less intense impressions and so are often ineffective.

Abstract: He argued that this nation could no longer accept poverty.

Concrete: Hungry children crying themselves to sleep, families evicted from their homes and sleeping in the streets, old people in cold-water flats surviving by eating cat food—these are conditions, he argued, that we as Americans can no longer tolerate.

Abstract: Immigrants came to America in search of a better life.

Concrete: Immigrants came to America to farm their own land, to earn a living wage, to put a roof over their heads and food in their stomachs, and to speak and believe as they wished without fear of being thrown in jail.

Abstract: One reason supermarkets began to replace ma-and-pa grocery stores is that they offered more variety.

Concrete: One reason supermarkets began to replace ma-and-pa grocery stores is that they offered not one brand of peas, but seven brands; not one kind of coffee, but six kinds; not one type of paper towel, but ten in five different colors—all under one roof.

214

Of course, abstract words do have a place in your writing. However, too many of them can create an impression of vagueness. When you do use abstract words, try to provide concrete examples to make their meaning vivid. Compare the following pairs of sentences. The second sentence in each pair contains a concrete example that clarifies the meaning of the abstract word or words in the first sentence.

> Hating people is self-destructive.
>
> Hating people is like burning down your own house to get rid of a rat.
>
> HARRY EMERSON FOSDICK

> Circumstance makes heroes of people.
>
> A light supper, a good night's sleep, and a fine morning often made a hero of the same man who by indigestion, a restless night, and a rainy morning would have proved a coward.
>
> EARL OF CHESTERFIELD

> Americans are absorbed in the present but are unaware of the past.
>
> We Americans are the best informed people on earth as to the events of the last twenty-four hours; we are not the best informed as to the events of the last sixty centuries.
>
> WILL and ARIEL DURANT

Exercise. Each of the following sentences is vague or unclear. Rewrite each sentence, replacing general and abstract words with specific or concrete ones.

1. Some people were hurt by floods.
2. Owning a pet may be good for your health.
3. The artist uses a lot of color.
4. Greed is harmful.
5. Hope is a basic requirement of human life.
6. They were requested by the court to leave their apartment.
7. A snowstorm can cause a lot of damage.

8. This is an interesting book with an exciting story line and good people.

9. Scrooge was mean and took no joy in life.

10. After he talked while under oath, he was accused of lying.

37c Denotation and connotation

Besides their **denotation,** or basic dictionary definition, many words also have **connotations**—associations that the word brings to mind and emotions that it arouses. Words that have the same dictionary meaning may have quite different connotations. For example, consider the following two sentences.

The clothes at this boutique are quite **cheap.**
The clothes at this boutique are quite **reasonable.**

Both *cheap* and *reasonable* have the dictionary meaning of "not expensive." However, *cheap* carries a negative connotation of low value, while *reasonable* carries a positive connotation of fair value.

When you write, you must choose words with the appropriate connotations.

Inappropriate: The quality of **childish** innocence shines through her poetry.
Appropriate: The quality of **childlike** innocence shines through her poetry.

Inappropriate: The editorial praised the candidate for being a rugged **egocentric.**
Appropriate: The editorial praised the candidate for being a rugged **individualist.**

Inappropriate: In 1873 the Supreme Court prevented Myra Bradwell from becoming a lawyer, since it did not consider the law an **effeminate** profession.
Appropriate: In 1873 the Supreme Court prevented Myra Bradwell from becoming a lawyer, since it did not consider the law a **ladylike** profession.

Some words have such strong connotations that they are said to be *loaded*. When used, they go off with a deafening emotional bang. For example, the words *slumlord, witch-hunt,* and *imperialism* are all loaded. Their connotative effect drowns out their denotative meaning. Be careful of loaded words, since they can make your writing appear biased.

Exercise. In each of the following pairs, the words have the same or almost the same denotative meaning but different connotations. Write a sentence for each word that shows you understand its connotative value. You may use your dictionary to help you.

1. talkative/effusive
2. mature/old
3. bookish/studious
4. ingenuous/unaffected
5. smell/scent
6. brainy/bright
7. petite/little
8. unctuous/earnest
9. grin/smirk
10. artful/guileful

37d Wordiness and repetition

Write as concisely as possible. Do not use five words where one will do. Avoid using empty words and unnecessary repetitions. Conciseness gives vigor to your style.

One way to achieve conciseness is to eliminate wordy expressions. Notice how each of the following phrases can be changed to a single-word equivalent.

Wordy	**Concise**
at all times when	whenever
at this point in time	now
at that point in time	then
because of the fact that	because
bring to a conclusion	conclude
by means of	by
due to the fact that	because
during the time that	while
in the event that	if

Wordy	Concise
in spite of the fact that	although
make reference	refer
be of the opinion that	think
on a great many occasions	often
prior to this time	before
until such time as	until
have a conference	confer

You can also make your writing more concise by deleting superfluous words, using exact words, and reducing larger elements to smaller elements. Notice how the following sentence is improved by the deletion of unnecessary words (deadwood), the use of exact words, and the reduction of larger elements such as clauses to smaller elements such as single words.

Wordy: In the month of April in the year 1984, men who were flying in space on board the spaceship that was named *Challenger* made an attempt to catch hold of and perform a repair job on a satellite that had been disabled.

Concise: In April 1984 astronauts on board the spaceship *Challenger* attempted to grab and repair a disabled satellite.

The words *the month of* and *in the year* add nothing to the meaning of the sentence; they simply fill up space and can be deleted. The noun phrase *men who were flying in space* can be replaced by one exact noun—*astronauts*. The words *that was named* are also deadwood. The phrase *made an attempt* can be reduced to the more direct *attempted*, *catch hold of* to *grab*, and *perform a repair job on* to *repair*. The clause *that had been disabled* can be reduced to the single word *disabled*.

Wordy: A man named Allan Dwan, who was a pioneer in the field of filmmaking, began his career as a director in the year 1910.

Concise: Allan Dwan, a pioneer filmmaker, began directing in 1910.

Wordy: The film that is called *The Birth of a Nation* and that was made by D. W. Griffith has caused a lot of controversy among people.

Concise: D. W. Griffith's film *The Birth of a Nation* is highly controversial.

Using the active voice instead of the passive voice will usually make a sentence more concise. Sometimes the passive voice is the simplest and most concise way to express an idea. For example, the sentences *Her husband was killed in Vietnam* or *The President is inaugurated on January 20* would be much wordier and more awkward if they were rewritten to make the verbs active. In general, however, the passive voice is wordier than the active voice. Notice how the following sentences are improved by changing the passive voice to the active voice and eliminating other kinds of wordiness.

Wordy: Studies **are being undertaken** by doctors who specialize in psychology to find out what effects the divorce of two parents has on the children of the two parents.

Concise: Psychologists **are studying** the effects of divorce on children.

Wordy: According to the author, whose name is Freeman Dyson, *Weapons and Hope* **was chosen** by him as the title for his book because a desire **was felt** by him "to discuss the gravest problem facing mankind, the problem of nuclear weapons."

Concise: Freeman Dyson **titled** his book *Weapons and Hope* because he **wanted** "to discuss the gravest problem facing mankind, the problem of nuclear weapons."

Wordy: Advice about gardening **is given** every day by Blair Michels, and this advice **is printed** on page 13 of this newspaper.

Concise: Blair Michels **gives** daily gardening advice on page 13 of this newspaper.

Try to avoid the constructions *it is*, *it was*, *there is*, and *there was*. Like the passive voice, these constructions are sometimes useful and appropriate, but often they are an unnecessarily wordy way of introducing an idea. Notice how the following sentences are improved by eliminating them.

Wordy: It is known that there is a need for security in children.
Concise: Children need security.

Wordy: It is a fact that the painting is a forgery.
Concise: The painting is a forgery.

Wordy: There is a need among modern people to gain an understanding of the risks of modern technology.
Concise: We need to understand the risks of modern technology.

Another cause of wordiness is redundant elements, words or phrases that unnecessarily repeat the idea expressed by the word to which they are attached. For example, the phrase *to the ear* is redundant in the expression *audible to the ear* because *audible* itself means "able to be perceived by the ear." Here is a list of some other common expressions that contain redundant elements.

Redundant	Concise
and etc.	etc.
bibliography of books	bibliography
mandatory requirements	requirements
refer back	refer
tall in height	tall
collaborate together	collaborate
visible to the eye	visible
repeat again	repeat
advance forward	advance
negative complaints	complaints
humorous comedy	comedy
close proximity	proximity
expensive in price	expensive
past history	history
continue to remain	remain
component parts	components

Not: The plot of Le Carré's **fictional novel** *The Little Drummer Girl* involves the **emotionally passionate** claims of the Israelis and the Palestinians.

But: The plot of Le Carré's **novel** *The Little Drummer Girl* involves the **passionate** claims of the Israelis and the Palestinians.

Not: The **consensus of opinion** is that the **true facts** of the **fatal assassination** may never be known.

But: The **consensus** is that the **facts** of the **assassination** may never be known.

Not: Copies of the **biography of his life** quickly **disappeared from sight** on the shelves, although the book was **large in size** and **heavy in weight.**

But: Copies of the **biography** quickly **disappeared** from the shelves, although the book was **large** and **heavy.**

Repetition has an important place in writing. It can be used effectively to emphasize a point or to complete a parallel structure. However, needless or excessive repetition weakens your writing. You can eliminate it by deleting the repeated words or by substituting synonyms or pronouns for them.

Not: Lady **Macbeth** urges **Macbeth** to murder the **king** so that **Macbeth** can become **king.**

But: Lady **Macbeth** urges **her husband** to murder the **king** so that **he** can gain **the crown.**

Not: One admirer of the rock group Devo has found similarities between **the works of Devo** and the **works** of the Dadaists.

But: One admirer of the rock group Devo has found similarities between **their works** and **those** of the Dadaists.

Not: After they decided to shoot the movie in a **shopping mall,** they examined thirty-five **shopping malls** until they found the right **shopping mall.**

But: After they decided to shoot the movie in a **shopping mall,** they examined thirty-five **malls** until they found the right **one.**

37e Flowery language

Wherever possible, use simple and direct words and phrases instead of showy and pretentious ones.

Flowery: Travelers on the road of life cannot help looking back and considering the possibility of whether any companion on this lonely journey will remember them after they have passed from this vale of tears.

Direct: People cannot help wondering whether anyone will remember them after they die.

Flowery: Even a person who passes his daily hours by contemplating the strange little tricks played on unsuspecting victims by cruel and relentless fate receives a jolt that shakes him to the depths of his being when, at the Huntington Library, he sets his eyes upon the pass that Lincoln inscribed in his own hand to allow his trusted bodyguard to be absent from his side on that fateful night of April 14, 1865.

Direct: Even people who appreciate the ironies of life receive a jolt when, at the Huntington Library, they see the pass that Lincoln wrote for his bodyguard to have the night off on April 14, 1865.

Flowery: The streets of this fair city were graced on this day of May 19, 1984, by the arrival of Hank Morris, an artist of more than well-deserved distinction.

Direct: The distinguished artist Hank Morris arrived in town on May 19, 1984.

Exercise. Revise each of the following sentences to eliminate wordiness, needless repetition, or flowery language.

1. The owner of a bicycle should have the bicycle inspected every year.

2. People who smoke are becoming more aware of the rights of people who do not smoke.

3. A story about ghosts that many critics feel has not been surpassed by any other story about ghosts was written by a writer who was an American and who was named Henry James, and it was called *The Turn of the Screw.*

4. It has been noted that many movies that have been made in recent years have a plot that involves the trials and tribulations of a made-up fictitious character who dresses up and wears the clothes of a person of the sex to which this character does not belong.

5. At every point in time that he was in close proximity to cats, our poor hero felt a fear that was not normal.

6. It is interesting and enlightening to compare and to show the

similarities between the writer Edgar Allan Poe's "The Oval Portrait" and the writer Oscar Wilde's *The Picture of Dorian Gray*.

7. A stranger who is unknown to the people in town helps the people in the town to feel less ridden by fear and more full of courage.

8. A flaw is shown by Billy Budd that mars his otherwise perfect beauty; his flaw is that at each time that he is confronted by a situation that makes him feel upset and ill at ease, he experiences an interruption in his speech, a spasmodic hesitation or prolongation of sounds.

9. The vitamin supplement that was to be added to the diet of the dog to improve the luster of the coat of the dog was recommended by the doctor who specializes in the treatment of animals.

10. In Gina Berriault's *The Infinite Passion of Expectation*, it is shown that the happiness and contentment of a person must come from the inside of the person; this "passion of expectation" gives to the person the ability to continue to go on.

37f Figurative language

Franklin P. Jones once quipped, "You're an old-timer if you can remember when setting the world on fire was a figure of speech." In a **figure of speech,** or **figurative language,** words are used in an imaginative and often unusual way to create a vivid impression. For example, as a figure of speech, *setting the world on fire* means "doing something astounding that gains recognition." Literally, of course, setting the world on fire means burning it. Most figures of speech make a direct or indirect comparison between two things that are essentially unlike each other. Three common types of figures of speech are simile, metaphor, and personification.

A **simile** uses the word *like* or *as* to make a direct comparison between two essentially unlike things: for example, "He was like a lion in the fight." Here are some other examples of simile.

> The land was perfectly flat and level but it shimmered like the wing of a lighted butterfly.
>
> EUDORA WELTY

223

He wore faded denims through which his clumsy muscles bulged like animals in a sack.

ROSS MacDONALD

Art is like a border of flowers along the course of civilization.

LINCOLN STEFFENS

The man's tie was as orange as a sunset.

DASHIELL HAMMETT

He [Monet] paints as a bird sings.

PAUL SIGNAC

A **metaphor** is an indirect comparison between two essentially unlike things that does not use the word *like* or *as*. In a metaphor the writer says or implies that one thing *is* another: for example, "He was a lion in the fight." Here are some other examples of metaphor.

Advertising is the rattling of a stick inside a swill bucket.

GEORGE ORWELL

His elegance was the thorn. And he was well aware that his aversion to coarseness, his delight in refinement, were futile; he was a plant without roots.

MISHIMA YUKIO

Roads became black velvet ribbons with winking frost sequins. Pines became whispering flocks of huge, dark birds and the hilltop and pasture cedars were black candle flames.

HAL BORLAND

He gave her a look you could have poured on a waffle.

RING LARDNER

A California oak is a tough, comforting thing—half tree, half elephant—its gray, baggy elbows bending solicitously close to the ground, following the contours of the hill.

PHYLLIS THEROUX

Personification is the attributing of human qualities to inanimate objects or abstract ideas. You may have noticed the word *solicitously* in the last example of metaphor above. This is an example of personification, since an oak cannot be solicitous; solicitousness is a human quality. Here are some other examples of personification.

His clothes were dark and a white handkerchief peeped coyly from his pocket and he looked cool as well as under a tension of some sort.

RAYMOND CHANDLER

A painting in a museum hears more ridiculous opinions than anything else in the world.

EDMOND DE GONCOURT

In all its career the Rio Grande knows several typical kinds of landscape, some of which are repeated along its great length.

PAUL HORGAN

I am for an art that is political—erotical—mystical, that does something other than sit on its ass in a museum.

CLAES OLDENBURG

A **mixed metaphor** is one that is not logically consistent. Complete your figurative comparisons appropriately.

Not: The river was a giant **snake** that **galloped** through the valley. (*Snakes cannot gallop.*)

But: The river was a giant **snake** that **slithered** through the valley.

Not: The bill **rolled** through the House with little opposition, but it **ran aground** in the Senate. (*Something that is rolling cannot run aground, since one action occurs on a solid surface and the other on water.*)

But: The bill **rolled** through the House with little opposition, but it **hit a stone wall** in the Senate.

Or: The bill **sailed** through the House with little opposition, but it **ran aground** in the Senate.

Not: Her **shallow** arguments were easily refuted by the more **solid** reasoning of her opponent. (*You cannot contrast something shallow with something solid;* shallow *refers to depth, whereas* solid *refers to firmness.*)

But: Her **shallow** arguments were easily refuted by the more **profound** reasoning of her opponent.

Or: Her **flimsy** arguments were easily refuted by the more **solid** reasoning of her opponent.

Exercise. Use figurative language to complete each of the following items in a vivid and consistent manner.

1. The approaching storm was . . .

2. Against the backdrop of the night sky, the building . . .

3. The old man lay in bed like . . .

4. The dog growled at the intruder . . .

5. With their opened umbrellas the people on the crowded street looked like . . .

6. The ticking of the clock seemed as loud as . . .

7. Her arms were as comforting as . . .

8. When he discovered he had passed the test, he felt . . .

9. The rainy weather was . . .

10. His pent-up anger was . . .

37g Clichés

A **cliché** is an overused phrase or figure of speech that has lost its freshness and its ability to express thoughts exactly. Clichés bore the reader and give the impression that the writer is lazy or unimaginative. Avoid staleness in your writing; strive for freshness and originality. Eliminate all clichés.

The following is a list of clichés. Avoid them and others like them.

shadow of a doubt	all walks of life
busy as a beaver	as luck would have it
bee in your bonnet	the crack of dawn
babbling brook	green with envy
depths of despair	take the bull by the horns
face the music	the acid test
bite the bullet	as happy as a lark
to the bitter end	in the nick of time
a thinking person	as sly as a fox
never a dull moment	as proud as a peacock
in the final analysis	callow youth
a crying shame	fly in the ointment
a bundle of joy	out of the woods
as quick as a wink	count on one hand
by the skin of our teeth	by hook or by crook

interesting to note	in the blink of an eye
slowly but surely	by the seat of my pants
in his heart of hearts	the depths of her soul

Clever writers or speakers often use clichés in an original way.

> Marriage is a great institution, but I'm not ready for an institution, yet.
>
> MAE WEST

> There nearly always is a method in madness. That's what drives men mad, being methodical.
>
> G. K. CHESTERTON

> Life is just a bowl of pits.
>
> RODNEY DANGERFIELD

> Ecologists believe that a bird in the bush is worth two in the hand.
>
> STANLEY C. PEARSON

37h Euphemisms

Euphemisms are words that disguise seemingly harsh or offensive realities. Euphemisms are quite rightly used in many situations to be polite or to avoid giving offense. There is nothing really wrong with referring to old people as *senior citizens* or to dead people as having *passed on*. However, many euphemisms have become clichés; they also tend to be wordy and to give writing a timid quality. In addition, euphemism can be improperly used to cover up the truth. Euphemism is commonly used in this way in gobbledygook.

> **Not:** The employees who had been notified of an interruption in their employment were referred to their outplacement manager.
>
> **But:** The laid-off employees were told to speak to the person who would try to help them find new jobs.
>
> **Not:** The official acknowledged that he had misspoken when he said the troops had not engaged in any protective-reaction missions.

But: The official admitted that he had lied when he claimed the troops had not engaged in any offensive missions.

Or: The official admitted he had been lying when he claimed the troops had not attacked any enemy positions.

Not: The prisoner's life will be terminated at dawn.
But: The prisoner will be shot at dawn.

Exercise. Rewrite each of the following sentences to eliminate clichés and euphemisms.

1. The army completed the pacification of the village.

2. He passed the test by the skin of his teeth.

3. The funds came through in the nick of time.

4. Although the interment of his bosom buddy upset him, he knew that into each life some rain must fall.

5. The company announced that it was relocating to another state and releasing its employees.

6. A good time was had by all at the party to mark the entrance into this world of a little bundle of joy.

7. He experienced a temporary setback to his earning potential.

8. Although she felt as fit as a fiddle, she was disturbed by the appearance of a large beauty mark on her left cheek.

9. Residents in this correctional facility dine on Salisbury steak every Monday.

10. It was raining cats and dogs when the government tested its new antipersonnel device.

38 Correct word choice

A **malapropism** is a word or expression that sounds unintentionally humorous when it is used in place of the similar-sounding one that the writer intended. The term is derived from Mrs. Malaprop, a pretentious character in Richard Sheridan's eighteenth-century play *The Rivals*, who uses near-miss words with a hilarious effect. For example, she refers to an "allegory [*rather than* alligator] on the banks of the Nile" and to another character's "historical [*rather than* hysterical] fit."

Do not be a Mrs. Malaprop. If you are not sure of the meaning of a word, look it up.

Not: Women charged with witchcraft were often accused of using spells and **incarnations** to cause their neighbors misfortune.

But: Women charged with witchcraft were often accused of using spells and **incantations** to cause their neighbors misfortune.

Not: At the end of the book are several helpful **appendages.**

But: At the end of the book are several helpful **appendixes.**

Not: The author argues that environmental damage is not necessarily a **coronary** of industrial development.

But: The author argues that environmental damage is not necessarily a **corollary** of industrial development.

Exercise. Choose the word in parentheses that sensibly completes each of the following sentences. Use your dictionary where necessary.

1. Regular exercise is especially important for people who have (sedentary/sedimentary) jobs.

2. Nicaragua argued that the mining of its harbors was a (flagrant/fragrant) violation of international law.

3. An extraordinary (prodigy/progeny), Mozart began composing and performing in public at the age of five.

4. An almost (palpable/palatable) air of crisis hung over Washington during the Watergate hearings.

5. *Main Street* expresses Sinclair Lewis's (aversion/inversion) to the constricted values of small-town America.

6. One panel of the altarpiece depicted the saved enjoying their heavenly reward; the other, the damned suffering (restitution/retribution) for their sins.

7. The editorial (deplored/implored) the governor's veto of the bill, calling him a political coward and a tool of lobbyists.

8. Patients recovering from surgery are urged to get back on their feet as soon as possible to prevent muscle (apathy/atrophy).

9. Daniel Webster was (excoriated/exonerated) by abolitionists for supporting the Compromise of 1850, which they considered a concession to slaveholders.

10. Most of Brazil's population is concentrated along the coast, and some interior areas are almost (uninhabited/uninhibited).

THE PROCESS
OF
WRITING

THE PROCESS OF WRITING

39 Preparation for writing

A few people can pick up a tennis racket for the first time and nail a perfect serve across the net without thinking. Fortunately for the rest of us, such competence is rare, and the same is true among writers. Like the tennis serve, writing requires a combination of skills perfected over time. It requires coordination of thought, language, and hand, and most of us are no more naturally adept at making the three work together than we are at making our arm muscles, our eyesight, and a racket put a tennis ball where we want it. To arrange words on paper so that they convey the message we want to send takes practice. To write easily and well, therefore, write frequently. Make writing a regular activity, not just a chore to be performed only when it is required of you. Three activities are especially useful as training for writing: keeping a journal, reading, and writing letters.

39a Keeping a journal

A journal differs from a diary because it goes beyond recounting the events of the writer's day to recording what the writer *thought* about the events or about some information. For example, a diary entry might read:

> *May 17*
>
> Met Juanita at the ice cream parlor yesterday p.m. She had a bandaged knee from falling off her bicycle and couldn't keep our date for the dance. Ralph's girlfriend offered to call a friend of hers for me, but I stayed with Juanita and went with her to a movie and Burger King instead.

A journal entry, on the other hand, might read like this:

> Juanita had to break our dance date the other night because she had damaged her knee in falling off her bike. She piled up, of course, because she was riding no-hands the way she always does on her heavy class days. Nothing I say seems to convince her that a backpack would be much better for hauling her books around than four texts under each arm and a prayer that God will steer and brake for her. She says the backpack would look sloppy, and I have to admit she dresses well. But why wear a boutique on your shoulders and live dangerously? I suppose there is something to be said for going in style, but she ought to realize as well that pride goeth before a fall.

The beauty of a journal is that you need not keep it on a daily basis; the obligation of a journal is that you must keep it with some regularity if you are to gain any benefit from it. The journal gives regular practice in coordinating thought, language, and hand; it also provides a reservoir of ideas for future writing. In the sample entry above, there is an abundance of raw material to develop into an essay: the sacrifice of safety and practicality to appearance, the futility of arguing for a change in a person's basic values, the theme of pride leading to a fall. That great authors like Henry David Thoreau, F. Scott Fitzgerald, Henry James, George Sand, and many, many others kept journals is no accident. The practice of thinking things out in a journal is invaluable writing preparation.

39b Reading

Travel with a book. When you are stuck in traffic, waiting for a bus, or standing in line at the bank or the supermarket, improve the time by reading. Read everything—books, newspapers, magazines, poems, billboards. Learn through reading what others have experienced and learned. What you read becomes part of your own experience for later use.

As you read, do more than absorb information; think about the way the author writes, about the turns of phrase, about the rhythm of sentences and how the author avoids—or fails to avoid—a monotonous delivery. Try to store up particularly effective passages as models for your own prose. Read critically. Learn to argue with the printed word. A disagreement with another's point of view is a potential starting point for an essay. Read looking for grammatical mistakes and errors of punctuation. If you can spot the faults of others, you will proofread your own work more accurately. Read to discover the author's tone and purpose, and how they complement each other. Use your journal to record what you think about what you read.

39c Writing letters

Writing letters to friends and relatives is excellent writing practice. The recipient of a letter is a clearly defined audience for the writer, and we usually adjust our letters consciously or unconsciously to the likes and dislikes of the person we are writing to. Think of the adjustments you find yourself making in such letters. Ask yourself why you wrote to Great-Uncle Herman about the "minor automobile accident" that prevented you from attending Gretchen's wedding, and why you described the same occurrence as "a stupid fender-bender" to your friend Dee. Work at making your letters entertaining. Invent new ways of saying "nothing much has happened here"—and remember, something always has.

Exercise 1. Set yourself the goal of writing at least 150 words a day for a month. The writing can be of any sort as long as it is not required academically or professionally. It must be coherent, that is, it must be about a topic and in connected sentences. Count personal letters and journal entries as part of the exercise. By all means write more than 150 words if you like, but don't write a thousand words on Tuesday evening and call it a week's work.

Exercise 2. Keep a record for one week of everything you read. (Don't count advertisements and notices.) At the end of the week, review your record and select the piece of reading that sticks most clearly in your mind. Write a brief discussion of your choice, explaining why you remember it so well. Look at it again and evaluate the way it is written. Is there anything in the author's writing that makes the piece stand out?

40 The process of writing: first draft

The finished essay is the product of the writer's work, and that work consists of interrelated and interwoven actions that are collectively called a process. It is a complex process whose parts are unpredictable, because writers tend to develop their own distinct processes as they grow in experience. And it is a process that shapes itself as it goes.

If you set out to make a box, you begin with a clear mental picture of what a box is and can easily follow a simple process of construction that will give you a product with a bottom, four sides, and a lid connected at right angles. But when you decide to write, your image of the product is vague or perhaps nonexistent. You might, for example, begin with the idea of saying something about air pollution and find yourself discussing alternative forms of energy production, only to discover that what you really feel strongly about is the possible danger of nuclear reactors. The process of writing is likely to produce such discoveries. Because the process may loop back on itself or even change direction altogether, it is partly misleading to present it as a series of steps that are completed and cemented in place one on top of another.

But familiarity with some of the typical steps in the writing process will help you understand the process as a whole and give you freedom to apply it as you find best in your case. The actions most writers find necessary in the process of writing are *prewriting*, *drafting*, *revision*, and *proofreading*.

40a Prewriting

Prewriting is the writing activity that precedes a first draft. It is what the writer may do to find a topic and to refine that topic into a thesis. During prewriting, the writer may also make some preliminary decisions about the purpose for writing, the audience to be addressed, the tone of the writing, and the basic plan for the essay.

In the following pages you will find a number of suggestions for prewriting. Do not regard them as a prescription, every element of which must be used. Experiment until you find the practices that work for *you*. If some do not help, do not frustrate yourself by following them.

Invention

When the task of writing an undefined essay falls on a blank mind confronted with a blank piece of paper, the writer must get a topic into one and onto the other. Several tactics are useful for discovering a topic.

Freewriting

If you are at a loss for an idea, try **freewriting.** Set yourself a time limit of, say, ten minutes and write down anything that comes into your head during that time. No restrictions apply as far as content is concerned. The only rule is that your pen or pencil must keep moving on the page for those ten minutes. This is a sample of one writer's freewriting:

On the mark - ten minutes. Find something to
say. Find something to fix your mind on. What's
on the desk here? Brother's photograph. Some
sort of Middle Eastern pot with two pencils
and a letter opener in it. Sundial I never
fixed up in the yard. (Think my brother gave
me that two years ago.) Why did I never put
that thing to use? Is it something about an
unwillingness to face passage of time? Timeless
society. Aging without counting. How long does
it take to put a sundial on a post? If
I did put it up, would I look at it?
What's the point of a sundial in today's world
of quartz watches? A timeless way of keeping
time? Why are sundials in the Northern
part of U.S. different from those in the
South? Something to do with the angle of
the sun, I guess.

Go back to the sundial and time.

Remember verse I once saw on a sundial.
Something about "I record only sunny hours."
The sundial is an attractive anachronism
because it is a timeless way of telling time
and counts only hours in the sun.

This writer filled an empty mind by fixing quickly on an object
to think about. Another thrashed about by starting with
"freewriting" itself.

Freewriting for ten minutes! What's "free" about
that? Freewriting should include freedom not
to write at all. I don't intend to make my liv-

ing like Hemingway, and I bet he didn't have to spend time free-algebraing. This assignment is about as fair as required military service. Do what you aren't inclined to for your own good. Develop writing habits. Develop writing rabbits! New breakthrough in veterinary medicine — or would that be behavioral psychology? See the writing rabbit autograph a lettuce leaf!

This is getting nowhere.

In fact, this writer found two or three openings for an essay: the freedom exercised by saying no, the fairness of required military service, and the merit—or lack of merit—in being made to do something distasteful for one's own good.

Brainstorming

Another tactic of invention is **brainstorming.** A writer can undertake brainstorming alone or as part of a group. Obviously, the results of a group's brainstorming will be more diverse than the products of a single imagination, but the object in either case is the same: to generate as many topics as possible for exploration. In the first stage of brainstorming, keep the topics to simple nouns and noun phrases. Set a goal of ten different topics for a start, such as the following:

gun control	nuclear disarmament
vocational training	new roles for women
parades	military conscription
drunken driving	drug abuse
environmental pollution	regulation of the automobile industry

Before choosing a topic to explore, weigh the popularity of each entry. Consider, for example, how much has already been written about gun control. The more popular a topic is among journalists and other writers, the harder it will be to say anything new about that topic in a short essay. And the attempt to say something new will probably require some research. The more familiar a topic is, the more it demands from the writer.

The second stage of brainstorming is similar to the first, but the object is to write down as much as you can think of about the topic selected. Here is a sample of brainstorming on the topic "parades."

"I Hate a Parade" is the reverse of the popular song title "I Love a Parade." Why do people love parades? Band music is stirring. Costumes are colorful. Parades are festive, nationalistic, patriotic, symbols of rejoicing or of united purpose. Common cause.— COMMON CAUSE—relation between protest marches and parades.

FAMOUS PARADES: July 4th, St. Patrick's Day, Memorial Day, Thanksgiving, May Day, trooping the color, Bastille Day.

BIG CITY PARADES/SMALL TOWN PARADES.

Components of a parade: high school bands, floats, dignitaries, firefighting equipment, civic groups, majorettes—teenage bunnies, color guards, national guard, entertainment stars, helium balloons, child spectators with flags, flag and button sellers, policemen's benevolent association, police controlling the crowd, excuses for drinking, cheering.

PARADES IN HISTORY—Roman triumphs: barbaric display of captives. Shows of force—German marches down Champs Elysées during occupation of France in WW II.

THE DOWNSIDE OF PARADES: Disruption of traffic. Too many parades—meaning lost. Parade meaningless to many paraders. Big parades much alike. Progress slow. Exhibitionism. A parade or a mob? Military parades at least precise and prompt; civilian parades more like strolls. Mess to clean up. Bands always play two blocks from your position. Crowds.

SCENES I REMEMBER: Columbus Day parade—Catholic girls' school marching to "Scotland the Brave" with grim faces. St. Patrick's Day and advocates of terrorism. Freezing and unable to get close enough to see at Thanksgiving Day parade. Little girls twirling dummy rifles painted white. Twenty-minute halts during Memorial Day parade. Fire engines overheating because pace so slow. Marching to rock music. Televising the Thanksgiving Day parade and the strain on the commentators to keep saying something. Never seen a big parade end to end. (Big parades like bad stories—they have a middle but no beginning or end.)

If brainstorming one topic does not produce an adequate range of thoughts, try another topic.

Clustering

A variation of brainstorming is **clustering.** Write the topic in the middle of a piece of paper. As ideas related to the topic occur to you, place them randomly around the topic. Then study the related ideas and see what kinds of connections you can find among them. Draw lines between connected ideas. Then, on another page, write the topic in the middle again and arrange potentially related ideas in clusters around it.

On the opposite page is an example of clustering around the topic of parades.

Other ways of finding a topic

If freewriting and brainstorming fail to produce a workable topic for an unspecified essay, try these other approaches.

1. If you keep a journal, page through it for a thought or impression you can enlarge.
2. Open a newspaper or magazine at random and read the first piece of article your eye falls on. Keep trying until something inspires you to state an opinion about it.
3. Start a sentence with "I think" and make an outrageous statement. Then see how far you can go in defense of it.

> I think all drivers should be drunk. Drunken drivers so often walk away unscathed from the accidents they have caused that we must assume their intoxicated state of muscle relaxation has something to do with survival. If all drivers were tanked, the highway death toll would decline.

Sometimes such a preposterous position leads to a satiric essay developing the wrongheaded idea; more often, the mental tussle with an impossible proposition stimulates a novel approach to the defensible view.

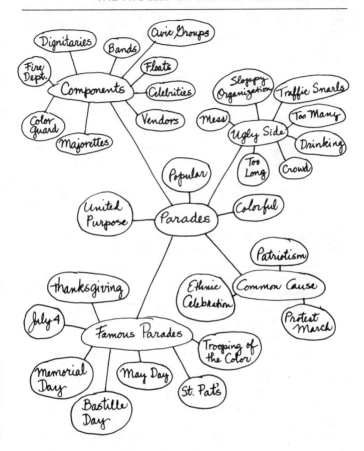

Finding a purpose

The purpose of an essay is not the same thing as the reason for writing an essay. An error in your telephone bill gives you a reason to write to the telephone company, but the purpose of your letter will be to *inform* the company it has made a mistake and to *persuade* it to make a correction in your favor. Once you have found a topic, a preliminary decision on your purpose in writing about that topic will help you shape your essay. You may choose to inform or to persuade or to do any of the following:

- *to record* your thoughts on a topic. Most journal entries are written to record.
- *to entertain* an audience. In entertaining essays the writer embellishes the topic with wit, humor, word play, and action.
- *to instruct*, to tell someone, for example, how to connect a printer to an Apple IIc computer. Such essays are often called process papers because they describe a process.
- *to analyze* a topic, that is, to examine the parts of the topic and the way they relate to one another. Essays about literary works are often analytical; they probe the author's performance to understand its effect.
- *to argue* a point. Such an essay must take both sides of an issue into account while favoring one of them.
- *to express* an opinion.
- *to reveal* the writer. A job application letter is written not only to describe the applicant's qualifications but also to reveal the applicant's character through the manner of its describing.
- *to evaluate* a work or item. Criticism evaluates a play.

This list is not exhaustive, but it includes the primary purposes. Two or more purposes may characterize the same essay: for example, an argumentative essay may be entertaining, and an evaluative paper may include the writer's expression of opinion and an analysis of the topic. When planning an essay, however, you will probably find it most helpful to decide on a single purpose and let subordinate purposes arise as you develop your thesis.

Reviewing brainstorming and clustering

As part of finding a purpose for your topic, study your brainstorming and/or clustering. In brainstorming the topic "parades," the writer began with the song "I Love a Parade" to question why people love parades and then developed six categories of ideas about parades: the attractions of parades, famous parades, big-city and small-town parades, parades in history, the ugly side of parades, and scenes of parades remembered. A number of purposes can be derived from these categories:

1. To describe famous parades
2. To compare big-city and small-town parades
3. To trace the history of parades
4. To analyze the good and bad aspects of parades
5. To narrate personal experiences at parades

The basic purpose formula

You may be able to establish a preliminary purpose by filling out the following formula:

In this essay I will _____.

Fill in the blank with statements such as *record my impressions of* (the topic); *express my opinion that* (the topic) *is or is not* _____; *argue that* (the topic) *should or should not be approved; analyze* (the topic) *to show that* _____; *instruct my audience how to* _____. You need not use exactly these phrases, but do give yourself something specific to achieve in the essay.

The journalist's formula

As a way of defining what you know about your topic (or need to know) in order to state a purpose, you can use **the journalist's formula:** Who? What? When? Where? Why? How? For example, here is how the journalist's formula might be applied to the topic of parades.

Who takes part in parades?
What happens at parades?
When do parades take place?
Where are parades held?
Why do people like parades?
How do parades affect people and communities?

Burke's pentad

The rhetorician Kenneth Burke proposes a refinement of the journalist's formula in his **pentad**, a series of five categories for inquiry about a topic: action, agent or actor, agency or method, scene, and purpose. Burke's pentad might be applied to the topic of parades in the following way:

Action: What takes place during a parade?
What happens around the parade among spectators and in the neighborhood?

Agent: Who takes part in parades?
Of what else is a parade composed?
What kind of people watch a parade?
What is the spirit of a parade?

Agency: How do parades interest people?
How are parades assembled?
How do I/we react to parades?

Scene: When and where are parades presented?
What is the setting for a parade like?

Purpose: Why are parades held?
Why do I like or dislike parades?

The journalist's formula and Burke's pentad do not in themselves establish a purpose for the writer. They help the writer to focus methodically on components of the topic in order to discover an aspect of it that can be developed into a purpose. For example, after answering the questions the pentad has suggested and reviewing them, the writer might return to the basic purpose formula to complete it like this:

In this essay I will analyze parades to show what the spirit of parades is and why people are attracted to it.

After further thought, the writer might restate the purpose like this:

In this essay I will express my opinion that the spirit of parades appeals to our sentimentality.

Or like this:

> In this essay I will argue that parades are frivolous extravagances.

The rhetorical modes

One other way to establish a purpose is by writing four paragraphs about the topic, choosing for each paragraph a purpose based on one of the classic **rhetorical modes**: *description, narration, exposition,* and *argument.* A descriptive paragraph tells what the topic is like; a narrative paragraph tells what action occurs in relation to the topic; an expository paragraph explains why the action takes place; and an argumentative paragraph states the writer's reasons why that action should occur or not occur again. Here is how the rhetorical modes might be applied to the topic of parades:

Description

A parade consists of floats, civic groups, marching squads, bands, vintage automobiles, and young women and men in various costumes. The parade is often filled out with firefighting equipment from neighboring communities. A dozen fire engines add considerable length and turn what might be mistaken for repertory theater revue into a genuine parade—a long string of persons and machinery moving in one direction past a lot of other persons for the pleasure and inspiration of all.

Narration

Deputy Mayor Caleb Nordstrom agreed to ride a horse in the Fourth of July parade as long as the parade marshals found him a gentle horse. They did. The Bit and Crupper Riding Stable produced Snowball, a plodding gray gelding of twenty-five whose sagging underlip showed his extended teeth. Snowball had one gait, a limp shuffle, and patrons of the stable well knew that whip and spur had no effect on him. Indeed, Snowball under stimulus was inclined to lie down wearily and look quizzically at his displaced rider over his shoulder. And that is exactly what he did under Deputy Mayor Nordstrom when the band struck up "The Star-Spangled Banner" at the review stand.

Exposition

The fundamental appeal of parades must go back to the tribal dance for rain, plentiful crops, victory in war, or the expulsion of evil spirits. In such rituals, the individuals of the tribe came together in a single blended purpose and became, in their repetitive actions, essentially one body. Today, the parade's infinite variety—from juggling acts to marching banjo bands—seems to belie the underlying principle of common cause. But it is the parade's ability to mix such disparate participants into the performance of a single event that achieves the tribal aim. The message of a parade is: We're all in this together.

Argument

For a space of five hours the city has been diverted by an apparently endless stream of bands, floats, police benevolent associations, and sauntering dignitaries. The crowd has waved its arms off and left with its throats sore from cheering. Now, looking down at the rubbish in the parade's wake, we can ask ourselves if the expenditure necessary to let the populace make fools of themselves, either as actors or spectators, is really worth it. Have we achieved anything permanently uplifting? Have we experienced the catharsis of tragedy or the release of comedy? No, we have simply watched a mob pass formed in roughly regular lines and stepping to a cacophony of badly played and hysterically mixed music. We have not attended an event; we have watched a piece of traditional foolishness—and probably been soaked to the skin while we did it. Yet given the choice of feeding several thousand starving Ethiopians or gawking at a parade, we fall in with the parade every time. When humanity decides the proper value of expensive trivia in ritual jubilation, there will be some hope for us.

Like Burke's pentad, the modes of rhetoric force the writer to think a topic through. Description and narration are relatively easy steps to accomplish; exposition and argument require analysis and originality.

Note that the rhetorical modes build on each other: the narration paragraph includes description of Snowball; the expository paragraph includes description of the modern parade and narration of the history of parades; while the argumentative paragraph includes description of the parade that has passed, narration of what the crowd did, exposition of what the spectators have experienced—or not experienced—and argument in the conclusion that humanity ought to revise its priorities. In an essay expressing a complicated point of view, the modes will be intermixed, as in the last paragraph. Think of the rhetorical modes as a series of concentric circles.

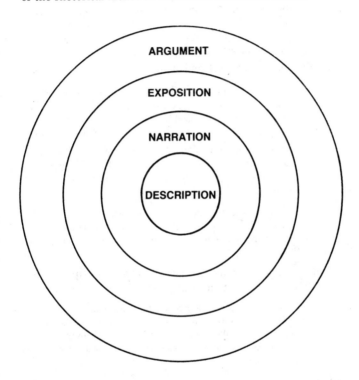

Defining an audience

Every writer of an essay should answer the question "With whom do I want to communicate?" The question should be reasked and reanswered frequently as the writing goes on and after each draft is finished. Experienced writers not only define their audience, they *envision* it as they write—a single person or group personified in the imagination.

247

After identifying an audience, a writer must analyze that audience to determine how to write effectively for it. For good reasons, you do not usually write the same essay for your classmates, your boyfriend or girlfriend, your parents, the general public, a potential employer, an examination committee, a fellow hacker with an IBM PC, and the town council. Each audience requires a difference in the writer's performance—sometimes a subtle difference, sometimes a dramatic one. In analyzing an audience, ask and answer the following questions:

1. How much is the audience like me? If its age, experience, and style of living are very close to mine, I can write in a relaxed and casual style and be reasonably sure that what I say and how I say it will be understood. If the audience is different from me in these respects, then I must expect it to be unfamiliar with some things I take for granted. For example, I might describe a new restaurant in town to a group of local friends this way:

   A restaurant has just opened on Academy Drive next to the Ball and Gutter. The menu is longer than a term paper and all in French, but if you ask for a cheeseburger and fries, they bring you the right thing.

   Reviewing the same restaurant in a newspaper with a fairly wide circulation, I might write this:

   Parkersville now boasts a French restaurant at 316 Academy Drive. In this unlikely location between a car wash and the Ball and Gutter bowling alley, patrons will find a surprisingly extensive sampling of genuine French cuisine as well as a solid base of good American cooking.

2. How much does the audience know about my topic? If it is well informed, I can, and perhaps should, use precise terminology without definition. If the audience is largely unfamiliar with my topic, I must explain more and define technicalities in common terms. For students of the history of marine architecture, I could write this:

   American shipwrights in the early nineteenth century tended to follow French or Spanish patterns. They constructed hulls characterized by minimal sheer, low angle of dead rise, and a relatively high ratio of beam to length.

But for the general reader, the following would be more appropriate:

American shipbuilders in the early nineteenth century copied the French and Spanish vessels of the time. Their ships showed almost flat in profile with little rise at either end, and the stern, or rear, tapered gradually to a point below the waterline, rather than coming abruptly to a blunt end as it did in English and Dutch craft. American ships were also narrower than English ones.

3. How interested is my audience in my topic? Will I have to stimulate interest by writing with humor or emotion or dramatic action? Or can I proceed straight to my point as simply as possible? The journalist reporting a fire can count on an attentive audience and will try to state the facts plainly. The same journalist writing an editorial opinion must use more art to arouse interest.

4. What relationship do I want to create between my audience and me? Do I want an informal, friendly relationship? Is it proper for me to take the role of instructor to pupil? Should I treat the reader with special respect as my superior? Should I be impersonal and formal? To appreciate the different relationships involved, imagine writing a letter to a friend, a letter to a younger relative who has asked for advice, a letter to a manager for whom you would like to work, and a letter asking for information about a company's product. Although essays are not letters, imagining the audience of your essay as the recipient of a letter will help you develop the relationship you want.

Before starting your first draft, try to complete this formula:

I am writing this essay to (this person/these persons): _____.

The blank can be filled with the name of an individual you think stands for the audience as a whole or with a more general description such as *my colleagues at work, my classmates, people who don't know me but know my topic, someone who has probably read a lot of essays like mine before.*

Setting a tone

Tone cannot be determined by completing a formula; sometimes it cannot be determined until the first or even the third draft of the essay is complete. But some decision on tone before the writing begins will help you keep a consistent delivery and find the right tone for the finished essay.

Tone is the result of word choice based on attitude—on how the writer feels about the subject, on how the writer feels about the audience, and on how the writer wants the audience to feel about the writer and the subject. The writer's purpose will influence decisions on all three points, but especially on the last.

Consider the different way two writers handled the same subject in the following sentences:

> The city planning board has apparently surpassed its usual high standard of idiocy and irresolution by willfully ignoring the menace of increased and uncontrolled heavy vehicle traffic on Prospect Avenue.

> The city planning board may have shown poor judgment in making no plans for controlling the number of trucks using Prospect Avenue.

Both sentences say essentially the same thing. The second, however, has an almost neutral tone. We cannot say much about how the author sounds, except to say he sounds mildly concerned. His audience could be anyone he does not want to offend, his subject is of minor importance to him and his audience, and his purpose is to call attention gently to a situation that may need correction at some time in the distant future.

The tone of the first sentence, on the other hand, is full of sounds. We might even call it strident. The author has loaded the statement with scorn (*apparently surpassed*), sarcasm (*high standard of idiocy*), accusation (*willfully ignoring*), foreboding (*menace*), and—overall—anger. But the author is doing more than venting wrath at the city planners. For that effect she might have written:

> Those lunkheads on the planning board really loused up when they forgot to put a "No Trucks" sign on Prospect.

But if she had written that, she would have written without considering her audience. (Are we moved by someone who writes "lunkheads"?) She would also have written without considering her purpose. (The tone calls attention to the writer, not to how the writer wants us to respond.) Instead, she chose an almost literary tone. She determined that this subject and her feelings called for formal language (*irresolution, vehicle, increased and uncontrolled*) and stylistic devices (scorn and sarcasm) to show that she was angry at the city planners and that her intelligent readers would agree with her. The choices may not be entirely successful, but we can see that they were made consciously.

Tone is like fire: a good servant and a bad master. To control it, the writer must have a good sense of subject and purpose and must keep a constant vision of audience in mind. To make a preliminary choice of tone, try to answer these questions:

1. What is my attitude to my topic? (Am I enthusiastic? Am I bitter? Am I cynical? Am I concerned? Many other attitudes are possible.)
2. How deeply do I feel this attitude?
3. How do I want my audience to perceive my attitude?
4. How closely do I want my audience to feel my presence as writer? (Talking directly individual to individual? Talking from the front of the room to a group? Talking from a distance via radio?)
5. What response do I want from my audience? (Amusement? Agreement? Action?)

Remember that the audience senses the writer through tone. Writers must learn to hear themselves in their tone if they want to sound natural, for although writing and speaking differ, the essay tone of an experienced writer reflects rhythms and word choices of the writer's speaking habits. Such a tone reads more naturally than an assumed or forced one does. *As you write, ask yourself: "Would I say that if I were talking?" If, in all honesty, you doubt that you would, consider carefully whether you want to keep the construction you have used or to replace it with a more familiar expression.*

Stating a thesis

Before starting your draft, you may want to summarize your prewriting to this point by stating your thesis succinctly. The **thesis statement** is a phrase, preferably a complete sentence, composed before the draft begins. It encapsulates the point the essay will make. As you think of a thesis statement, keep three things in mind.

1. Do not try to put your thesis statement into words appropriate to the style and tone of your finished essay. Make the plainest possible declaration of what you want to achieve. One good formula to begin with is the following:

   I think ____(topic)____ is _____

   shows _____

   should or should not _____

   because _____.

2. Do not assume your thesis statement is a fixture. If work on your essay proves that the thesis statement is indefensible or that some other aspect of your topic is more appealing, more interesting, or more controversial, restate your thesis to meet the new developments. Remember you are experimenting with an idea in the rough. You have several drafts in which to test the idea for validity.

3. If you are stuck for a thesis statement, simply begin to write. Move on to *priming writing*, which is explained in the next section.

If you use the formula recommended, take the product another step before beginning to write. *Make sure that your thesis statement does more than merely announce your topic.*

Topic: A Brooklyn neighborhood

Formula:	I think my Brooklyn neighborhood is unique because diverse cultures form a unique identity.
Thesis Statement:	My own neighborhood, Bay Ridge, shows how diverse ethnic cultures combine to give the area a unique identity.

Build on the formula to include specific nouns, verbs, adjectives, and adverbs. The more specific you are, the more guidance you will have in writing your essay.

Topic:	Drivers' responsibilities
Formula:	I think young drivers are unaware of the responsibility involved in operating a car.
Thesis Statement:	A person of seventeen seldom fully appreciates the responsibility of operating an automobile.

A thesis statement should make a *vigorous* statement; it should assert the topic in a context that demands explanation, expansion, analysis, or defense.

Bland:	Those who argue for abortion on demand sometimes also argue against capital punishment.
Vigorous:	Those who argue for abortion on demand are inconsistent when they also argue against capital punishment.

A good test of a thesis statement is to ask: Could I state the opposite and make a case for that point of view? If you can answer yes, you probably have a workable thesis statement.

The thesis statement will usually emerge in the finished essay as a thesis sentence, but let the essay's development determine how and where the thesis sentence appears.

Priming writing

If a thesis statement does not occur to you at the start, try **priming writing.** Set a goal of 150–250 words and start writing about the topic from any angle. Try to produce connected sentences with some coherence, that is, with details or subordinate points to support generalizations. The purpose of this writing is to prime the pump, to get your mind and fingers working with your topic and into the mood to write.

The following is an example of priming writing on the topic of parades.

The idea of A PARADE is part of the American heritage. Communities large and small seem addicted to the process of stringing people and things over a few miles of principal street and moving them slowly past spectators as a way of commemorating almost any public occasion. Humanity has been fascinated by the pomp of parades probably since the first tribe went to war against its neighbor. The parade was a way of getting the population together before the fight and a way of letting it know the outcome afterwards. Triumphs for Roman generals were the biggest formal parades of the time.

During its evolution, the parade seems to have moved in two directions. In one way it has become a strictly formal military affair, such as trooping the color in Britain or the May Day parade in Moscow. Other parades have concentrated on civilian participation, as in China, France, and the United States, where an offshoot of the parade is the protest march. This division of the parade has produced a pageant of military precision, on the one hand, and something resembling a circus on the other. The only difference

254

between a U.S. civilian parade and a protest march is
the mood. Sometimes the absence of music is another
distinguishing aspect of the protest march. In its
"celebration" aspect, the parade is a motion of organized rabble for the pleasure of a disorganized
rabble.

Although the priming writing contains no specific thesis statement, it reveals to the writer an attitude about parades. The
modern civilian parade seems to be "a motion of organized
rabble for the pleasure of a disorganized rabble." This rather
exaggerated statement should give the writer a clue to filling
the thesis statement formula:

> I think a modern parade is (vulgar/frivolous/meaningless/a waste
> of time) because it is disorganized and far removed from its
> original purpose of uniting people in spirit.

A more explicit thesis statement derived from the formula
might be:

> The modern American parade has lost the parade's historic sense
> of purpose and become a meaningless collection of unrelated
> groups who have nothing in common but motion in the same
> direction.

Outlining

An outline provides a framework for a first draft and helps
prevent organizational blunders. There are two main kinds of
outlines. The first, and the most practical for a short essay, is
the sentence outline; the second is the formal outline. In a
sentence outline, the writer states each subordinate topic of
the thesis as a sentence and arranges the sentences in the
order of development that the essay will follow. Usually, but
not always, each sentence of the sentence outline is the topic
for a paragraph of the essay.

I Hate a Parade

1. On every conceivable excuse, every American city sponsors a parade consisting of as many high school bands, civic groups, old cars, and police departments as the city can get together.

2. Historically the parade was associated with war or the people's welfare.

3. The modern civilian parade in America has lost most of its military or communal heritage and has become a circus carnival.

4. This strange mob of a parade is falsely justified by a superficial appearance of innocence.

5. Although parades involve ugly undercurrents, they are grim enough as "clean" fun to raise questions about their merit.

The **formal outline,** by comparison, is more complicated and requires detailed thought about content. It is arranged in descending order from major topic through lesser subtopics in a rigid system of indentation and symbol.

I Hate a Parade

Roman numeral:	I. The Character of Parades
Capital letter:	A. Occasions
Arabic numeral:	1. Columbus Day
	2. Memorial Day
	3. July Fourth
	4. St. Patrick's Day

Capital letter:	B. Components
Arabic numeral:	1. Bands
	2. Floats
	3. Police department
	4. Vehicles
Lower-case letter:	a. vintage cars
	b. firefighting equipment
Arabic numeral:	5. Civic groups
Capital letter:	C. Big-City Parades
Arabic numeral:	1. Length
Lower-case letter:	a. beginning
	b. end
	2. Expense
Roman numeral:	II. The History of Parades

And so on. Obviously, the writer who chooses a formal outline as a start must think the topic through thoroughly and develop working notes *before* trying to outline. For a long essay, such as a research paper, the formal outline is valuable; for a short essay it is probably too cumbersome.

The formal outline *is* useful in the preparation of a short paper *after the first draft is complete.* If the content of your first draft cannot be arranged systematically in a formal outline, there is a good chance that something in the draft is irrelevant or out of place. Always consider using the formal outline for revision.

One traditional rule for the formal outline is that a topic divided into subtopics must be divided into at least two such subtopics. In other words, there must be a subtopic B if there is a subtopic A, or a subtopic 2 if there is a subtopic 1. If you are using a formal outline to help you get started, do not worry about this rule. The outline is an aid, not an end in itself.

40b Writing the first draft

Having selected a topic; defined it; settled on purpose, audience, and tone; established a thesis sentence; and planned your essay, you are ready to write a first draft.

But take a breather for a moment. All those prewriting steps, or some of them, may well help you get started; however, there is such a thing as getting bogged down in the preliminaries. Another way of getting started is to write the first draft without making any of the preparatory efforts. It is not a crime to plunge straight in and see what happens. *What is a crime is to plunge in under the impression that the first draft will become the final draft with only a bit of light tinkering.*

Whether you make a careful prewriting preparation or let the essay happen as it may from your pen, you *must* regard your first draft as a throwaway—as something that will be only vaguely related to the finished essay. Always think of it as something to be broken down and rearranged, as prose to be thoroughly rewritten until it is right, as something far beneath your potential. If you can think of the draft this way, you will have no self-esteem invested in it that will suffer if the work is cut up or even thrown out.

Keeping in mind that the first draft is only the first stage of an essay, follow these guidelines in writing it:

1. Write the first draft well before the finished essay is due. A week in advance is desirable; a twenty-four-hour lead is essential. *Don't wait until the last minute—ever.*
2. Write the first draft as rapidly as possible. You want to capture ideas rather than form.
3. Ignore spelling and punctuation questions as you write. If you are uncertain of one or the other at any point, mark the place and write on. Any signal will do. Use a wavy line under the doubtful place or circle it, but don't stop to look things up. Do that *after* the first draft is complete.
4. Minimize your investment. Cut regular-size sheets of paper in half and start every paragraph on a new half-page. The less writing you have on a piece of paper, the easier it will

be to move that writing around in the essay or to discard it altogether.

5. Write double or even triple space. Leave room to insert.
6. Cross out; don't erase. And when you cross out, let what you have crossed out show through. You might want to go back to that wording later.
7. Be sloppy! Discourage yourself from even *thinking* of the draft as finished work.
8. Write the draft where you cannot be interrupted. You want a free, sequential flow of ideas. Work in a place where you can stop and pace the floor if you have to, but not where friends can drop in and knock an hour off your concentration.
9. Don't worry about intriguing openings and watertight conclusions. Keep your mind on your thesis, the main points supporting it, and the details that support the main points. Lay a foundation and leave architectural refinements for a later stage.
10. If you find your first draft wandering from your thesis or suggesting more interesting developments, stop. Weigh the merits of starting over to get back to the thesis against the possible value of constructing a new thesis. *At this stage nothing is permanent.*

41 The process of writing: revision

The process of writing does not consist of a series of finite steps, that is, of stages that have defined beginnings and ends. When you have once stated a thesis, you are not then done with the thesis. The first draft and subsequent revisions may substantially alter your thesis as you discover more about your relation to your topic while you write about it. You may also find that your purpose, audience, and tone change as you work. You may even find yourself going back to the prewriting activities after a first draft—or even after a second one— because you have found a new topic or a radically different aspect of the original one during the process of writing. You must not, therefore, think that the separation of first draft and revision shown here represents a true sequence of events. It is true only insofar as revision, by definition, follows a first attempt.

41a Revision is re-vision

Revising a draft is a matter of seeing again the topic, purpose, audience, and tone. To revise you must probe to discover possible new insights and overlooked opportunities, and you must test what you have written to discover whether it says what you finally want it to say. Revision requires detachment, critical and analytic attention, invention, ruthlessness, and self-discipline.

Detachment: The effort of writing leaves most of us too closely involved with what we have put on paper to judge the result immediately; therefore, put distance between you and your work. Wait several hours or a few days before revising. The difference between an impression of a draft upon its completion and the impression of it a week later is often startling. If you cannot wait or doubt your objectivity, have a friend read your draft and criticize it.

Critical and analytic attention: Revision is not only a search for a way to express a point better; it is a search for the best possible point. The critical revision question is not "Could I have put that better?" but "Does what I say truly reflect what I feel *now* about my topic?" The analytic revision question is not "Do my sentences and paragraphs flow smoothly from my thesis to my conclusion?" but "Can I disprove or refute anything I have said?" Some other questions to ask when revising critically and analytically are the following:

- If someone else had written this, what would my impression be of that person and his or her opinions?
- Can I make a formal topic outline of this draft in which all the headings are orderly and related?
- Do the thesis statement and the conclusion match? If they do not, which should I choose as the guide to my revision?

- Does everything in the draft relate to my thesis and my conclusion? Is each point a development toward the conclusion, or is it a digression?
- Is each generalization developed with adequate specific facts, illustrations, or examples? Can I think of exceptions to my generalizations that I have not anticipated in my argument?
- Who is my audience? How will he or she respond to my points?
- If I were to start this paper over from scratch, what would I do differently?

Invention: Revision should not be restricted to what is in the draft. It should include all aspects of the topic treated— even if these aspects did not occur to you in the first trial. If review of the draft suggests new departures, explore them. Do not abandon new ideas because the first set is on paper and the new ones are not. The more you work with a topic, the more thoughts on the topic you will gather. Let those thoughts occur to you; seek them out; brainstorm again while revising.

Ruthlessness: Cross out and rewrite freely. If the change you have in mind will not fit in the space available, cut the draft apart with scissors and tape it back together with the addition inserted. *Assume from the start that the draft is ailing and will need surgery to recover.* But do not throw away what is good. Critical revision should discover merits as well as faults in a draft.

Self-discipline: Seeing yourself as others see you is part of revision. Ask a friend to read your draft and give you an opinion. If what you have written is clear to you but unintelligible to someone else, you need to express yourself better.

Do not be lazy. Revision is part of the creative process. It deserves at least as much effort as a first draft—usually more. When revising, resist the temptation to proofread for spelling and punctuation faults. Save that step for later. Revision is the time to test the essay for coherence and to refine your tone so that it serves the content instead of directing it. Revision is the time to suit your diction to your topic, purpose, and audience; it is not the time to worry about comma splices or pronoun reference.

41b Sample first draft

The following is the first draft of an essay on parades, with the author's original spelling and punctuation.

1   The civic leadership of most American towns and cities has one answer for celebrating an occasion of significance, a parade. On Columbus Day, Memorial Day, July Fourth, Thanksgiving Day, St. Patrick's Day, Labor Day, and a dozen other days important to one group or another, each center of population gathers together a quorum of high school bands, the Masonic Lodge, the fire department and as many fire engines as it can muster, a company of the National Guard, a rythm dance squad, any vintage automobiles in the neighborhood, a trailor-load of pretty young women, assembles all the above into a long line and moves them slowly down the main street in front of a crowd of onlookers. The bands play, the fire engines sound their sirens, children on the curb wave flags and buy balloons from vendors, and after the last contingent of the parade has passed, everyone drifts home. The larger the city, the more numerous and varied the parade components. In New York, Philadelphia, and Los Angeles, a parade lasts several hours and often leads spectators to think it is an incomplete work. The

middle is obvious, but the beginning and end seem elements of pure theory.

2   Historically, the parade is a military event. The war dance a tribe performed before attacking another tribe was a form of parade. It got the group united in purpose, and the parading of prisoners after the fight showed the results to the noncombatants. The triumphs awarded victorious Roman generals were among the biggest parades ever sponsored, and they probably satisfied the egos of the participants in proportion. The parade of military pomp survives today in Britain for the Queen's birthday and the opening of parliament; the parade of military might survives in Russia, where the latest in tactical nuclear missiles rumble past the Kremlin every May Day. The military parade may be criticized for its belicose spirit, but it is at least a recognizable form carried out with relative precision, and, as a rule, it keeps moving.

3   The civilian parade is by contrast a curiosity. It moves at a crawl because it has children in it and because each component must stop and perform before the reviewing stand. It's military heritage appears faintly in the uniforms of the school bands, the occasional civilian uniformed force--such as the sanitation workers, and in the shambling efforts of

its participants to keep step. In all other respects it reflects a past of circus processions and traveling mummers shows. It is a carnival on the hoof. The very music of the "march" is more often than not adapted popular rock or jazz. Incongruity is an essential quality, and the picture of a Catholic girls school high-stepping grimly to the strain of "Scotland the Brave" in celebration of America's discovery by the Spanish-backed Italian Christopher Columbus is only one example of the parade organizer's motto: "Get as much in as possible and hang the relevance."

4   The indiscriminate mingling that characterizes these civilian parades might be taken for a charming democratic innocence. Unfortunately, the atmosphere of the affair is often tainted by mature ideas of pleasure. High school bands are marshalled by majorettes in short skirts and accentuated busts—budding bunnies of the male's female ideal. Many parades coincide with justification for good old-fashioned boozing—much of which takes place on the fringe of the parade. And some parades, St. Patrick's Day's, for example, have come to symbolize strife and violence, or at least a potentially inflamatory nationalism. Under that face of fun and high spirits, the parade suggests a license for unprincipled, if not lawless, behavior.

5   One famous parade, however, is founded entirely

on childish innocence and an unbelievably just
world. It is, of course, the Macy's Thanksgiving Day
Parade that brings Santa Claus and a host of other
myths right down New York's Fifth Avenue. Can we find
any dark side to an event like that? Perhaps we cannot—if we overlook that the whole purpose behind the
affair is to stimulate spending for the holiday season; if we ignore the fact that Thanskgiving is a nondenominational celebration while Santa Claus is em-
phatically Christian; if we dismiss the number of
police necessary to keep order in the crowd and to
minimize the success of pickpockets; if we disregard
the televising of the parade and the blizzard of com-
mercials that relieve the desparate commentators grop-
ing for words to fill in the interminable minutes
between the passage of units; and if we convince
ourselves that a spectacular display of crass commercial hooplah is genuine folk art. With a bit of self-
deception, the Thanksgiving Parade can pass as a
pretty wholesome business.

6   But even the best civilian parade is a sloppy
pageant. In the small town, the slow pace of the
walkers—marchers they never are—inevitably causes
the police chief's car or the prize pumper to boil
over and produce a complete halt. In the big city,
the bands always play two blocks away, never where you

265

are standing. The first rank of spectators is always composed entirely of football players and basketball teams. Bored children drip melting ice cream onto silk dresses and with sticky hands attach themselves to strangers mistaken for parents. Cab drivers refuse to accept passengers on the excuse that they cannot drive across town. The weather is too hot, too cold, or raining. When the last contingent has passed, the crowd breaks up, revealing a street littered with paper cups, broken flags, burst balloons, abandoned ice cream cones, cigarette butts, bumper stickers, bottles in paper bags, and wilted flowers.

7   Is it any wonder that a parade and a stiff drink so often go together?

Criticizing the draft

Returning to the draft after several days had passed (Detachment), the author of the parades essay made the following comments:

1. I began with the thesis "I hate a parade," and I have shown that I do. But I have not achieved any purpose, that is, I haven't shown my readers why they should share my dislike of parades. The lack of any real conclusion shows this lack of purpose. I have done little more than wallow in personal disgust.
2. Most people like parades. If I want to make a case for my disliking them, I need to show more respect for the good points of parades. My first paragraph, for example, almost takes it as given that parades are dreary. Look at my opening sentence—"one answer for celebrating"—and my weary "everyone drifts home." Would it be better to start with a more upbeat

opening and then show how my point of view sees through the celebration to the darker side?

3. The first paragraph has too much in it. Isn't that stuff about large cities and long parades really better somewhere else? The sentence beginning "On Columbus Day . . ." is entirely too long.

4. Do I really know enough about the history of parades to write about it? I think I might do better to concentrate on the difference between military parades and civilian ones. Sentence beginning "Incongruity is an essential . . ." is too long.

5. Paragraphs 4 and 5 move from generalizations about parades to the analysis of a particular parade. If I revamp the first paragraph to stress the good points of parades, would I do better to reverse the order of 4 and 5 so that the good aspects of the Macy's Thanksgiving parade precede the gloom about parades in general?

6. If I make paragraph 4 the next-to-last paragraph, am I going to be setting the stage too dark for paragraph 6, which is really a review of petty irritations associated with parades? I think paragraph 6 shows me that I can't be too serious about parades. Now that I've written about them, I don't think they're worthy of heavy criticism. See about playing down paragraph 4 (to be paragraph 5).

7. Points to reconsider:

    Do most American towns and cities really have as many parades as I've implied in the first paragraph?
    Keep "belicose"?
    Countries with military parades are warlike countries?
    Keep "sanitation workers"?
    Why "democratic innocence"? Do I know what I mean?
    "mature ideas of pleasure"? (bit pompous)
    "In . . . skirts and . . . busts"? Can someone be *in* a bust?
    "Coincide with justification"? (wordy?)
    Does the Macy's parade go down Fifth Ave.? (check)
    How about that long sentence beginning "Perhaps one cannot . . ."? Is that a piece of overdone rhetoric?

8. Who is my audience? "Parades" can't be called a controversial issue, so I can't assume my reader is motivated by my topic. I see him or her as something of a browsing reader who'll be interested to see if a flat topic can be given some new meaning by the writer. What does that information do to my tone, my topic, and my purpose?

41c The intermediate draft

Having reviewed his first draft, the author of the parades essay
wrote a second draft. As his view of his topic was clearer, he
used the second draft to experiment with different phrasings.
The following excerpt shows the deletions and additions that
occurred during the writing after several rereadings of the
work.

4   By contrast, the parade organized in the interest

of civic festivity is a sloppy pageant. Its military

heritage ~~is~~ shows faintly in the uniforms of the

school bands, the occasional uniformed civilian force,

and in the shambling efforts of its participants to

keep / step. But the ~~resemblance~~ ~~military~~ warlike
    in

vestige ends there. The pace is a ~~drawl~~ leisurely

stroll because children are walking. The components
                  full scale

are randomly mixed. A / parade in a city like Los An-

geles or New York ~~is~~ ~~generally~~ ~~so~~ ~~long~~ ~~that~~ ~~it~~ looks

incomplete; ~~to~~ ~~the~~ ~~spectator~~ ~~having~~ ~~only~~ it has a mid-

dle, but no beginning or end. The very music is ~~more~~

~~often~~ ~~than~~ ~~not~~ adapted rock or jazz instead of

Sousa. Starting from a distant military ~~base~~ origin,

the civilian parade has incorporated elements of reli-

gious processions, ~~carnival~~ circus arrivals, mummers
                          sales

shows, and ~~other~~ snake oil ~~shows~~ until ~~the~~ ~~descendant~~

~~is~~ ~~untraceable~~ line of descent is ~~almost~~ ~~obli-~~

~~terated~~ lost. The modern civilian parade is a carni-

val on the hoof. Incongruity is ~~an~~ essential

~~quality~~. The Catholic girls' school high-stepping
grimly to the strains of "Scotland the Brave" in
~~celebration~~ commemoration of America's discovery by
the Spanish-backed, Italian-born Columbus typifies the
parade organizer's creed: "Get as much in as possible
~~regardless of~~ and hang the relevance."

5   This meandering clutter of ill-matched units endears itself by its surface of innocent good fun. ~~The~~
~~Thanksgiving Day Parade held in a dozen major cities~~
Embodying the myths and fairy tales of childhood, no
parade better exemplifies this innocence than the
Macy's Thanksgiving Day Parade in New York that brings
Santa Claus and a ragtag of other fictitious characters
right down Broadway into the start of the holiday season. ~~What could be sweeter than that? Can anyone find~~
Surely nothing could be more harmless than that, and
nothing ~~is~~ seems so—if we ignore the purpose behind
the affair, which is to stimulate spending; if we overlook the Christmas centerpiece in this celebration of a
nondenominational event; if we discount the number of
police required to keep the crowd orderly and the pickpockets ~~minimal~~ at bay; if we disregard the television
version with its blizzard of advertisements; if we can
put up with the ~~professional~~ commentators ~~struggling to~~
~~fill the gaps/in/the/parade with babble~~ babbling until
the next commercial relieves them; and if we convince

269

ourselves that a spectacular display of big—business
hoopla passes for folk art—if we can do all that, then
the Thanksgiving Parade wins a rating of "pretty whole—
some."

41d The final draft

Here is the final draft of the essay on parades. Notice that it
has been proofread for spelling and other errors.

The Great American Parade

1   In the sharp spring sunshine, people line both
sides of Main Street expectantly. Girls and boys
clutch small bright flags just bought from the man
moving down the curb with a cluster of helium—filled
balloons, a tray of buttons and noisemakers, and a bag
of miniature Old Glories. The elderly sit in chairs
moved down from porches, and their younger relatives
stand behind and around them forming a crowd of family
groups. Greetings, good—natured jibes, laughs, repri—
mands to children crackle in the clear air. At last a
police siren a few blocks away gives a warning wail
that is picked up by a dozen other sirens. And then,
here it comes, turning into Main Street down by
Corell's Drugstore. The police car crawls forward,
howling. Behind it trail loosely a company of the
National Guard, the Masonic Lodge, the first of three

high school bands, Chester Gould's 1933 Packard, a
bunting-covered tractor towing a wagonload of pretty
young women, another high school band, the volunteer
fire brigades in uniform with all their equipment, a
deadly serious rhythm squad stomping intricately in
unison, the mayor in a 1955 Cadillac convertible, the
Black Powder Club in Civil War outfits, the third high
school band, and--bringing up the rear--the League of
Women Voters and the town council. The Memorial Day
parade is under way.

2   Across the United States in cities large and
small, the same thing is going on, and the same thing
will go on July Fourth, Veteran's Day, Columbus Day,
Thanksgiving, St. Patrick's Day, and every other day
that offers an excuse. America does indeed love a
parade.

3   This love of ours has produced a unique species
among parades. In Britain and France, the parade
tends to be an affair of military pomp and precision
with an emphasis on formation and martial music. The
Soviet Union adds a dimension of military might by including nuclear missiles, while China takes the military style and fits drilled civilians into it. By
contrast, the American parade of civic festivity is a
hybrid pageant. Its military heritage shows in the
uniforms of the bands and civic organizations; it

shows in the shambling efforts of the participants to keep step; it shows in the flags and their color guards. But the military vestige ends there. Rarely does an American parade include regular members of the armed forces. Instead of a crisp march, the pace is a stroll to accommodate the children who take part. The music is adapted rock or jazz rather than Sousa. Components are mixed at random. Above all, the parade is as long as possible. Full-scale parades in Philadelphia, Los Angeles, and New York are so immense that they seem incomplete; the spectator often sees a middle but no beginning or end.

4   Starting from a military origin, our contemporary parade has incorporated elements of religious processions, circus arrivals, mummers' shows, Olympic Games, fashion promenades, and snake-oil sales until its line of descent is almost lost. The American parade is a carnival on the hoof. The Catholic girls' school high-stepping grimly to the strains of "Scotland the Brave" in celebration of America's discovery by the Spanish-backed, Italian-born Columbus epitomizes the parade organizer's creed: "Get as much in as possible and hang the relevance."

5   This meandering clutter of ill-matched units endears itself by its surface of innocent good fun. Embodying the myths and fairy tales of childhood, the

Macy's Thanksgiving Day Parade in New York City typifies this innocence as it brings Santa Claus and a ragtag of other fictitious characters right down Broadway into the holiday season. Surely nothing could be more harmless than that. And nothing is—if we ignore the purpose behind the affair, which is to stimulate spending; if we overlook the Christmas centerpiece in this nondenominational event; if we discount the number of police required to keep the crowd orderly and the pickpockets at bay; if we disregard the television version with its blizzard of advertisements; if we can put up with commentators babbling until the next commercial relieves them; and if we convince ourselves that a spectacular display of big-business hoopla passes for folk art. If we can do all that, then the Thanksgiving parade wins a rating of "pretty wholesome."

6   Other parades and some features common to all parades assert a less clear-cut innocence. Why in the name of innocent fun are majorettes dressed in the shortest of skirts and tightest of tunics? Is it innocence that accentuates the thighs and busts of these budding bunnies of machismo fantasy? Why do politicians wheedle their way into parades that have no political significance? Why do so many parades excuse good old-fashioned boozing—much of which takes place

on the fringe of the parade? Can the St. Patrick's Day parade disassociate itself from advocates of terrorism? Under its face of fun and high spirits, many a parade suggests license for unprincipled behavior, if not for something worse.

7   But there is no need to probe so deep to wonder at the popularity of parades. To experience one is enough. The unbearably slow pace comes to a complete standstill when the fire department's prize pumper boils over because its motor has no air flow. The band plays two blocks from where you are standing, never in front of you. Football and basketball teams seem inevitably to get the front spectator positions. Bored children drip ice cream on silk dresses and with sticky hands attach themselves to strangers mistaken for parents. Cab drivers refuse fares on the ground that they cannot drive across town. The weather is too hot, too cold, or rainy. And when the last contingent has crept past and the crowd drifted home, the street reveals its pitiful litter of paper cups, broken toy flags, burst balloons, soggy ice cream cones, cigarette butts, bumper stickers, election fliers, empty bottles in paper bags, and crushed flowers.

8   Yes, we Americans are right to _love_ our parades. These shows inspire neither patriotic fervor nor admiration. They appeal because they are respectably dis-

solute, because they collect a community in a bit of

condoned foolishness that allows children to pretend

to be adults and adults to delight in childishness.

They deserve affection the way old shoes do; they fit

the random and mildly illicit urges of behavior as an

old shoe fits corns and bunions. So let us love them

sentimentally as we love our disreputable old tomcat.

They are too silly to hate, too irresponsible to de-

spise, and too frivolous to resent.

41e Components of the essay

In the process of writing, the writer should be concerned primarily with generating ideas and shaping them for expression. The "form" of the essay should develop naturally during this process, and worrying about parts of the form in isolation is often counterproductive. Toward the end of the composing process, however, an awareness of the parts of the essay may help in revising and polishing. The parts that most often come under consideration are the title, the thesis sentence, the opening, the body, and the conclusion.

Title

Wait until the essay is in almost final draft or completely finished to pick a title. When you do choose a title, search for a word or phrase—the briefer, the better is the rule—that suggests the topic, the tone, and perhaps the purpose of the essay. Alternatively, you may want to use a title that does none of these things but that challenges interpretation. Suzanne Britt Jordan, for example, used the title "I Wants to Go to the Prose" for her essay on the failures of some educational reforms of the 1970's.

Thesis sentence

Much ink has been spilled in arguments over the importance of the thesis sentence. Sometimes the thesis statement inserted in almost unchanged form in the essay is an aid to both writer and reader; sometimes it is simply a burden. As a rule of thumb, the more complex the topic is and the more serious the discussion of it is, the more value a thesis sentence will have. The lighter the topic and treatment, the less significant a detailed thesis sentence is. In "The Great American Parade," the thesis sentence is barely recognizable as the last sentence of the second paragraph: "America does indeed love a parade."

You may find it helpful in your first draft to insert your thesis statement into the first paragraph, but be critical of it in every revision and see that it is modified as necessary to suit the essay.

Opening

In a short essay, the opening is usually restricted to the first paragraph. The opening is important because it shapes the reader's first impression and may be a deciding factor in whether the reader goes beyond it. The opening sets the tone of the essay, establishes the writer's relation to the reader, and indicates the direction the essay will take.

Openings can take many forms to achieve a variety of effects:

- An opening can be a straight piece of narrative that sets the scene for the reader and gives information necessary to an understanding of the essay's thesis.
- An opening can be a personal anecdote or invented piece of fiction to arouse the reader's interest or entertain as a way of leading to the thesis sentence.
- An opening can consist of a joke or an inflated treatment of a minor issue to amuse the reader.
- An opening can begin with a paradoxical statement, one that seems to contradict itself: "Most law-abiding citizens break at least three laws a day." Or the writer may use

the opening to take a position toward the subject that is the opposite of the position to be developed in the paper. Such openings surprise readers or intrigue them.

- An opening can lead with a contradiction of a popular assumption as a challenge to the reader: "Cats and dogs are by nature affectionately drawn to each other. Unfortunately, dogs like playing tag and cats don't."
- An opening can employ a famous quotation or a piece of dialogue as a means of establishing the thesis.

An opening can also, of course, simply identify the topic to be addressed, as is the case with this opening for a paper on young drivers:

> When we obtained our first driver's licenses at sixteen, seventeen, or eighteen, few of us paused before hitting the accelerator to think that we were about to solo in a machine with the destructive power of four sticks of dynamite and a record for manslaughter three times greater than that of the notorious handgun.

Or an opening may be a focus of inquiry. An essay on legalized abortion, for example, might begin with an explanation of the views in opposition over the topic.

As a general rule, avoid attempts at a striking opening in your first draft. Shape the final opening against the structure and tone of the essay. An opening that is too contrived in the early stages is likely to dominate what follows it; the opening should introduce an essay, not lead it.

Body

The body of an essay consists of everything between the opening and the conclusion. In the body, the writer develops the thesis with facts, examples, and specific points so that the reader fully understands or accepts the writer's position. Every part of the body must not only relate to the essay's thesis but also increase readers' understanding of the problem being explored or their appreciation of the thesis.

A finished essay should balance generalization and specific information. The thesis of the essay is a generalization, that is, a statement that includes all conditions or circumstances indicated by a given set of evidence. You, the writer, have arrived at your thesis generalization by considering the evidence. In your body of your essay, you must retrace your steps to your generalization to demonstrate the truth of it to your reader. In most essays, this demonstration follows a pattern of a broad generalization (thesis) supported by a series of narrower generalizations that are supported in turn by reference to facts, examples, specific details, or other information that confirms or strongly suggests the truth of the generalization. This pattern of generalization, narrower generalization, and specific detail need not emerge in the finished essay as a rigid A-because-B-because-C formula, but the principle of it should influence the overall content of the essay.

Consider the final draft of the sample essay "The Great American Parade." The final thesis is "We Americans should love our parades despite their vulgarity." The writer's obligation to the reader is to demonstrate that parades are vulgar and, at the same time, justifiably lovable. But the writer does not use the formal structure of a logical geometric proof; some of the supporting generalizations are implied rather than stated, and much of the specific detail is given without a "therefore . . . because" structure. The demonstration is nonetheless quite complete.

To show the popularity of parades, the writer begins by describing in folksy detail what a typical small-town parade is like. He does not prove that such parades go on across the United States because he believes this is common knowledge.

The third and fourth paragraphs follow a more conventional pattern. They open with the generalization that American parades are a unique species, which is supported by the comparison with parades of other countries and the description of comparatively unusual elements found in American parades.

In the fifth paragraph, the writer introduces another generalization: that the average parade looks innocent on the surface but has a darker side. By analyzing the Macy's parade and the less innocent characteristics of other parades, the writer supports this statement.

Having made a case for a highly critical attitude toward parades by the end of the sixth paragraph, the writer faces a problem in proving his ultimate thesis that parades are lovable. His solution is an implicit generalization, a seventh paragraph devoted to showing that objections to parades are as petty as the vulgarity of parades themselves. The implied generalization of the next-to-last paragraph is not that experiencing a parade is enough to demonstrate how bad parades are but that silly objections to parades are silly. This paragraph establishes the grounds for concluding in the last paragraph that parades are not so obnoxious that we cannot find a soft spot in our affections for them.

Coherence: The essence of the body of the essay is **coherence,** the quality of rightness and fit in all the essay's elements that produces the connection of thoughts between them. This quality depends not only on the relevance of detail and the transitional devices of language, but on an agreement of tone, subject, purpose, and audience. All the parts of the essay should have meaning within the context of the essay. In the first draft of "The Great American Parade," the attempt to summarize the history of parades had no real meaning in the essay's development, and it was abandoned during the revision process. In a coherent essay, the reader should be able to follow the writer's thought without having to ask "Why is that here?" or "How did I get here from there?"

Conclusion

The Latin word *concludere*, from which *conclusion* derives, means "to shut up closely." An essay should not just stop; it should conclude, that is, it should end by emphasizing the point the writer has made.

The conclusion of an essay ought to reflect the essay's thesis in some way. In "The Great American Parade," the thesis is unstated in the essay but expressed as a proved point in the conclusion. As that example shows, the conclusion of an essay is not necessarily a restatement of the thesis, but it ought to be a statement that summarizes and reaffirms the main argument of the essay.

When writing a conclusion, remember to look back. The final paragraph or final sentence should not contain arguments, perceptions, expansions, or ideas that are not already present in the essay. Although a conclusion may contain a prediction for the future or a suggestion for future action, it may include such an element only if the preceding content of the essay clearly establishes the ground for it. In other words, the conclusion should refer to "what I have said" rather than to "what I can say next."

As a general rule, avoid phrases like "in sum," "to conclude," and "in conclusion" when closing your essay. A good conclusion does not need to be announced.

41f Proofreading

The last stage of writing is proofreading. As proofreading is a noncreative, mechanical duty, it is not an optional part of the writing process. There is no choice about proofreading. Spell *separate* as *seperate* and your paper will strike someone as flawed, however ingeniously it is constructed.

In proofreading, look up in this handbook or a dictionary every point in your essay you have marked for spelling or punctuation questions.

Read your final draft backwards. You may find spelling errors you miss reading the normal way.

Check each pronoun carefully. Can it possibly refer to the wrong antecedent?

Read each sentence critically. Have you by chance used a singular verb form with a plural subject, or vice versa?

Read your essay aloud. Where you make pauses to make the sense clear, have you used a punctuation mark?

Be careful of possessives. Have you used all the apostrophes you should?

If you know you are weak in punctuation or spelling, persuade a friend who is strong in these niceties to proofread for you. After being corrected half a dozen times, you'll learn to correct yourself.

Correct mistakes in your final draft neatly in ink, or use a correcting tape and retype the error. Check with your instructors to find out how they regard handwritten corrections in a final paper. Some require a perfect typescript; others accept neat corrections.

Keep essays returned to you by your instructor. Where you have made a mistake before, you are likely to make one again. Look for similar situations in your current essay and see if the same red pencil marks apply to it.

If an essay is returned to you with mistakes marked, go through it and correct each mistake. Look up the rule that covers the error and be sure you understand it. If you don't, ask someone to explain it until you do. Write out misspelled words twenty times, using the right spelling. Remember that coordination of language, hand, and thought builds correct habits.

42 Writing coherent paragraphs

A **paragraph** is a group of sentences that develops an idea about a topic. The word *paragraph* comes from an ancient Greek word referring to the short horizontal line that the Greeks placed beneath the start of a line of prose to indicate a break in thought or a change in speaker. This convention of marking the places in a written work where the sense or the speaker changed was followed by medieval monks, who used a red or blue symbol much like our modern paragraph symbol ¶ in their manuscripts. Today, we indicate such a change in thought by indenting the first line of each new paragraph.

While a paragraph is usually self-contained, at the same time it is usually part of a larger work, such as an essay or a research paper, and depends on the paragraphs before and after it. For example, look at the following three paragraphs.

There seems to be no limit to the number of individuals a single person is capable of recognizing. An adult living in a large city probably sees millions of faces over a lifetime, and can recognize thousands of them, even if he cannot assign names to them. Not even the passage of decades clouds the memory for faces. Psychologists have shown people photographs cut out from their high school yearbooks 15 years after graduation, and they were able to match 90 percent of the faces with the correct names. Nearly fifty years after graduation the accuracy only dropped to 70 percent.

Identifying and remembering faces is a mental process that takes place in the cerebral cortex, the most highly evolved area of the brain, where thinking occurs. Neurologists in France made this discovery in the nineteenth century, when they found that injuries to certain parts of the brain could cause a total loss of the ability to recognize people visually, including family and even one's own reflection in a mirror. This rare condition, called prosopagnosia (literally, not knowing people), usually occurs when the lesion is in the right temporal lobe, the portion of the cortex behind the ear (although injuries in the left hemisphere can produce the same symptoms). To a prosopagnosic, people look like cubist Picassos, with the features in the wrong positions, or the entire face appears out of focus. Those with the condition have difficulty reading expressions as well as identifying faces.

Learning to recognize people is a process that starts at birth and isn't complete until adulthood. For the past 20 years psychologists have been trying to find out how babies first acquire this ability, but their quest hasn't been easy. They can't ask an infant, "Have you ever seen this face before?" Instead, the researchers make use of curiosity. A baby's heartbeat will often change at the sight of a new object; babies spend extra time studying new things, as well as those that are vaguely familiar (moderately discrepant stimuli, in psychology jargon), whereas they will soon turn away in boredom from anything they already know. The general procedure in recognition studies is to show a baby a photograph of a face, then sometime later show the same face alongside another, and observe which one evokes the greater response.

SHANNON BROWNLEE
"What's in a Face"

Each of these paragraphs develops its own point. This point, which guides the paragraph, is often referred to as the **controlling idea.** The controlling idea of the first paragraph is that a human being is capable of recognizing an unlimited number of people. This idea is supported by examples of people recognizing a great number of faces. The controlling idea of the second paragraph is that the process of identifying and remembering faces takes place in the cerebral cortex. This idea is supported by an explanation of how this discovery was made by nineteenth-century French neurologists. The controlling idea of the third paragraph is that for the past twenty years, psychologists have been trying to answer a difficult question: how do babies learn to recognize people? This idea is supported by an explanation of how they have used a baby's natural curiosity to help them answer this question.

Although each of these paragraphs is controlled by its own idea, the three also work together. The second picks up the general subject discussed in the first paragraph but focuses on a single aspect of it. Whereas the first paragraph was concerned with the fact that faces are recognized, the second is concerned with the part of the brain that controls recognition. The third paragraph then picks up the general subject discussed in the first paragraph and focuses on another aspect. While the second paragraph was concerned with where the process occurs, the third paragraph is concerned with how it is developed. Therefore, we can say that although a paragraph is largely self-contained, its general subject and controlling idea must conform to the objectives of the larger work of which it is a part.

A paragraph is made up of individual sentences, but these sentences must cohere, or fit together, in order to be effective. Three interrelated qualities contribute to the coherence of a paragraph: unity, a consistent method of development, and clear transition from one idea to another.

42a Unity

Unity in a paragraph means that all the sentences in the paragraph relate to and develop the controlling idea. In other words, no sentences digress, or go off the track. Unity can be achieved through the use of a topic sentence and of relevant support.

The topic sentence

A paragraph develops a controlling, or main, idea, which is often summarized in a **topic sentence.** Functioning in a paragraph as a thesis statement functions in an essay, a topic sentence establishes the direction for the paragraph, with all the other sentences in the paragraph supporting and developing it.

A topic sentence most often appears at the beginning of a paragraph, although it may also be placed in the middle or at the end. When it is placed at the beginning of the paragraph, the rest of the sentences support the topic sentence, and the paragraph is developed deductively. In other words, the main idea is presented first, and then the information supporting this idea is given. For example, the following paragraph is about the British composer Peter Maxwell Davies. The controlling idea, or the idea to be developed, is that he had a difficult time winning recognition both at home and abroad.

> **For Davies, winning recognition wasn't easy, at home or abroad.** He was born near Manchester, a grim industrial city. The son of working-class parents, he taught himself composition by studying scores in the library. When he asked to study music at his grammar school, in preparation for the O-level exams given all British students, the headmaster scoffed. The faculty at the Royal Manchester College of Music and at Manchester University, where Davies subsequently studied, proved to be hardly more enlightened. It was the mid-fifties, and the Austrian moderns—Mahler and Bruckner—were still highly suspect. So, in fact, was anyone but such homegrown products as Sir Edward Elgar, Ralph Vaughan Williams, and Charles Villiers Stanford. Davies wanted none of it. Along with a group of other students, including Harrison Birtwistle, who were eager to hear the new European music, he began listening to Stravinsky and Schoenberg.
>
> ANNALYN SWAN
> "A Visionary Composer"

Sometimes the topic sentence is expressed in the form of a question. When this is the case, the rest of the paragraph answers the question. For example, the following paragraph is about the black artist's obligations to the black community.

The controlling idea is that a certain kind of art fulfills these obligations. The rest of the paragraph explains what kind of art this is.

What kind of art meets the Black artist's obligations to the community? First, these obligations require an art that is functional, an art that makes sense to the audience for which it was created. They also require a highly symbolic art that employs the symbols common to Black lives. Next, art by Black Americans should reflect a continuum of aesthetic principles derived from Africa, maintained during slavery, and emergent today. The art that the Black artist produces should also be relatively inexpensive to buy. This does not mean, as one might suppose, that only drawings and prints rather than paintings and sculpture should be produced. It does, however, mean that volume production at a low cost is a primary consideration. Black art should also help enrich the physical appearance of the community. This does not mean uncontrolled graffiti and fanciful false facades on buildings. It does mean the use of legitimate opportunity to enhance the quality of the environment. Finally, the obligations of the Black artist require a diverse art: an art that explores every avenue of search and discovery, an art that exploits every possible quality of individual difference in the artist who produces it.

SAMELLA LEWIS
Art: African American

A paragraph that begins with a topic sentence sometimes ends with a concluding statement that restates the controlling idea, or summarizes or comments on the information in the paragraph. For example, the following paragraph is about wolves. The controlling idea is that they are Holarctic. The topic sentence is printed in **boldface** and the concluding statement is in *italics*.

Wolves, twenty or thirty subspecies of them, are Holarctic—that is, they once roamed most of the Northern Hemisphere above thirty degrees north latitude. They were found throughout Europe, from the Zezere River Valley of Portugal north to Finland and south to the Mediterranean. They roamed eastern Europe, the Balkans, and the Near and Middle East south into Arabia. They were found in Afghanistan and northern India, throughout Russia north into Siberia, south again as far as China, and east into the islands of Japan. In North America the wolf reached a southern limit north of Mexico City and ranged north as far as Cape Morris Jesup, Greenland, less than four hundred miles from the North Pole. *Outside of Iceland and North Africa, and such places as the Gobi Desert, wolves—if you imagine the differences in geography it seems astonishing—had adapted to virtually every habitat available to them.*

> BARRY HOLSTUN LOPEZ
> *Of Wolves and Men*

Sometimes the topic sentence occurs at the end of the paragraph. When this is the case, the topic sentence provides the focus for the sentences that lead up to it. The paragraph is developed inductively; that is, the evidence is given first and then the conclusion derived from this evidence is given. For example, the following paragraph is about the Hill Country in Texas. The controlling idea, or the idea that the rest of the sentences lead up to, is that to the early settlers, this country seemed like a paradise.

> And the streams, these men discovered, were full of fish. The hills were full of game. There were, to their experienced eyes, all the signs of bear, and you didn't need signs to know about the deer—they were so numerous that when riders crested a hill, a whole herd might leap away in the valley below, white tails flashing. There were other white tails, too: rabbits in abundance. And as the men sat their horses, staring, flocks of wild turkeys strutted in silhouette along the ridges. Honeybees buzzed in the glades, and honey hung in the trees for the taking. Wild mustang grapes, plump and purple, hung down for making wine. **Wrote one of the first men to come to the Hill Country: "It is a Paradise."**

> ROBERT A. CARO
> *The Path to Power*

Sometimes the topic sentence is delayed until the middle or near the middle of the paragraph. When this is the case, the topic sentence serves as a bridge between the information in the first part of the paragraph and the information in the second. The following paragraph is about King Richard III of England. The controlling idea of this paragraph is that the traditional view of Richard III has been obstinately opposed over the years.

> History is always written by the victors. The basic Tudor picture of Richard as a bloodthirsty tyrant was handed down through the standard histories of England and the school textbooks for five centuries. **There has been an obstinate opposition, however.** Beginning with Sir George Buck in the 17th century, a series of writers and historians have insisted that Richard was not getting a fair break, that the Tudor version was largely fabrication: far from being a monster Richard was a noble, upright, courageous, tenderhearted and most conscientious king. This anti-Tudor version reached its definitive statement in the work of Sir Clements Markham, a 19th-century eccentric who spent years of passionate research trying to prove that crimes attributed to Richard were either outright libels by, or the actual work of, a pack of villains, most notably including Cardinal Morton and Henry VII.
>
> ROBERT WERNICK
> "After 500 Years, Old Crookback Can Still Kick Up a Fuss"

Sometimes a topic sentence is really two sentences. The first sentence states the controlling idea and the second sentence clarifies or restricts the controlling idea in some way. The controlling idea in the following paragraph is that the content of coffee-table art books is changing.

> **The topography of the coffee-table art book is changing.** *Each year, it seems, larger and more daunting mountains of text rise from the lush lowlands of visual reproduction, obliging the reader to sit up and take notice.* It used to be commonly accepted that the text of a large-format art book was a joke—a harmless effusion of bold type between the title page and the color reproductions—but these days you are likely to find yourself scaling craggy massifs of prose by some well-known scholar or art historian. My own feelings about this are ambivalent. Art scholarship takes it out of you under the best of circumstances. It also tends to make you suspect that the reproductions in a book are a very far cry from the original paintings—which is true, of course, but not necessarily what you long to hear when you have just paid seventy-five dollars plus tax for the book in question. The fact that books of this calibre have to be read at a desk or a

table—they are too cumbersome for all but world-class laps—adds to the inner conflicts that they set up. Objects that used to be associated with conspicuous display or with sybaritic leafing-through are coming to be associated increasingly with hard work.

CALVIN TOMPKINS
"Heavyweights"

Sometimes a topic sentence is not used and the controlling idea is left unstated, or implied. This is especially the case when the paragraph elaborates on or continues a discussion started in a preceding paragraph. When there is no topic sentence, the details in the paragraph should be so clear and well organized that it is easy to state the implied main idea for yourself. The implied main idea of the following paragraph is that the population of wolves in North America has dwindled.

Mexico still has a small population of wolves, and large populations—perhaps twenty to twenty-five thousand—remain in Alaska and Canada. The largest concentrations of wolves in the lower forty-eight states are in northeastern Minnesota (about one thousand) and on Isle Royale in Lake Superior (about thirty). There is a very small wolf population in Glacier National Park in Montana and a few in Michigan's Upper Peninsula. Occasionally lone wolves show up in the western states along the Canadian border; most are young animals dispersing from packs in British Columbia, Alberta, and Saskatchewan.

BARRY HOLSTUN LOPEZ
Of Wolves and Men

Support

Support your controlling idea with specific information—facts, statistics, details, examples, illustrations, anecdotes—that backs it up. Consider the following paragraph.

Oranges and orange blossoms have long been symbols of love. Boccaccio's *Decameron*, written in the fourteenth century, is redolent with the scent of oranges and orange blossoms, with lovers who wash in orange-flower water, a courtesan who sprinkles her sheets with orange perfume, and the mournful Isabella, who cuts off the head of her dead lover, buries it in an ample pot, plants basil above it, and irrigates the herbs exclusively with

288

rosewater, orange-flower water, and tears. In the fifteenth century, the Countess Mathilda of Württemberg received from her impassioned admirer, Dr. Heinrich Steinbowel, a declaration of love in the form of a gift of two dozen oranges. Before long, titled German girls were throwing oranges down from their balconies in the way that girls in Italy or Spain were dropping handkerchiefs. After Francis I dramatically saved Marseilles from a Spanish siege, a great feast was held for him at the city's harborside, and Marseillaise ladies, in token of their love and gratitude, pelted him with oranges. Even Nostradamus was sufficiently impressed with the sensual power of oranges to publish, in 1556, a book on how to prepare various cosmetics from oranges and orange blossoms. Limes were also used cosmetically, by ladies of the French court in the seventeenth century, who kept them on their person and bit into them from time to time in order to redden their lips. In the nineteenth century, orange blossoms were regularly shipped to Paris in salted barrels from Provence, for no French bride wanted to be married without wearing or holding them.

JOHN McPHEE
"Oranges"

The controlling idea of this paragraph is contained in the first sentence. Notice all the details McPhee gives to support his controlling idea. First he tells us about oranges and orange blossoms in Boccaccio's *Decameron*. Then he tells us about Countess Mathilda in the fifteenth century and how the gift of oranges from her admirer led to the custom of German girls throwing oranges from their balconies. Next he tells us how Francis I was pelted with oranges as a token of love, and how Nostradamus published a book on how to prepare cosmetics from oranges and orange blossoms. Finally, he tells us that in the nineteenth century a French bride would not want to be married without holding or wearing orange blossoms. Notice how fully he treats these details. He tells you not only that Boccaccio wrote about oranges and orange blossoms in the *Decameron* but also what he said about them—the lovers, the courtesan, the mournful Isabella.

Notice all the supporting details Peter Steinhart uses to develop his controlling idea in the following paragraph.

Adobe is an ancient material. Peruvians and Mesopotamians knew at least 3,000 years ago how to mix adobe—three parts sandy soil to one part clay soil—and box-mold it into bricks. The Walls of Jericho, the Tower of Babel, Egyptian pyramids, and sections of China's Great Wall are adobes. So are more modern structures like Spain's Alhambra, the great mosques of Fez and Marrakesh, and the royal palace at Riyadh.

PETER STEINHART
"Dirt Chic"

Not only must a paragraph contain support for its controlling idea, but this support must be relevant. Consider the following paragraph:

Several writers have used San Francisco as a backdrop for their novels. Kathryn Forbes's novel *Mama's Bank Account*, on which the movie *I Remember Mama* was based, is set in San Francisco. The immigrant family lives on Steiner Street, in a big house in the middle of the city that Mama loved so well. Jack London's novel *The Sea Wolf* is enriched by its vivid depiction of San Francisco, the city in which London grew up. London set what is perhaps his most famous novel, *The Call of the Wild*, in the Klondike, however. Dashiell Hammett's detective, Sam Spade, lives and works in San Francisco. As he solves his cases, Spade reveals to us the seamy underbelly of the city, which challenges his ideals and forces him to develop a mask of cynicism. Other writers reveal to us the corrupt side of city life, too. For example, in his short novel *Maggie: A Girl of the Streets*, Stephen Crane shows us the lower depths of New York's Bowery and the effects of this environment on the destiny of a young girl, Maggie Johnson.

The paragraph above lacks unity. The controlling idea is that several writers have used San Francisco as a backdrop for their novels. However, the paragraph contains three sentences that do not relate to this main idea. The fifth sentence is a digression because it does not develop the idea of novels set in San Francisco. The last two sentences also wander off the track. The next-to-last is not limited to San Francisco, and the last deals with New York City.

Digressions weaken your paragraphs. Eliminate or rewrite any sentences that do not develop the controlling idea. Notice how the sample paragraph is improved by removing the digressions.

> Several writers have used San Francisco as a backdrop for their novels. Kathryn Forbes's novel *Mama's Bank Account,* on which the movie *I Remember Mama* was based, is set in San Francisco. The immigrant family lives on Steiner Street, in a big house in the middle of the city that Mama loved so well. Jack London's novel *The Sea Wolf* is enriched by its vivid depiction of San Francisco, the city in which London grew up. Dashiell Hammett's detective, Sam Spade, lives and works in San Francisco. As he solves his cases, Spade reveals to us the seamy underbelly of the city, which challenges his ideals and forces him to develop a mask of cynicism.

42b Development

A paragraph should be developed and organized in a purposeful way to assist the reader in following your argument or line of reasoning. The paragraph's organization should depend on your overall aim in the particular section of your essay. Sometimes a method of development will come to you naturally, without thought; at other times you will have to choose deliberately from a variety of options.

General to specific

Arrange your information from general to specific when you want to present a general idea first and then supply specific examples, details, or reasons to support your idea. The following paragraph is organized in a general to specific pattern. Notice how the information in it becomes more and more specific.

> As of now, the biological productivity of the lower Hudson is staggering. Fishes are there by the millions, with marine and freshwater species often side by side in the same patch of water. All told, the population of fishes utilizing the lower Hudson for spawning, nursery or feeding grounds comprises the greatest single wildlife resource in New York State. It is also the most neglected resource; at this writing, not one state conservation department biologist is to be found studying it regularly. Besides

sea sturgeon, the river is aswarm year-round or seasonally with striped bass, white perch, bluefish, shad, herring, largemouth bass, carp, needlefish, yellow perch, menhaden, golden shiners, darters, tomcod, and sunfish, to cite only some. There is the short-nosed and round-nosed sturgeon, officially classified by the Department of the Interior as "endangered," or close to extinct, in the United States. Perhaps it is extinct elsewhere along the Atlantic Coast, but not only is the fish present in the Hudson, but occasional specimens exceed the published record size in the scientific literature. The lower Hudson also receives an interesting infusion of so-called tropical or subtropic fishes, such as the jack crevalle and the mullet, both originally associated with Florida waters.

ROBERT H. BOYLE
The Hudson River

Specific to general

Arrange your information from specific to general when you want to present specific details first and then lead up to a generalization about them. The following narrative paragraph is organized in a specific to general pattern. The paragraph starts with a specific description of the birds' behavior, which leads up to a generalization about their behavior: they were anting, or deliberately covering themselves with ants.

As he walked in an orange grove behind Trinidad's Asa Wright Nature Centre, Ray Mendez noticed a pair of birds that were behaving strangely. The birds—violaceous trogons, judging from the ring of bright orange around their eyes—were preoccupied with something, so preoccupied that they seemed to have lost their usual bird sense. They appeared fascinated, expectant, oblivious. Mendez drew close and watched. Suddenly one of the trogons broke from its perch and flew a hard flat line at an ants' nest hanging from a tree branch. The bird crashed into the nest, held on, and then shoved itself in headfirst, allowing *Azteca* ants to cover its body. It flittered its wings a moment and the *Azteca* boarded them too. Then the trogon flew back to a safe perch, and Mendez, entranced by the mystery of these events, suddenly saw the simple answer. The trogons were anting.

DAVID WEINBERG
"Ant Acid Spells Relief"

The following paragraph is also organized in a specific to general pattern. The author first gives the evidence supporting his argument and then concludes the paragraph with a general statement of his position.

> American workers understand that the manufacturers of arms have been the bulwark of the capitalist system in the United States, as well as of the communist Soviet Union. In their bones these workers sense that what financial security they have—little enough—is tied to the billions of dollars invested in the arms race. Where would America's "free enterprise" be without that ongoing safety net? Some of us—the more privileged—can afford not to wonder. But most cannot. It wouldn't hurt the peace movement if we found a better way to reach out to this less affluent majority, if we coupled our opposition to nuclear weapons with a clear and compelling program for economic reform.
>
> ROBERT COLES
> "The Doomsayers: Class Politics and the Nuclear Freeze"

Climactic order

Arrange your information in climactic order when you want to begin by supporting your generalization with the least important information and build up to the most important. The following paragraph is organized in climactic order. It starts with the least important criterion for judging a behavior as conscious and builds up to the most important.

> What criteria lead us to judge that a particular behavior is conscious? What is the difference between the eight-month baby who clumsily knocks over its milk, and the two-year-old who obviously does it on purpose? Several things incline us to judge that another being is acting consciously: if it studies its goal before acting, if it chooses one of a very flexible set of behaviors, or even a novel behavior with detours to reach the goal. Conscious purpose seems especially likely if some learned symbol like "No! Naughty!" communicates the situation to the aggravated parents. Finally, if there is misdirection—hiding or lying—it seems likely that the creature has formed some conception of other animals' intentions and awareness.
>
> ALISON JOLLY
> "A New Science That Sees Animals as Conscious Beings"

Comparison and contrast

Arrange your information through comparison and contrast when you want to show the similarities and/or the differences between two things. The following paragraph contrasts two things—the child of fifty years ago and the child of today—by alternating between them.

> The most disquieting aspect of the silicon chip is not that it distances us from nature; even before the Industrial Revolution, man was trying to do that. The more troubling fact is that electronic developments distance us from understanding. Any child of fifty years ago looking inside a household clock, with its escapement and weights or spring, could see in a few minutes how it worked. A child of today peering at a digital watch can learn nothing. Yesterday's children could appreciate that pushing a switch on a television set meant completing a circuit. Today's children, using remote control devices based on ultrasound or infrared radiation, can scarcely comprehend what they are doing. The real danger of the microelectronic era is posed by what was called, even in the days of macroelectronics, the black box mentality: passive acceptance of the idea that more and more areas of life will be taken over by little black boxes whose mysterious workings are beyond our comprehension.
>
> BERNARD DIXON
> "Black Box Blues"

The following paragraph compares the National Aeronautics and Space Administration's lunar explorations to the voyages of Christopher Columbus.

> Both NASA and Columbus made not one but a series of voyages. NASA landed men on six different parts of the moon. Columbus made four voyages to different parts of what he remained convinced was the east coast of Asia. As a result both NASA and Columbus had to keep coming back to the Government with their hands out, pleading for refinancing. In each case the reply of the Government became, after a few years: "This is all very impressive, but what earthly good is it to anyone back home?"
>
> TOM WOLFE
> "Columbus and the Moon"

Cause and effect

Arrange your information through cause and effect when you want to discuss the causes behind certain effects or the reasons for certain results or consequences. The following paragraph gives the result first—the tartan was transformed into an instrument of Scottish nationalistic ideology. Then it provides the reasons or causes that brought about this result.

> A cluster of events transformed the tartan into an instrument of nationalist ideology. In the wake of the great defeat of Bonnie Prince Charlie in 1745, the British banned Highland wear, including tartans and the kilt, under penalty of six months in prison for a first offense and seven years' transportation for a second. The elder Pitt simultaneously formed the Highland regiments for service abroad. They alone were permitted to wear the plaid and the kilt, both for reasons of esprit de corps and, no doubt, to impede desertion: a man running about in a skirt south of the border or in France was a conspicuous object. This is, most likely, when tartans peculiar to certain regiments became established. Finally, Scottish nationalism, seeking to extirpate both Irish and Lowland roots of the culture, turned to the literal invention of an ancient Highland culture, kilt and all. The final triumph came when Lowland Scotland, offered this bogus tradition, eagerly accepted it.
>
> ALEXANDER COCKBURN
> "The Origin of the Kilt"

The next paragraph gives the cause first—people have a stake in seeing themselves as different from computers. Then it describes the effects brought about by this cause.

> But despite these encouragements to personify computers, people have a stake in seeing themselves as different. They assert this difference, much as we saw children do. They speak of human love, sensuality, and emotion. They speak of the computer's lack of consciousness, originality, and intention. In the end, many sum up their sense of difference in the statement "Computers are programmed; people aren't," or "Computers only do what they are programmed to do, nothing more, nothing less." This last response has a history. It is associated with Lady Ada Lovelace, a friend and patroness of Charles Babbage, inventor of the "analytical engine," the first machine that deserves to be called a

295

computer in the modern sense. In a memoir she wrote in 1842 she became the first person known to go on record with a variant of "Computers only do what you tell them to do."

SHERRY TURKLE
The Second Self: Computers and the Human Spirit

Time order

Arrange your information in time order when you want to explain a sequence of events or tell a story. The details in the following expository paragraph are organized according to time order.

Jesuit missionaries stationed in China were probably the first voyagers to bring soybeans to Europe, in the seventeen-thirties, and there, like potatoes before them, the beans were considered a horticultural curiosity. Specimens were planted at the Jardin des Plantes, in Paris, in 1739, and in London's Kew Gardens—these probably from India—in 1790. (As early as 1712, a German botanist, Engelbert Kämpfer, who had visited Japan in the sixteen-nineties, published a recipe for soy sauce; that may have been the first time any Europeans were informed that the bean was in any respect edible.) Benjamin Franklin has been credited, perhaps apocryphally, with having espied soybeans at the Jardin des Plantes and bringing a few home. He would have been a logical courier, for he was acquainted with the head of the Jardin. In any event, there were soybeans in the United States—brought over from China by clipper ship—in 1804, at which time an admirer wrote, "The Soy-bean bears the climate of Pennsylvania very well. The bean ought therefore to be cultivated." Whether or not Pennsylvania farmers followed that advice is uncertain; it is known that a botanical garden in Cambridge, Massachusetts, had some soybeans on display—once more, merely as a rare exhibit—in 1829. They were written up in the *New England Farmer* that October. Soybeans enjoyed another brief flurry of notice in 1854, when Commodore Perry brought some back from Japan. In 1879, they were being grown at the Rutgers Agricultural College Farm, and ten years later at the Kansas Agricultural Experiment Station. They also began to be scrutinized by botanists at Cornell—among them Edward Lewis Sturtevant, later the author of "Sturtevant's Edible Plants of the World," who in 1882 appraised soybeans as "of excellent promise as a forage plant" but added, as he doubtless would not have when he got to know them better, that "the beans are not acceptable to the palate."

E. J. KAHN, JR.
"Soybeans"

Spatial order

Arrange your information in spatial order when you want to explain or describe the relative physical positions of people or objects. The details in the following descriptive paragraph are organized according to spatial order.

Greenwich Village is a mass of "little twisted streets that crossed and recrossed each other and never seemed to get anywhere. . . ." In its center is Washington Square, a stretch of green, bordered by a number of park benches, where one can sit and read, talk, or do nothing at all. In the background of Washington Square looms New York University. Before Washington Square became a park in 1827, it had been "in successive decades Potter's Field, parade grounds, place of executions. . . ." During Millay's time, little delicatessens and coffee shops helped to create an old English atmosphere in the Village.

ANNE CHENEY
Millay in Greenwich Village

Definition

Develop your paragraph through definition when you want to clarify a term, assign a particular meaning to a word, or discuss a concept from a special or unusual point of view.

What is war? It is not weapons or warheads or even military force itself; these are only "the *means* of war." According to Clausewitz, war is simply "an act of force to compel our enemy to do our will." That is precisely what the Vietnamese are attempting to do to the Cambodians, what Iraq tried to do to Iran, what Somalia is striving to do with Ethiopia, what Israel attempted to do in Lebanon, and why Soviet troops are in Afghanistan.

COLONEL HARRY G. SUMMERS, JR.
"What Is War?"

Classification

Develop your paragraph through classification when you want to group information into types in order to find patterns or similarities. The following paragraph classifies ranks within a troop of rhesus monkeys.

> The core of the troop's structure is a series of matriarchies. A mother ranks above her own daughters until she becomes very, very old. She supports them in fights, so her offspring rank just below her and thus above all the other matriarchies that she can dominate. Young males commonly migrate to other troops. A male's adult rank depends on his own fighting prowess and on his charm—much of his status depends on whether the females of his new troop back him up. A female, on the other hand, is usually locked for life into the nepotistic matrix of her kin. Her adult rank is roughly predictable the day she is born. But female status changes do occasionally happen, and it is worth a young female's while to test the system. In the wild, predation and disease knock out relatives at random, so there is more flexibility than we see in our well-tended captive colonies. Wild or captive, kinship is still the major fact of female social life. A baby learns early those situations when its relatives will come and help—and when they won't.

> ALISON JOLLY
> "A New Science That Sees Animals as Conscious Beings"

Explanation of a process

Develop your paragraph through explanation of a process when you show how something is done or how something works. The following paragraph explains how the heart works.

> With its valves, tubing, electrical system and four chambers, the heart looks for all the world like a simple pump. First, it collects the oxygen-depleted blood from the body in its right upper chamber, or right atrium, while receiving a fresh supply of oxygen-rich blood from the lungs in its left upper chamber, the left atrium. Then as the heart's natural pacemaker, a small lump of tissue called the sinoatrial node, fires an electrical impulse, the atria contract, the valves open, and the blood rushes into the two lower chambers, the ventricles. Another electrical signal then causes the ventricles to contract, forcing the oxygen-poor blood from the

lower right ventricle into the lungs and the oxygenated blood in the lower left ventricle to all the other parts of the body. It all happens in a second, this heartbeat.

PATRICK HUYGHE
"Your Heart: A Survival Guide"

42c Transition

Even if all the sentences in a paragraph relate to a controlling idea and follow an organized method of development, it is often helpful to the reader's understanding to link sentences with transitional devices that provide smooth passage from one idea to the next. These devices include transitional words and expressions, pronouns, repetition of key words and phrases, and parallel grammatical structure.

Transitional words and expressions

Transitional words and expressions show the relationship of one term to another term, one sentence to another sentence, one idea to another idea, and even one paragraph to another paragraph. They serve as signposts that direct the reader through the passage.

Below are some common transitional words and expressions and the relationships they may indicate:

Addition
again, also, and, besides, equally important, finally, first (second, third, etc.), furthermore, in addition, last, likewise, moreover, next, too

Similarity
in a similar fashion, likewise, moreover, similarly, so

Contrast
although, but, even so, for all that, however, in contrast, nevertheless, on the contrary, on the other hand, still, yet

Time
afterward, at the same time, before, earlier, finally, in the past, later, meanwhile, next, now, previously, simultaneously, soon, subsequently

Place or direction

above, beyond, here, in the distance, nearby, opposite, overhead, there, to the side, underneath

Purpose

for this purpose, to this end, with this object in mind

Result

accordingly, as a result, consequently, hence, then, therefore, thus

Examples or intensification

for example, for instance, indeed, in fact, in other words, that is

Summary or conclusion

finally, in brief, in conclusion, in short, in summary, on the whole, to conclude, to sum up

In the following paragraph, the transitional words and expressions are printed in **boldface.**

> There were other important applications of new technology that looked ahead to the future, **too.** Thaddeus Lowe was by no means the first to fly in lighter-than-air balloons, but he was the first to use these craft for doing reconnaissance work on enemy positions. **Likewise,** the telegraph had been around for some years, but the Civil War was the first war in which it played a crucial role. **So, too,** railroads were already enjoying a robust adolescence, but it was during the Civil War that they found themselves making a major contribution. Barbed wire entanglements were **also** used for the first time in the Civil War, **as** were land and water mines.
>
> ARTHUR M. SCHLESINGER, JR.
> *The Almanac of American History*

Pronouns

Pronouns link sentences by referring the reader to their antecedents. In the following excerpt, notice how the pronouns in the second and third sentences link these clauses and sentences to the first sentence.

> There is always a teahouse wherever you go in the Orient. **Some** are big with red pillars and gleaming orange-yellow roofs;

many have tables in a garden among scented flowers and lotus ponds; a **few** are huge houseboats carved to look like dragons floating on the water. But **most** of them are just plain, unornamented regular restaurants.

MAI LEUNG
The Chinese People's Cookbook

Repetition and parallel structure

Repetition of key words and phrases and the use of parallel grammatical structure provide emphasis and clear transition from one thought to another. In the following paragraph, notice how the repetition of the word *know* drives home the author's point. Notice also that the last three sentences are in parallel form: each is made up of a clause beginning with *if* followed by a clause beginning with *you will*. This structure, along with the transitional words *then* and *Next* at the beginning of the second and third sentences, makes it easy for the reader to follow the progression of ideas from one sentence to the next.

But I am wandering from what I was intending to do; that is, make plainer than perhaps appears in the previous chapters some of the peculiar requirements of the science of piloting. First of all, there is one faculty which a pilot must incessantly cultivate until he has brought it to absolute perfection. Nothing short of perfection will do. That faculty is memory. He cannot stop with merely thinking a thing is so and so; he must **know** it; for this is eminently one of the "exact" sciences. With what scorn a pilot was looked upon in the old days, if he ever ventured to deal in that feeble phrase "I think," instead of the vigorous one "I **know**!" One cannot easily realize what a tremendous thing it is to **know** every trivial detail of twelve hundred miles of river and **know** it with absolute exactness. **If** you will take the longest street in New York, and travel up and down it, conning its features patiently until you **know** every house and window and lamp-post and big and little sign by heart, and **know** them so accurately that you can instantly name the one you are abreast of when you are set down at random in that street in the middle of an inky black night, **you will** then have a tolerable notion of the amount and the exactness of a pilot's knowledge who carries the Mississippi River in his head. And **then** if you will go on until you **know** every street crossing, the character, size, and position of the crossing-stones, and the varying depth of mud in each of these numberless places, **you will** have some idea of what the pilot must **know** in order to keep a Mississippi steamer out of trouble. **Next, if** you will take half of the signs in that long street, and *change their places* once a month, and still manage to **know** their new positions accurately on dark nights, and keep up with these repeated changes without making any mistakes, **you will** understand what is required of a pilot's peerless memory by the fickle Mississippi.

MARK TWAIN
Old Times on the Mississippi

42d Transitional paragraphs

A transitional paragraph consists of one or two sentences whose purpose is to carry the reader from one paragraph to another. Usually a transitional paragraph sums up or emphasizes the thoughts in the preceding paragraph and announces the idea to be developed in the next paragraph. Notice how a quotation is used as a transitional paragraph in the following passage.

I got back into the car with my escort, a former Viet Cong captain, and we drove south, down the road that my battalion had swept for mines each morning. I pointed out a narrow gravel road and we followed it through the paddies toward the mountains. Where a refugee camp had been, there was now a cemetery for the war dead, filled with hundreds of graves, each marker bearing, in Vietnamese, the word *hero*. I stopped two old men who were walking along the road. One of them had been the president of the Viet Cong in a nearby village. "All this was a no-man's-land," he said, gesturing around the paddies and hills I knew so well. "We were very strong here. We lived underground right next to the American base on Hill 10. Our best fighters worked for the Americans; at night they joined us."

Then a woman came up the road. Her name was Dong Thi San. I asked her if she had been here during the war. "Of course," she said. "I was the wife of a guerrilla. He was killed in Bo Ban hamlet by an American Marine patrol in 1969. And he left four children." She looked at me with steady eyes. In 1969 I had commanded a platoon of young Americans, their average age less than twenty. We had been through Bo Ban hamlet and had set out ambushes there. My platoon could have—I could have—killed her husband.

"But life goes on," she said. "The war is over now."

The last Americans fled Vietnam ten years ago this April, but for us the war never really ended, not for the men who fought it, and not for America. It was longer than the Civil War, the First World War, and the Second World War put together. We spent $140 billion and suffered 58,022 Americans killed, another 303,000 wounded. Perhaps a million and a half Vietnamese died. The war shook our confidence in America as a nation with a special mission, and it left the men who fought it orphans in their own country. It divided us then, and its memory divides us now. The debate over when and how to commit American power abroad is really a debate over how to avoid, at all costs, another Vietnam.

WILLIAM BROYLES, JR.
"The Road to Hill 10"

Exercise 1. The following passage actually consists of three paragraphs. Read the passage carefully and decide where each new paragraph should begin.

The next issue that confronts the Bible translator is that of the textual basis for the translation. We have no original text of any biblical book, and some books may have circulated in more than one version almost from the beginning of their existence as written documents. One theory has it that in the case of a number of Old Testament books three distinct texts emerged between the fifth and first centuries B.C., among the Jews of Palestine, Egypt, and Babylonia, respectively. Later, when ancient Jewish and Christian authorities defined the limits of the biblical canon, they did not fix the precise text of each individual book. To further complicate matters, all the books of the Bible have to some degree suffered the textual corruption that is the inevitable by-product of two to three thousand years of manuscript copying and recopying. How, then, do Bible translators establish reliable working texts of the books that they are to translate? Even the assumption that a given book had a single prototype, an *Urtext*, is itself questionable and unprovable. What scholars can do is try to reconstruct, from surviving manuscripts, the earliest stage of the text that can be established with confidence. This is an extraordinarily tangled problem, one that requires scholars to sift through a prodigious mass of data. In some instances where the text of a verse is obviously corrupt, half a dozen plausible reconstructions of the verse have been proposed. Such conjectural solutions to textual cruxes are often quite ingenious. The job of a Bible translator is—or should be—to choose the most probable reconstruction, to discriminate between what is merely ingenious and what is in fact likely. Establishing a good critical text for the New Testament is a less severe task than establishing a text for the Old. Most of the books of the New Testament were composed in the second half of the first century; a few—Jude and 2 Peter, for example—may stem from the second century. We possess complete manuscripts of the Greek New Testament that date from the fourth century, as well as copies of individual books that may be as early as the second century in origin. Therefore, the oldest surviving copies were made a maximum of three centuries after the books were originally written. Thanks to the existence of these early manuscripts, New Testament scholars, unlike their Old Testament colleagues, have been able to reach something resembling a consensus on the matter of a critical text. That something is a work entitled *The Greek New Testament*, published by the United Bible Societies. It contains a critical text of the New Testament, prepared by an international, interdenominational panel of specialists and intended especially for translators.

BARRY HOBERMAN
"Translating the Bible"

Exercise 2. Identify the topic sentence in each of the following paragraphs. If the topic sentence is not stated, write your own sentence expressing the main idea.

1.   Dirt turns out to be a miracle roofing compound. Its natural milieu is exactly that harsh environment that wreaks such havoc with roofs. Consider: dirt is composed of small particles; it can flow. It moves when vent pipes or other obstructions expand and contract, keeping tight contact. Dirt dampens the swings in temperature that crack roof materials. Farmers well know how long dirt takes to warm up. And dirt reduces oscillations between wet and dry, maintaining a more constant moisture. A layer of dirt protects the roof itself from wind abrasion and keeps sunlight from reaching any plastic membrane underneath.

JOHN P. WILEY, JR.
"Phenomena, Comment, and Notes"

2.   In the 1630s Descartes visited the royal gardens at Versailles,

which were known for their intricate automata. When water was made to flow, music sounded, sea nymphs began to play, and a giant Neptune, complete with trident, advanced mechanically. Whether the idea was in his mind before this visit or not, Descartes's philosophy, which he supported with his mathematics, became that the universe and all the things in it also were automata. From Descartes's time to the beginning of this century, and perhaps because of him, our ancestors began to see the universe as a Great Machine. Over the next three hundred years they developed science specifically to discover how the Great Machine worked.

GARY ZUKAV
The Dancing Wu Li Masters

3.   Maya art provided more puzzles than answers. Sites were full of stone carvings—upright slabs, or stelae; door lintels; occasional wall panels—that showed elaborately dressed individuals, usually in formal poses. The carvings seemed to be full of religious symbols and sometimes included fantastic, obviously mythological animals, such as the two-headed serpent that writhes through the sky in some compositions. Were the individuals portrayed the kings, chieftains, and sages that Stephens had imagined, or were they instead priests dressed for ceremonies— or perhaps the gods themselves?

T. PATRICK CULBERT
"The Maya Enter History"

4.   Freud's isolation during these years is part of his legend. His colleagues, the story goes, shunned him; his revolutionary ideas fell on deaf ears. These letters suggest that this view needs some revision. While he was, indeed, isolated in these ways, there is now evidence that this was to some degree his own doing, as Frank Sulloway, the historian, has suggested.

DANIEL GOLEMAN
"New Insights into Freud: From Letters to a Friend"

5.   What are the United States' economic interests in the region? U.S. trade with East Asia and on the Pacific is greater than U.S. trade with any other region of the world. Japan is the second most important trading partner of the United States, after Canada. More than ten percent of U.S. foreign investment goes to the region, principally to Japan and Australia, though the proportion going to the Southeast Asian nations is growing. The growth of

all the East Asian nations (China excepted) has been based upon a high volume of international trade. Japan in particular is totally dependent upon imports for its raw-material resources. Thus the security of the sea-lanes of East Asia, and in particular those of Southeast Asia (through which most of Japan's energy resources pass), is vital for the economic well-being of East Asia and the Pacific.

STEPHEN J. MORRIS
"Vietnam's Vietnam"

6. A British doctor who gave physical examinations to many of the Asians who served in France during the First World War as members of the Chinese Labor Corps was impressed by the fine condition of their teeth. He attributed the good dental health to soybeans, and later, during a visit to China, he also attributed to them the absence of rickets in Chinese children at a time when, he said, perhaps eighty per cent of the elementary-school students in London had at least a trace of it. Doctors in Moscow have prescribed soybeans as a cure for rickets. Chinese physicians, for their part, have long had a high regard for the soybean's restorative powers. They use it as a remedy for ailments of the heart, liver, stomach, lungs, kidneys, bladder, bowels, and nerves, and recommend it for improving the complexion and stimulating hair growth. Yellow soybeans are favored for overcoming underweight (to soybeans of all colors is attributed the fact that the Chinese are, on the whole, less afflicted than other races with obesity), and for cooling the blood; black soybeans were often fed to horses before a long journey, to augment endurance. In Japan, doctors have urged soy milk—which has more iron and less fat than cow's milk—upon diabetics and arteriosclerotics; and in some circles there the ingestion of at least one bowl of miso soup every day is considered a way of averting stomach cancer and ulcers.

E. J. KAHN, JR.
"Soybeans"

Exercise 3. Reread the paragraph by John McPhee on pages 288–289. Can you find a statement in this paragraph that does not develop the controlling idea? Do you think the inclusion of this sentence affects the power of the paragraph? What reason might McPhee have had for including this sentence?

Exercise 4. Read the following controlling idea and the sentences that follow it. Indicate which sentences develop this controlling idea and which do not.

Controlling idea: People devised several ways of keeping track of the passage of time before the invention of the clock.

The earliest device for tracking the passage of time was the sundial, which measured the sun's shadow. Many homes today have a decorative sundial in their garden. Sundials can be found among the remains of the ancient Egyptians, Greeks, and Romans. The water clock was an improvement over the sundial, since it did not depend on the sun. I think it would be very annoying to go to bed hearing the dripping of water through a water clock. The use of water clocks was widespread in the ancient world; cultures as diverse as the Chinese and the Romans depended on them to keep track of the passage of hours. The ancient Egyptians devised their water clock at Thebes so that it divided night and day into equal units, making the hour a changeable unit dependent on the length of the day and of the night. Obviously, this type of clock would not be very useful today. The perfection of the art of glassmaking brought with it the invention of the hourglass, which marked the passage of time with sand. Today we use clocks and watches to measure time, and these have been perfected to measure not only hours and minutes, but also seconds and divisions of seconds.

Exercise 5. Discuss the method of development used for each of the following paragraphs.

1. The new breed of training institutes offer something special: individual attention for each member. No one is admitted to the high-tech centers without first undergoing thorough testing. Based on the results, a customized exercise program is drawn up, geared to the individual's needs and goals. In effect, it is a sports training prescription. If you are overweight and in danger of a heart attack, a gradual running, biking or other cardiovascular program will be emphasized, combined with nutritional guidance; if you want to simply strengthen your upper torso, a system of weight lifting will be developed for you. And to make sure you achieve these goals—to encourage, to chastise and, above all, to explain the proper way to work out efficiently and without hurting yourself—a personal trainer (a licensed physical therapist or

exercise physiologist) is assigned to accompany you as you exercise.

ROBERT GOLDBERG
"Tailor-made Fitness Training"

2.   Domestic play looks remarkably alike for both sexes at age three. Costumes representing male and female roles are casually exchanged. Everyone cooks and eats pretend food together. Mother, father, and baby are the primary actors, but identities shift and the participants seldom keep one another informed. Policemen sweep the floor and dress the baby, and mothers put men's vests over negligees while making vague appointments on the telephone. If asked, a boy will likely say he is the father, but if he were to say mother, it would cause little concern. It can be a peaceful place, the three-year-olds' doll corner, even if monsters and superheroes enter, for the cooking and dressing and telephoning are usually private affairs.

VIVIAN GUSSIN PALEY
"Superheroes in the Doll Corner"

3.   After the Prophet's death, Islam (the word is Arabic and means "submission" or "surrender") was ruled by a series of caliphs ("successors") selected by the family of Muhammad and the men around him. At the death of the fourth caliph—Ali, the Prophet's son-in-law—there was a dispute among factions, and two lines of succession were established. The Sunni line—to oversimplify—eventually petered out, ending ambivalently in the twentieth century with the end of the Ottoman Empire in Turkey. The Shia line ended, after a fashion, most Shias believe, in 873 A.D., when the Twelfth Imam ("leader") died or disappeared mysteriously. "The Hidden Imam" became an omnipresent factor in Shiism: "We are waiting for you, Twelfth Imam" was a revolutionary slogan in Iran, and Ayatollah Khomeini (or Imam Khomeini; the title applies to all Shia leaders) wore, for many, the mantle of the Hidden Imam. That connection gave Khomeini a temporal power over many people that it would be virtually impossible for any Sunni leader to accumulate.

RICHARD REEVES
"Journey to Pakistan"

4.   Rum found a major competitor as settlement spread to the frontiers. Both molasses and finished rum were too bulky and expensive to ship far inland, and as the eighteenth-century

settlement line advanced, frontiersmen shifted their loyalties to grain whiskies. Indeed, whiskey was particularly suited to the frontier. Grain was plentiful—much more was harvested than farmers could eat or sell as food—and a single bushel of surplus corn, for example, yielded three gallons of whiskey. This assured a plentiful liquor supply for Westerners and gave them a marketable commodity, which both kept longer and was easier to transport to market than grain. The advantages of whiskey were, therefore, such that it rapidly eclipsed rum as the staple drink in the Back Country. The arrival of the Scotch-Irish, who flocked to the frontier beginning in the 1730s, dealt rum a further blow. These immigrants had enjoyed reputations as whiskey lovers in their northern Irish homes, and they brought their distilling skills across the Atlantic with them. By the later 1700s, they had given American grain spirits a new quality in taste.

MARK EDWARD LENDER and JAMES KIRBY MARTIN
Drinking in America: A History

5.   The new research shows, for the first time in a convincing, repeatable way, that our behavior can be shaped by perceptions, experiences, and memories of which we have no conscious knowledge. In one striking example, people who had undergone surgery were found to have unconscious memories of the things they heard under anaesthesia. In another, amnesiacs and the partially blind seemed to have uncanny unconscious abilities to remember and see. The work also shows that certain apparently voluntary actions, like simple movements of the hand, may be initiated unconsciously even before we're aware of our decision to make them.

KEVIN McKEAN
"In Search of the Unconscious Mind"

43 Crafting sentences

Writing "correct" sentences is a mechanical process of applying rules, but writing *effective* sentences is an art that takes creative effort. To make a strong impression on the reader, you need to use your ear as much as your eye; that is, you need to listen to your sentences as well as read them. One essential tool of the sentence-writing craft is effective diction, or word choice; others include variety of structure, directness of assertion, and emphasis on important elements.

43a Variety of sentence structure

As a writer, you have a responsibility to hold your reader's interest. One way to do this is to vary your sentence structure. Just as the speaker who talks in a monotone will quickly lose the listener's attention, the writer who uses only one sentence structure will soon lose the reader's attention.

The following passage has been rewritten in a monotonous style. Notice that most of the sentences are short and choppy and that all begin with the word *you*.

> You see things vacationing on a motorcycle in a way that is completely different from any other. You are always in a compartment in a car. You are used to it. You don't realize that through that car window everything you see is just more TV. You are a passive observer. You are bored by everything moving by you in a frame.
>
> You lose the frame on a cycle. You are completely in contact with it all. You are *in* the scene. You are not just watching it anymore. You are overwhelmed by the sense of presence. You know that the concrete whizzing by five inches below your foot is the real thing. You know it is the same stuff you walk on. You see it is right there. You can't focus on it because it is so blurred. You can, however, put your foot down and touch it anytime. You are always immediately conscious of the whole thing. You are conscious of the whole experience.

Consider how the passage is improved by varying the sentence structure.

> You see things vacationing on a motorcycle in a way that is completely different from any other. In a car you're always in a compartment, and because you're used to it you don't realize that everything you see is just more TV. You're a passive observer and it is all moving by you boringly in a frame.
>
> On a cycle the frame is gone. You're completely in contact with it all. You're *in* the scene, not just watching it anymore, and the sense of presence is overwhelming. That concrete whizzing

by five inches below your foot is the real thing, the same stuff you walk on; it's right there, so blurred you can't focus on it, yet you can put your foot down and touch it anytime, and the whole thing, the whole experience, is never removed from immediate consciousness.

ROBERT M. PIRSIG
Zen and the Art of Motorcycle Maintenance

Do not be afraid to make your sentences long enough and complex enough to express complex ideas. When several short sentences are used to state what is really one complete thought, the effect is choppy and disjointed. Such writing gives the reader no clue to what is more important and what is relevant, but less important. For example, read the following paragraph.

Francis opened the trunk lid. An odor filled the attic air. It was the odor of lost time. The odor was a cloying reek of imprisoned flowers. It unsettled the dust. It fluttered the window shades.

Now read how the novelist William Kennedy combined the ideas in these short, choppy sentences into a single sentence.

When Francis opened the trunk lid the odor of lost time filled the attic air, a cloying reek of imprisoned flowers that unsettled the dust and fluttered the window shades.

WILLIAM KENNEDY
Ironweed

Notice that the ideas in the second and third sentences of the paragraph form the main clause of Kennedy's sentence (*the odor of lost time filled the attic air*), while the ideas in the other sentences are expressed as subordinate clauses and appositives. Thus the idea of the odor filling the air is given the most importance, while the other ideas are given less emphasis.

Many professional writers use short, clipped sentences to create a sense of urgency or suspense in narrative writing. In most of the writing you will do for school or other purposes, however, you will often need to use longer, more complex sentences to express your ideas. As you write and as you revise your earlier drafts, think about whether two or more short sentences might be more effective if they were combined into one. Among the ways in which you can combine sentences are by the use of appositives; adjective and adverb clauses; and prepositional, verbal, and absolute phrases.

Appositives

An appositive is a word or group of words that defines or renames the noun that precedes it. Notice how the choppy sentences in the following examples can be combined through the use of appositives.

> **Separate:** The ailanthus was brought to America by a distinguished Philadelphia importer. His name was William Hamilton.
>
> **Combined:** The ailanthus was brought to America by a distinguished Philadelphia importer, William Hamilton.
>
> **Separate:** The ailanthus grows in the most meager of environments. Its name means "the tree of heaven."
>
> **Combined:** The ailanthus, "the tree of heaven," grows in the most meager of environments.
>
> **Separate:** Beside the river was a grove of tall, naked cottonwoods so large that they seemed to belong to a bygone age. These cottonwoods were trees of great antiquity and enormous size.
>
> **Combined:** Beside the river was a grove of tall, naked cottonwoods—trees of great antiquity and enormous size— so large that they seemed to belong to a bygone age.
>
> WILLA CATHER
> *Death Comes for the Archbishop*

Adjective clauses

An adjective clause is a group of words with a subject and a predicate that modifies a noun or a pronoun. Usually, an adjective clause begins with a relative pronoun. Notice how the choppy sentences in the following examples can be combined through the use of adjective clauses.

> **Separate:** The birthplace of Jean Rhys is Dominica. Dominica is one of the Windward Islands.
>
> **Combined:** The birthplace of Jean Rhys is Dominica, which is one of the Windward Islands.

Separate:	William W. Warner described blue crabs as "beautiful swimmers." He wrote a study of the Chesapeake Bay. The book won a Pulitzer prize.
Combined:	William W. Warner, who wrote a study of the Chesapeake Bay that won a Pulitzer prize, described blue crabs as "beautiful swimmers."

Separate:	Holmes had been seated for some hours in silence with his long, thin back curved over a chemical vessel. In this vessel he was brewing a particularly malodorous product.
Combined:	Holmes had been seated for some hours in silence with his long, thin back curved over a chemical vessel in which he was brewing a particularly malodorous product.

SIR ARTHUR CONAN DOYLE
"The Adventure of the Dancing Men"

Adverb clauses

An adverb clause is a group of words with a subject and a predicate that functions as an adverb in a sentence. Usually, an adverb clause begins with a subordinating conjunction (such as *because*, *after*, or *so that*) that shows the relation of the adverb clause to the word or words it modifies. Notice how the choppy sentences in the following examples can be combined through the use of adverb clauses.

Separate:	He was never in a battle. Nevertheless, he wrote movingly about war.
Combined:	Although he was never in a battle, he wrote movingly about war.

Separate:	My wife and I both work at home. Quintana therefore has never had any confusion about how we make our living.
Combined:	Because my wife and I both work at home, Quintana has never had any confusion about how we make our living.

JOHN GREGORY DUNNE
"Quintana"

Separate: The purple and red jukebox belted accommodating rhythms. A couple slow-dragged. Billy spun yarns about his adventures.

Combined: While the purple and red jukebox belted accommodating rhythms, and while a couple slow-dragged, Billy spun yarns about his adventures.

> JAMES ALAN McPHERSON
> "The Story of a Dead Man"

Prepositional phrases

A prepositional phrase consists of a preposition, a noun or pronoun called the object of the preposition, and all the words modifying this object. Notice how the choppy sentences in the following examples can be combined through the use of prepositional phrases.

Separate: Jack London died at the age of forty. He had become an extremely popular writer.

Combined: Before his death at the age of forty, Jack London had become an extremely popular writer.

Separate: She had a genius for painting. She also had a talent for writing.

Combined: In addition to her genius for painting, she had a talent for writing.

Separate: His Royal Highness Prince Philippe gave me an audience. He was prince of Araucania and Patagonia. The audience was on a drizzling November afternoon. It was at his public relations firm. The firm was on the Faubourg Poissonière.

Combined: On a drizzling November afternoon, His Royal Highness Prince Philippe of Araucania and Patagonia gave me an audience at his public relations firm on the Faubourg Poissonière.

> BRUCE CHATWIN
> *In Patagonia*

Participial phrases

A participial phrase consists of a participle and all its modifiers and complements. Notice how the choppy sentences in the

314

following examples can be combined through the use of participial phrases.

> **Separate:**   Washington resigned as general. He then returned to his plantation.
> **Combined:** Having resigned as general, Washington returned to his plantation.

> **Separate:**   The producers planned a two-part miniseries. This miniseries would tell the story of the native American experience from the native American point of view.
> **Combined:** The producers planned a two-part miniseries telling the story of the native American experience from the native American point of view.
> **Or:**   The two-part miniseries planned by the producers would tell the story of the native American experience from the native American point of view.

> **Separate:**   We are given a thimbleful of facts. We rush to make generalizations as large as a tub.
> **Combined:** Given a thimbleful of facts, we rush to make generalizations as large as a tub.
> GORDON W. ALLPORT

Absolute phrases

An absolute phrase is a group of words with a subject and a nonfinite verb (a verb form that cannot function as a sentence verb). When the verb is a form of *be*, it is sometimes omitted but understood. Notice how the choppy sentences in the following examples can be combined through the use of absolute phrases.

> **Separate:**   The war was over. The nation turned its attention to reconstruction of the Union.
> **Combined:** The war being over, the nation turned its attention to reconstruction of the Union.
> **Or:**   The war over, the nation turned its attention to reconstruction of the Union.

> **Separate:**   The plane finally came to a stop. The passengers were breathing sighs of relief.
> **Combined:** The plane finally came to a stop, the passengers breathing sighs of relief.

Separate: Breakfast had been eaten. The slim camp outfit had been lashed to the sled. The men turned their backs on the cheery fire and launched out into the darkness.

Combined: Breakfast eaten and the slim camp outfit lashed to the sled, the men turned their backs on the cheery fire and launched out into the darkness.

JACK LONDON
White Fang

Exercise 1. Use appositives, adjective clauses, or adverb clauses to form one sentence from each of the following groups of sentences.

1. Wooden Leg fought against Custer at the Battle of the Little Bighorn. This battle is also known as Custer's Last Stand.

2. The painter is well known in China. He is unknown in the United States.

3. Licinius was defeated by Constantine. Licinius ruled jointly with Galerius.

4. Libya is situated in northern Africa. It was once an Italian colony.

5. The man believed he was hated. This made him act in a cruel and hateful way.

6. The Spanish writer's name is Cervantes. He wrote *Don Quixote*. *Don Quixote* is a satire.

7. Benvenuto Cellini was an Italian sculptor and goldsmith. In addition, he wrote an autobiography. His autobiography is considered an important work of literature.

8. The city of Antioch was founded in about 300 B.C. It was conquered by the Romans in 64 B.C.

9. In the tale Hercules kills the Hydra. The Hydra is a mythical monster. It has nine heads.

10. Columbus thought he had reached the East Indies. He mistakenly called the natives "Indians."

Exercise 2. Use prepositional phrases, participial phrases, or absolute phrases to form one sentence from each of the following groups of sentences.

1. The pioneers sought a better life. They moved westward over the mountains.

2. The party was over. The hosts relaxed.

3. He made his fortune in the new land. He sent money to his family so that they could join him.

4. She spent much time in his company. She came to appreciate his conversation and the quality of his mind.

5. He feared she would burn the poet's letters to her. Therefore, he broke into her apartment and searched for them.

6. Some people fear they will be disliked if they are successful. They seek failure.

7. The Chippewa fought with the French. They fought against the English. This was during the French and Indian Wars.

8. Eero Saarinen designed the Gateway Arch and the Dulles Airport terminal. The arch is in St. Louis. The airport is outside Washington, D.C.

9. Henry Lewis Stimson served as secretary of state. During this period he formulated the Stimson Doctrine.

10. The Vandals fled the Huns. During their flight they swept through Gaul.

Exercise 3. Revise the following passage by combining short, choppy sentences to form strong, effective sentences.

"Blind Girls" is a short story. It is in the collection *Black Tickets*. This collection is by Jayne Anne Phillips. In this story, the author creates a picture of two teenagers. They are named Jessie and Sally. These teenagers are drunk on their first wine. They are also drunk on their awakened desire. As they drink, they tell pornographic stories. They scare themselves with tales of lonely adults. These adults are attracted to the young. These tales are also of amputees. These maimed bodies lurk in the grass around parked cars. The passion of their fantasies and the intensity of their sexual fears finally overwhelm the teenagers. They know full well that the sounds outside their shack are simply from neighborhood boys. These boys have come to spy on them. They also want to scare them. However, knowing this, Sally whines when she hears them. She has to be led blindfolded through the field. She is led to her house.

These characters are unable to connect or to confront their own desires. This is characteristic of the stories of Jayne Anne Phillips. Another of her stories is called "Heavenly Bodies." In it, a father is unable to express his concern for his daughter directly. He can ask only about her car. The daughter's name is Jancy. Jancy can complain about her mother's emotional distance only by expressing concern about the distance the mother drives. These characters reach out. Their attempt is always incomplete. The father telephones. He wants to find out if Jancy is home. He doesn't speak. He only listens for her voice. Jancy telephones Michael. She wants to rekindle their romance. She cannot speak.

Like Sally who travels the path blindfolded, the father who once built roads, and the daughter who constantly travels on them, Jayne Anne Phillips's characters are always moving. They always move blindly. They have no place to go. Their loneliness and desperation reflect the alienation of modern American society.

43b Directness of assertion

In general, try to construct your sentences so that your ideas are expressed as forcefully and directly as possible. You can achieve force and directness by using action verbs and by writing in the active voice.

Action verbs

Action verbs give power and precision to your writing, whereas the overuse of the verb *be* weakens your writing. Note how the sentences in the following examples are strengthened when the verb *be* is replaced with an action verb.

> **Weak:** Her face **was** a wall of brown fire.
> **Strong:** Her face **flashed** a wall of brown fire.
>
> > JAMES ALAN McPHERSON
> > "The Story of a Scar"

> **Weak:** Everywhere, in the bathroom too, there were prints of Roman ruins that **were** brown with age.
> **Strong:** Everywhere, in the bathroom too, there were prints of Roman ruins **freckled** brown with age.
>
> > TRUMAN CAPOTE
> > *Breakfast at Tiffany's*

| Weak: | Their feet **were** no longer on firm sand but **were** on slippery slime and painful barnacled rock. |
| Strong: | Their feet **lost** the firm sand and **slipped** on slime, **trod** painfully on barnacled rock. |

MICHAEL INNES
The Man from the Sea

The active voice

As its name suggests, the active voice is usually more direct and forceful than the passive voice.

| Unemphatic: | Kronos **was overthrown** by Zeus, his son. |
| Emphatic: | Zeus **overthrew** Kronos, his father. |

| Unemphatic: | At the Rubicon a decision **was made** by Caesar. |
| Emphatic: | At the Rubicon, Caesar **made** a decision. |

| Unemphatic: | Infinitely less **is demanded** by love than by friendship. |
| Emphatic: | Love **demands** infinitely less than friendship. |

GEORGE JEAN NATHAN

If you wish to emphasize the receiver of the action instead of the agent, use the passive voice.

The father **was granted** custody of the child by the court.
The schools **were consolidated** in 1953.

43c Emphasizing important elements of a sentence

Construct your sentences to emphasize the important elements. You can achieve emphasis through careful choice of words, through proper subordination, and through any one of the following methods.

1. Achieve emphasis by placing important elements at the beginning or at the end of a sentence, particularly at the end.

| Unemphatic: | It is not known why more boys than girls are autistic. |
| Emphatic: | Why more boys than girls are autistic is unknown. |

Unemphatic: The trip was not as bad as, but worse than, I feared it would be.

Emphatic: The trip was not as bad as I feared it would be—it was worse.

Unemphatic: A bore is a man who tells you how he is when you ask him.

Emphatic: A bore is a man who, when you ask him how he is, tells you.

BERT LESTON TAYLOR

2. Achieve emphasis by changing loose sentences into periodic sentences. In a loose sentence, the main clause comes first; modifying phrases, dependent clauses, and other amplification follow the main clause.

Jane Eyre would not declare her love for Mr. Rochester, although the fortune-teller pressed her for the information when they were alone together on that dark and mysterious night.

In a periodic sentence, the main clause comes last.

Although the fortune-teller pressed her for the information when they were alone together on that dark and mysterious night, Jane Eyre would not declare her love for Mr. Rochester.

Periodic sentences are less commonly used than loose sentences and therefore are more emphatic. They give emphasis to the idea in the main clause by saving this idea for last.

Loose: The fortune-teller was really Mr. Rochester, although she claimed to be a gypsy from a nearby camp who had come simply to tell the ladies' futures.

Periodic: Although she claimed to be a gypsy from a nearby camp who had come simply to tell the ladies' futures, the fortune-teller was really Mr. Rochester.

Loose: It's easy to choose between love and duty if you are willing to forget that there is an element of duty in love and of love in duty.

Periodic: If you are willing to forget that there is an element of duty in love and of love in duty, then it's easy to choose between the two.

JEAN GIRAUDOUX

Loose: Emancipation will be a proclamation but not a fact until justice is blind to color, until education is unaware of race, until opportunity is unconcerned with the color of men's skins.

Periodic: Until justice is blind to color, until education is unaware of race, until opportunity is unconcerned with the color of men's skins, emancipation will be a proclamation but not a fact.

LYNDON B. JOHNSON

3. Achieve emphasis by writing balanced sentences. A balanced sentence presents ideas of equal weight in the same grammatical form, thus emphasizing the similarity or disparity between the ideas.

Unbalanced: Generally the theories we believe we call facts, and the facts that we disbelieve are known as theories.

Balanced: Generally, the theories we believe we call facts, and the facts we disbelieve we call theories.

FELIX COHEN

Unbalanced: Money—in its absence we are coarse; when it is present we tend to be vulgar.

Balanced: Money—in its absence we are coarse; in its presence we are vulgar.

MIGNON McLAUGHLIN

4. Achieve emphasis by inverting normal word order. In most English sentences, the word order is subject-verb-complement. Changing this order makes a sentence stand out.

Unemphatic: He gave his property to the poor.
Emphatic: His property he gave to the poor.

Unemphatic: Indiana Jones walked into the Temple of Doom.
Emphatic: Into the Temple of Doom walked Indiana Jones.

Unemphatic: Long hours of hard work lie behind every successful endeavor.
Emphatic: Behind every successful endeavor lie long hours of hard work.

Unemphatic:	The lens, which helps to focus the image, is in the front of the eye.
Emphatic:	In the front of the eye is the lens, which helps to focus the image.

Exercise. Revise each of the following sentences to make it more forceful or to emphasize important elements. Where appropriate, change the verb *be* to an action verb, change the passive voice to the active voice, place important words at the beginning or the end of a sentence, turn a loose sentence into a periodic sentence, turn an unbalanced sentence into a balanced sentence, and invert word order.

1. The eclipse of the sun will be viewed by many people.

2. Darkness was there in the beginning.

3. The theme of love and death is at the heart of many American novels.

4. We learn very little about his inner life, although he is the central character of the play.

5. The large painting is in the main hall of the museum.

6. To talk to the old woman is learning history first-hand.

7. The goal of the park service is to preserve the plant life of the island in a pristine state.

8. A diamond necklace of light is around the moon.

9. As usual, Jeeves, the soul of reason, steps into the confusion.

10. The young man rejects his community, since he feels it has rejected him.

44 Critical thinking

To write effectively, you need to think clearly and critically. Since the effectiveness of any assertion depends on the validity of the reasoning behind it, a well-written paper must of necessity be a well-reasoned one.

44a Inductive and deductive reasoning

The two major kinds of sound reasoning are inductive and deductive reasoning. **Inductive reasoning** is reasoning from the specific to the general. The word *inductive* comes from a Latin word that means "to lead into." In the inductive method, you observe a number of particulars or specifics, and these particulars lead you to a general principle or conclusion. For example, imagine you are studying folk medicine. For a year you live in a society that practices folk medicine, and you carefully observe the practices of the healers. You observe that they use a preparation made from a particular plant to treat boils. In all cases, the boil disappears within two days of the application of the plant. On the basis of your observations of these particular cases, you reason that this plant helps cure boils.

Deductive reasoning is reasoning from the general to the specific. The word *deductive* comes from a Latin word that means "to lead from." In the deductive method, you start with a general principle and apply it to specific instances. For example, imagine you are a doctor. As a general principle, you accept that penicillin is effective against the bacteria causing strep throat. When a patient with strep throat comes to you, you apply the general principle to this specific case and prescribe penicillin.

The deductive method can be expressed as a three-step process, called a **syllogism.** The first step, the general principle, is called the **major premise;** the second step, the specific instance, is called the **minor premise;** and the third step, the application of the general principle to the specific instance, is called the **conclusion.**

Major premise: Penicillin cures strep throat.
Minor premise: This patient has strep throat.
Conclusion: (Therefore) This patient will be cured by using penicillin.

Although inductive and deductive reasoning are powerful tools in writing, their misuse can lead to errors. To make effective use of the inductive method, make sure that you have made enough observations, that your observations are accurate and representational, that you have noted and accounted for any exceptions, and that your conclusion is derived from these observations. For example, suppose the plant mentioned above did not cure three cases of boils. If your conclusion is to be valid, you must note these exceptions and explain them in terms of the conclusion. Perhaps this plant will not cure boils in people who have been treated with it previously, or whose boils are especially severe. The more observations and information you accumulate, the more likely that your conclusion will be accurate.

To make effective use of the deductive method, make sure that the general principle you start with is true and that the situation to which you apply it is relevant. Note and account for any exceptions. For example, imagine that the bacteria in the strep throat patient mentioned above have developed an immunity to penicillin. Then the principle would not be applicable to this patient's case. The more information you have about the specific situation, the more likely you will be to apply the relevant principle.

44b Logical fallacies

All thinking is subject to **logical fallacies,** or errors in reasoning. Test your own writing to make sure you have avoided false analogies, overgeneralizations and stereotyping, unstated assumptions, appeals to the emotions, confusion of cause and effect, improper either-or thinking, non sequiturs, and circular reasoning.

False analogies

Analogies, which are used often in inductive reasoning, are comparisons. For an analogy to be sound, or true, the comparison must make sense; that is, the things being compared must correspond in essential ways, and the ways in which they do not correspond must be unimportant in terms of the argument or conclusion. Consider the following analogies:

These are not books, lumps of lifeless paper, but *minds* alive on the shelves. From each of them goes out its own voice . . . and just as the touch of a button on our set will fill the room with music, so by taking down one of these volumes and opening it, one can call into range the voice of a man far distant in time and space, and hear him speak to us, mind to mind, heart to heart.

GILBERT HIGHET

First the writer compares books with minds. These two things are alike in essential ways. Both contain the thoughts of a person, and from both these thoughts are communicated. Then the writer compares pushing the button on a radio with taking down a book from a shelf and opening it. These acts are alike, since both call into range the voice of a person who is not present.

Here are some other sound analogies:

News is the first rough draft of history.

BEN BRADLEE

The individual who pollutes the air with his factory and the ghetto kid who breaks store windows both represent the same thing. They don't care about each other—or what they do to each other.

DANIEL PATRICK MOYNIHAN

If a State can prescribe, as a rule of civil conduct, that whites and blacks shall not travel as passengers in the same railroad coach, why may it not so regulate the use of the streets of its cities and towns as to compel white citizens to keep to one side of the street and black citizens to keep to the other?

JUSTICE JOHN MARSHALL HARLAN

While analogies help readers to understand a point, they are not proofs of a conclusion. In fact, many analogies that appear in writing are misleading, or false. A **false analogy** does not make sense. Although the things being compared may correspond in some ways, they are dissimilar in other ways that are crucial to the argument or conclusion, or their similarities are blown out of proportion. Consider the following false analogy.

Buying a car is like buying a steak. You can't be sure how good the product is until you've bought it and used it.

325

This analogy is false because you can test-drive the car, but you cannot test-eat the steak; moreover, the economic difference between the items is so great that a comparison between the purchase of one and the purchase of the other has little meaning.

Exercise. Explain why the following analogies are false.

1. A nation's full use of its natural resources is as proper as an individual's full use of his or her talents.

2. A nation that can put a man on the moon can eliminate poverty.

3. Think of a job interview as a first date, where you're trying to make a good impression on someone.

Overgeneralizations and stereotyping

An **overgeneralization** is a conclusion based on too little evidence or on evidence that is unrepresentative or biased. For example, imagine you go to a major-league baseball game with your friends. You observe that attendance at this game is very low. On the basis of this observation, you conclude that attendance at major-league baseball games has fallen off drastically. This is an overgeneralization, since one observation—or even two or three—are not a sufficient number from which to draw a conclusion.

Now imagine that while you are visiting a large city for a week, you ride the subway every evening at nine. You find the ride quick and comfortable, since there are never any crowds and you always get a seat. On the basis of your observations, you conclude that the subway provides pleasant and reliable transportation. This is an overgeneralization, since your evidence is not typical of a commuter's ride on the subway during rush hour.

Here are some other examples of overgeneralization:

Since neither of my parents smokes, the number of adults who smoke must be rapidly diminishing.

Melinda and her friend had dinner at a new local restaurant. Melinda's steak was undercooked and her friend's chicken was cold. They concluded that the restaurant was poor.

A candidate for mayor makes a door-to-door survey of all the houses in his neighborhood to find out whether voters are willing to pay higher taxes to improve the public schools. Most of them express enthusiasm for the idea, and the candidate decides to campaign on this platform.

Stereotyping is overgeneralization about groups of people. **Stereotypes** are the standardized mental images that are the result of such overgeneralization. Almost everyone holds stereotypes about one group or another, and we encounter them every day in advertising, television programs, and other media. For example, we are all familiar with stereotypes like these:

Stereotype	Stereotyping
the absentminded professor	Professors are absentminded.
the dumb blonde	Blondes are dumb.
the genius with glasses	Geniuses wear glasses.
the passionate French lover	The French are passionate lovers.
the stoical male	Real men don't cry.
the man-hunting female	Every woman wants a man.

Because stereotypes of this kind are so widely recognized as such, you can easily avoid them in your writing. A greater danger is that you will develop your own stereotypes by treating an individual as representative of a group to which the individual belongs. Try to eliminate stereotyping not only from your writing but also from your thinking.

Unstated assumptions

An assumption is an idea that we accept as true without any proof. Sometimes unstated assumptions enter into our reasoning and confuse our thinking. Many of these assumptions are really stereotypes. For example, consider the following statement:

Her autobiography must be fascinating because she is such a famous actress.

This reasoning does not make sense. It is based on the unstated assumption that someone who has had a glamorous or exciting career will be able to write about it in an interesting way. That may be true in this particular case, but it cannot be assumed as a general principle.

Exercise. Identify the unstated assumption in each of the following statements.

1. If he is elected senator, he will work to help the poor because he was once poor himself.

2. We should not hire a young woman for this position because she would leave after a few years to start having babies.

3. You can sell the American public any product if you can get the children to want the product.

Appeals to the emotions

Do not draw a conclusion for yourself or tempt others into drawing a conclusion on the basis of an appeal to the emotions instead of reason. Writers use various techniques to arouse an emotional rather than a rational response. Among these are name-calling, using loaded words, creating a bandwagon effect, using flattery, and creating false associations.

Name-calling

Name-calling, which is sometimes referred to as the **ad hominem fallacy,** is an attempt to discredit an idea or conclusion by attacking not the idea or conclusion but the person presenting it.

> Griffin claims that the legal drinking age should be raised in order to reduce the incidence of drunk driving. Are you going to let someone who was once himself convicted of drunk driving tell you when you can take an innocent drink?

> Gardner claims that teaching is attracting mediocre people. Yet she herself is a hick from a backwater town. What can she know of quality?

> So what if Mr. Klein told you you shouldn't drop out of school? He's only an old man with old ideas. What does he know about youth and adventure?

If the nature kooks had their way, America would still be a wilderness from coast to coast.

HARLEY G. WALLER

Loaded words

Loaded words are highly charged emotional words that appeal to readers' prejudices. Readers who do not already share these prejudices are as likely to be irritated as to be convinced by the use of loaded words.

Because of this nation's **giveaway** policies, the **hardworking** man or woman lives in squalor while the **lazy bum** drives a Cadillac.

Democracy is a system in which the **screeching** and **caterwauling** of the **vulgar masses** drown the pronouncements of the enlightened few.

Our library shelves are **infested** by the **filth** of **effete intellectuals** who crave the **corruption** of the **innocent youth** of this country.

Bandwagon

The **bandwagon technique** attempts to influence people by encouraging them to put aside their own powers of reasoning and simply join the crowd.

Don't be left out—see the film that all America has been waiting for.

Everyone in the neighborhood is signing the petition. You're going to sign it, aren't you?

ColaRite is the most popular soft drink in the country. Buy some and join the fun!

Flattery

Flattery is often used to try to persuade a reader or listener to do something or to accept the validity of a conclusion.

The voters of this city are too intelligent to be taken in by my opponent's promises.

You're young. You're on top of things. And you want to stay on top. That's why you need *Lifestyle*, the magazine that helps you be what you want to be.

A person of your sensitivity could not help being moved by the plight of these unfortunate victims.

False association

False association, sometimes called the **association fallacy,** attempts to convince people of the strength or weakness of a conclusion by suggesting that by agreeing or disagreeing with it, they will become associated with other people doing the same.

Many people active in the movie and theater world belong to this health club. Since you are young and talented, you should join it, too.

All of the best people in town support this proposal. Of course, you must support it, too.

Only eggheads and clods belong to that fraternity. You're not planning to pledge it, are you?

Exercise. Each of the following statements contains a logical fallacy. For each statement, indicate whether this fallacy is a false analogy, an overgeneralization, an unstated assumption, or an appeal to the emotions.

1. Your roommate, who went to Harrold School, is somewhat of a snob. You conclude that students from Harrold School are snobs.

2. A father is seeking custody of his child. You conclude that he should not be granted custody, because he is a man.

3. The people need a ruler just as children need a parent.

4. After reading the first chapter of a long book, you conclude that it is boring, put it down, and never open it again.

5. Everybody who is anybody in this school is working to support Hendrick's candidacy.

6. Abbott recommends an increase in taxes, but how can we follow the recommendation of a man who was once accused of beating his dog?

7. Only a coward would pull out of the war now.

8. The lovely Bette Kiddington uses Youthful You face cream. Don't you think you should, too?

9. I bought this candy from a health food store. Therefore, I can eat as much of it as I want, since it won't make me fat.

10. In the capitalist system, a worker is nothing but a slave.

Faulty cause and effect

Do not assume that one event causes another event simply because it precedes the second event. Many superstitions are based on this error in reasoning.

> It didn't rain today because, for once, I brought my umbrella.

> He won the game because he was wearing his lucky T-shirt.

> I now have a cold because I forgot to take my vitamin pill this morning.

Either-or thinking

Either-or thinking is a type of oversimplification that assumes that there are only two alternatives in a situation when usually there are many possibilities in between.

> You are either with us or against us.

> We have to decide: do we want clean air and water or do we want a higher standard of living?

> Every woman today must make a choice. She can have a family or she can have a career.

Non sequiturs

The Latin words *non sequitur* mean "it does not follow." A **non sequitur** is a logical fallacy in which the conclusion does not follow from the premise.

> Many wild animals live longer in zoos than in the wild. Therefore, all wild animals should be placed in zoos.

> Since Henderson does not beat his children, he is a good father.

> It is important to honor our parents, and so we should actively participate in the celebration of Mother's Day and Father's Day.

Circular reasoning

Do not try to prove that something is true by merely restating it in other words. This error is called **circular reasoning** or **begging the question.**

> Public transportation is necessary because everyone needs it.

> The play is unsophisticated because it displays a naive simplicity.

> The vest will protect an officer against a person with a gun because it is bulletproof.

Exercise. Each of the following statements contains a logical fallacy. For each statement, indicate whether this fallacy is faulty cause and effect, either-or thinking, a non sequitur, or circular reasoning.

1. Death is inevitable because we all must die.
2. You can join our protest now, or you can sit back and do nothing.
3. She will have a successful career as a newspaper reporter because everyone has always liked her.
4. Since no one can live without hope, all human beings are optimists.
5. Hemingway is a great novelist because he led an exciting life.
6. We could not win the war, because the enemy was unconquerable.
7. Rodgers did not get the job because a black cat had walked across his path earlier in the day.
8. Computers are replacing slide rules because slide rules have become obsolete.
9. In today's world, either you vote with the future, or you become part of the past.
10. Anita is a great conversationalist; therefore, she should become an actress.

45 Writing the research paper

The word *research* comes from an Old French word meaning "to seek out" or "to search again." A research paper is one in which you seek out information about a topic from a variety of sources. However, a research paper should not be merely a recapitulation of the findings of others. It should also reflect your own ideas and understandings.

A research paper is both informative and objective. It seeks to provide information about a topic by examining a variety of sources objectively and by reaching a conclusion about the findings.

A research paper is formal. It contains little, if any, colloquial language or slang and few, if any, contractions.

45a Choosing and limiting a topic

What interests you? Since you will be spending several weeks researching your topic, make sure you choose one that appeals to you. Are you interested in finding information about any particular person? Andrew Johnson? Diane Arbus? Woody Allen? Gwendolyn Brooks? Are you interested in studying any particular place? Spain? Jupiter? The Great Plains? Grenada? Are you interested in exploring any particular time period? The turn of the century? The sixteenth century? The fifth century B.C.? The 1920's? Are you interested in examining any particular event? The Civil War? The birth of Christianity? The first space flight to the moon? The building of the first transcontinental railroad? Are you interested in studying any particular object or activity? Clocks? Vitamins? Jazz? Cooking? Are you interested in exploring any particular idea or doctrine? Rationalism? Buddhism? Transcendentalism? Dada? Are you interested in investigating a controversial issue? Abortion? Nuclear power? School desegregation? The military draft?

When faced with the task of writing a research paper, many students go blank; they can think of nothing that interests them. Some solve this problem by thumbing through magazines, newspapers, and encyclopedias. When Tim Rogers, the student whose paper is featured on pages 363–397, was assigned to write a research paper, he looked through an encyclopedia until he found a topic that interested him—hypnosis.

A typical research paper is between 2,000 and 3,000 words long. Therefore, after you decide on a topic you must limit it so that you can cover it effectively within these boundaries. What aspect of your topic do you wish to cover? Notice how the following topics were narrowed.

Woody Allen⟶his life⟶his life as an artist⟶his artistic output⟶his movies⟶*Annie Hall*⟶the making of *Annie Hall*

Grenada⟶the history of Grenada⟶the military history of Grenada⟶Grenada's strategic importance to the United States

the fifth century B.C.⟶the fifth century B.C. in China⟶religion in China in the fifth century B.C.⟶the teachings of Confucius⟶modern Chinese reaction to the teachings of Confucius

the Civil War⟶important generals of the Civil War⟶important Union generals of the Civil War⟶General Sherman's role in the Civil War⟶General Sherman's Atlanta campaign

vitamins⟶types of vitamins⟶the use of vitamin supplements⟶vitamin therapy⟶the controversy over megadose vitamin therapy

transcendentalism⟶New England transcendentalists⟶the influence of transcendentalism on the works of Henry David Thoreau⟶the influence of transcendentalism on *Walden*

Of course, limiting your topic is not always such a simple, straightforward process. It is more a trial-and-error procedure that is open to revision. In fact, Tim Rogers delayed the completion of the process until he was well into his research. He even made several false starts. Finally he narrowed his topic to *the acceptance of hypnosis as a healing tool.*

Be sure that your topic lends itself to research. If it is very narrow or very new, you probably will not be able to find sufficient information written about it. For example, the topic *the increase in popcorn consumption in the United States during the last six months* will most likely not lend itself to adequate research. It is too recent. The topic *why I like popcorn* calls for personal opinion, not research. It might be appropriate for an essay, but not for a research paper.

45b Doing research

After you have chosen your topic, the next step is to gather information. The best place to start is your library.

Finding information

Begin your research in the library's card catalog, which lists alphabetically on index cards all the books and magazines in the library. Usually the card catalog contains at least three cards for each book: a subject card, a title card, and an author card. (Often it contains more than one subject card.) Unless you have a particular title or author in mind, the best place to start is the subject cards, which are often grouped separately from the author and title cards. Tim Rogers started his research by looking in the card catalog under *hypnosis*. When he couldn't find any books under this subject, he looked under a synonym for *hypnosis*, which is *hypnotism*. There he found the subject was divided into many subcategories. Here is one card he found under the subject *Hypnotism—History*.

Subject card

Compare the subject card with the title and the author cards for this book.

Author card

```
JFE         Tinterow, Maurice M., 1917-     , comp.
71-192

            Foundations of hypnosis, from Mesmer to Freud, by
         Maurice M. Tinterow.  Springfield, Ill., C. C. Thomas
         [1970]

         xiii,    606 p.    illus.    24 cm.
         Bibliography:  pp. 569-587

         1.  Hypnotism--Hist.            I. Tinterow, Maurice M.

         1917

         NN*R 4.7 w/R   OC, 1b*          PC1, SL (LC1, X1)
```

Title card

```
JFE         Foundations of hypnosis, from Mesmer to Freud
71-192

            Tinterow, Maurice M., 1917-     , comp.
               Foundations of hypnosis, from Mesmer to Freud, by
         Maurice M. Tinterow.  Springfield, Ill., C. C. Thomas
         [1970]

         xiii,    606 p.    illus.    24 cm.
         Bibliography:  pp. 569-587

         1.  Hypnotism--Hist.            I. Tinterow, Maurice M.

         1917

         NN*R 4.7 w/R   OC, 1b*          PC1, SL (LC1, X1)
```

Today, in a large library, you may find that the drawers of catalog cards are missing. Instead, the catalog is kept in books, on microfilm, or on microfiche. If you cannot find the catalog or do not know how to use a microfilm or microfiche catalog, ask the librarian for help.

Here is a section from the New York (City) Public Library's catalog, which is in book form.

HYGIENE, RURAL.
Ehlers, Victor Marcus, 1884-1959. Municipal and rural sanitation. New York [c1965] 663p. 71-292878 **Fr MM-SCI** **[614-E] NYPL** **[628-E33 M5] BPL**

Health by the people /. Geneva [Albany, N.Y.] 1975. xii, 206 p., [5] leaves of plates : 80-20428 **[362.1-H] BPL** — library call number

HYGIENE, RURAL - ADDRESSES, ESSAYS, LECTURES.
Long, Ernest Croft. Health objectives for the developing society. Durham, N. C., 1965. xiv, 163 p. 80-146525 **[614.04-L849 H] BPL**

HYGIENE, SEXUAL. — subject heading
Airola, Paavo O. Sex and nutrition. New York [c1970] 220p. 71-60827 **Cn MM-POP** **[612.6-A] NYPL** **[613.95-A] BPL**

Bertocci, Peter Anthony. The human venture in sex, love, and marriage. New York [c1949] 143p. 70-261477 **MM-HSS** **[301.414-B] NYPL** **[392-B54] BPL**

Bieler, Henry G. Dr. Bieler's natural way to sexual health. Los Angeles [c1972] xix, 231 p. 73-300871 **MM-POP MM-SCI BLS** **[613.95-B] BPL**

Brenton, Myron. Sex and your heart. New York [c1968] 180p. 71-445708 **BLS** — author and title information **[613.95-B] NYPL** **[612.6-B839 S] BPL**

Busby, Trent. Be good to your body /. Secaucus, N.J. , c1976. 235 p. ; 77-128354 **BLS** **[613.0424-B] NYPL** **[613.954-B] BPL**

After using the card catalog, you may want to use periodical indexes to locate magazine or journal articles. The more current your topic, the more likely you will be to use magazine, journal, and newspaper articles for information on it. Probably, the index you will find most useful for locating articles is the *Readers' Guide to Periodical Literature*, which provides a monthly, quarterly, and annual index to almost 200 periodicals.

Here is the information Tim Rogers found when he looked up *hypnotism* in the 1982 volume of this guide.

subject heading—**Hypertrophy**
    See also
  Heart—Hypertrophy
Hyphomycetes, Aquatic. See Aquatic fungi
Hypnotherapy. See Hypnotism—Therapeutic use
Hypnotics
    See also
  Flurazepam

title of article—Why pills are becoming passé. Bus Week p 134
  O 11 '82
Hypnotism
    See also
cross reference—Forensic hypnotism

  Hypnosis: put your mind power to work. S. D.
    Bryant. Essence 12:52+ Ap '82
  Research through deception [P. Zimbardo's study
    of hearing loss and paranoia causes ethical
author of article—stir] M. M. Hunt. il por N Y Times Mag p66-
    7+ S 12 '82
description of—To trust, perchance to buy [successful sales
article   techniques are form of hypnotism] D. J.
    Moine. il Psychol Today 16:50-2+ Ag '82

            Police use
  Hypnosis: guilty of fraud? [unreliable memory
    of witnesses; study by Martin T. Orne] Sci
    News 121:42 Ja 16 '82
subheading—   **Therapeutic use**
  Hypnosis can increase antibodies [increase in
    lymphocyte count; research by Howard R.
    Hall] USA Today 110:8 Je '82
  Sci-fi images aid hypnosis [therapy for chil-
    dren; work of Bryan Carter and Gary El-
    kins] Sci Dig 90:91 N '82
  Spellbinders [teaching tales of M. Erickson] por
    Psychol Today 16:39-42+ F '82
Hypnotism, Forensic. See Forensic hypnotism
Hypo. See Sodium thiosulfate
Hypoglycemia
source So you think you have low blood sugar. . . W. A.
information   Nolen. il McCalls 109:44+ S '82
Hypophysectomy
  Virus-induced corticosterone in hypophysec-
    tomized mice: a possible lymphoid adrenal
    axis. E. M. Smith and others. bibl f il Sci-
    ence 218:1311-12 D 24 '82
Hypotensive agents. See Antihypertensive agents
Hypothalamic hormones
    See also
  Pituitary hormone releasing factors

  Central regulation of intestinal motility by
    somatostatin and cholecystokinin octapeptide.
    L. Bueno and J.-P. Ferre. bibl f il Science
    216:1427-9 Je 25 '82
  Circulating somatostatin acts on the islets of
    Langerhans by way of a somatostatin-poor
    compartment. K. Kawai and others. bibl f il
    Science 218:477-8 O 29 '82
cross reference—Hypothalamic neurons. See Nerve cells

Another useful index is *The New York Times Index*. Here is the information Tim Rogers found in the index for 1980.

HYPNOSIS. See also Crime — NJ, Ap 13. Kidnapping, Mr 8, 12. Murders — NJ, Sell, Jane, Ap 13, My 18
Jane E Brody article on hypnosis; discusses what it is, who should perform it and its value in treating pain and other medical and psychological problems (L), Jl 2,III,9:1; Jane E Brody, in 1st of 2 articles on hypnosis, focues on its growing acceptance among health practitioners as form of therapy to treat diverse medical problems; 1 of most dramatic psychotherapeutice uses of hypnosis is emotional catharsis through 'age regression', although experts say it is far less useful than other modes of hypnotherapy (L), O 7, III,1:5; Jane E Brody, in 2d article on hypnosis, discusses its use as tool by police in criminal cases; some experts charge that forensic use of hypnosis is rife with dangers and is often abused by well-meaning but poorly trained police officers (L), O 14,III,1:1

The following is a list of these and other useful indexes to periodicals.

General

Cumulative Index to Periodical Literature, 1959–
New York Times Index, 1851–
Nineteenth Century Readers' Guide to Periodical Literature, 1890–1899
Poole's Index to Periodical Literature, 1802–1906
Popular Periodicals Index, 1973–
Readers' Guide to Periodical Literature, 1900–

Special

Abstracts of Popular Culture, 1976–
Agricultural Index, 1916–1964
The American Humanities Index, 1975–
Applied Science and Technology Index, 1958–
Art Index, 1929–
Bibliography and Index of Geology, 1961–
Biography Index, 1946–
Biological Abstracts, 1926–
Biological and Agricultural Index, 1964–
Book Review Digest, 1905–

Business Periodicals Index, 1958–
Current Index to Journals in Education, 1969–
Economics Abstracts, 1969–
Education Index, 1929–
Engineering Index, 1906–
General Science Index, 1978–
Humanities Index, 1974–
Index to Jewish Periodicals, 1963–
Index to Legal Periodicals, 1908–
Industrial Arts Index, 1913–1957
International Index to Periodicals, 1907–1965
International Political Science Abstracts, 1951–
MLA International Bibliography of Books and Articles on the Modern Languages and Literatures, 1921–
Music Index, 1949–
Public Affairs Information Service (bulletin), 1915–
Social Sciences and Humanities Index, 1965–1974
Social Sciences Index, 1974–
United States Government Publications (monthly catalog), 1895–

Sources of information

The sources of information for a research paper can be divided into primary and secondary sources. A **primary source** gives you firsthand information about a topic. For example, for a paper on the use of hypnosis in medicine, a primary source would be an article by or an interview with a researcher who had used hypnosis as an anesthetic during dental surgery. For a paper on a literary subject, primary sources would include the literature itself and the writer's letters and diaries.

A **secondary source** gives you secondhand information about a topic. For example, for a paper on the use of hypnosis in medicine, a book in which the author summarizes the experiments of others into the effectiveness of hypnosis as an anesthetic during dental surgery is a secondary source. For a paper on a literary subject, secondary sources would include critical studies of the literature involved or a biography of the writer.

In your research, try to use as many primary sources as possible. However, for some topics, you should also use or have to use secondary sources. For example, when Tim Rogers was researching the history of hypnosis, he consulted encyclopedias and books summarizing the history. Remember, though, that in many cases the closer you are to the original source, the more accurate your information is likely to be.

Keep in mind the reliability of your sources. If the source is primary, ask yourself:

1. Is the source objective?
2. Is the source an expert in the field?
3. If the source reports the results of an experiment, did the experiment follow established procedures?
4. How recent is the information? (Obviously, this question is not important for all situations. Someone who worked with F. A. Mesmer and saw him experiment with "animal magnetism" is probably a good source of information, although not a recent one, for a paper on the use of hypnosis in medicine.)

If the source is secondary, ask yourself:

1. What is the author's reputation in the field?
2. What sources did the author use?
3. How sound are the author's conclusions?
4. How recent is the book or article? (Once again, in some situations, this will not apply.)
5. Was the book published by a reputable publisher or was the article in a reputable magazine? (An article in a scholarly journal is more likely to contain reliable information than an article in a magazine that seeks to entertain its readers.)

Of course, your choice of sources depends on your purpose. For example, when Tim Rogers wanted information about public fascination with the so-called mystical aspects of hypnosis, he turned to *Fate*, a magazine devoted to publishing accounts of supposedly supernatural events.

Sources of information can also be divided into the three categories of yourself, others, and written and broadcast materials. Your first source of information is yourself. What do you know about the subject? What experiences have you had that relate to the subject?

Your second source of information is other people. Interview people who have firsthand information about the topic. Attend discussions and lectures about the subject. Take an opinion poll. Conduct a survey. When Tim Rogers started working on his research paper, he took an informal survey of students at his school to find out their attitude toward hypnosis.

Your third source of information is books, magazine and journal articles, newspaper articles, films, and radio and television news programs and documentaries. Read as much about your topic as you can. View films and documentaries.

When you are beginning your research, you may find reference books helpful in getting an overview of your topic. Your library contains many general reference aids. Learn what they are and use them appropriately, but do not depend on encyclopedias or other general reference works for all your research. After getting an overview of your topic, you will need to consult more specialized books and articles for more detailed information.

The following is a sampling of general reference aids.

General encyclopedias

Collier's Encyclopedia, 24 vols.
Encyclopedia Americana, 30 vols.
The New Encyclopaedia Britannica, 32 vols.

Almanacs and yearbooks

Americana Annual, 1923–
Britannica Book of the Year, 1938–
Collier's Year Book (titled *National Year Book* before 1942), 1939–
Facts on File Yearbook, 1940–
Statesman's Year-Book, 1864–
United Nations Yearbook, 1947–
World Almanac and Book of Facts, 1868–

Art and architecture

Art Books 1876–1949: Including an International Index of Current Serial Publications, 1981

Art Books 1950–1979: Including an International Directory of Museum Permanent Collection Catalogs, 1979

Art Books 1980–1984, 1984

Cyclopedia of Painters and Paintings, 4 vols., 1969

Encyclopedia of World Architecture, 2 vols., 1979

Encyclopedia of World Art, 15 vols., 1959–1968; and supplement, 1983

A History of Architecture, 18th ed., 1975

Atlases and gazetteers

Columbia-Lippincott Gazetteer of the World, 1952; and supplement, 1961

Commercial Atlas and Marketing Guide, 1981

Hammond New Contemporary World Atlas, 1977

National Geographic Atlas of the World, 5th ed., 1981

Oxford Economic Atlas of the World, 4th ed., 1972

Biography

Contemporary Authors: A Bio-Bibliographical Guide to Current Writers in Fiction, General Nonfiction, Poetry, Journalism, Drama, Motion Pictures, Television, and Other Fields, rev. ed., 106 vols., 1967–1982

Current Biography, 1940–

Dictionary of American Biography, 20 vols., 1928–1936; and supplements, 1944–1981

Dictionary of National Biography (British), 22 vols., 1885–1901; and supplements, 1912–1981

McGraw-Hill Encyclopedia of World Biography, 12 vols., 1973

Webster's Biographical Dictionary, 1983

Who's Who (British), 1849–

Who's Who in America, 1899–

Business and economics

American Business Dictionary, 1957–

Encyclopedia of Banking and Finance, 8th ed., 1983
Encyclopedia of Computer Science and Engineering, 2nd ed., 1982
Encyclopedia of Computer Science and Technology, 15 vols., 1975–1980
Encyclopedia of Computers and Data Processing, 1978–
Encyclopedia of Management, 3rd ed., 1982

Education

Cyclopedia of Education, 5 vols., 1968, reprint of 1911 ed.
Encyclopedia of Educational Research, 4 vols., 5th ed., 1982
International Encyclopedia of Higher Education, 10 vols., 1977

History and political science

Cambridge Ancient History Series, 12 vols., 2nd ed., 1982
Cambridge Medieval History, 9 vols., 2nd ed., 1966
Concise Dictionary of World History, 1983
Cyclopedia of American Government, 3 vols.
Dictionary of American History, 8 vols., rev. ed., 1978
Dictionary of Political Economy, 3 vols., 1976, reprint of 1910 ed.
Encyclopedia of the Third World, 3 vols., rev. ed., 1981
Encyclopedia of World History, 5th ed., 1972
New Cambridge Modern History, 14 vols., 1957–1970

Literature, theater, film, and television

Bartlett's Familiar Quotations, 15th ed., 1980
Cambridge History of American Literature, 4 vols., 1943
Cambridge History of English Literature, 15 vols., 1907–1933
Cassell's Encyclopaedia of World Literature, 3 vols., 1973
Granger's Index to Poetry, 7th ed., 1982
International Encyclopedia of Film, 1972
International Television Almanac, 1956–
Larousse World Mythology, 1981
McGraw-Hill Encyclopedia of World Drama, 5 vols., 2nd ed., 1983

Mythology of All Races, 13 vols., 1964; reprint of 1932 ed.
Oxford Companion to American Literature, 5th ed., 1983
Oxford Companion to Classical Literature, 2nd ed., 1937
Oxford Companion to English Literature, 4th ed., 1967
Play Index, 1949–
Short Story Index, 1900–

Music

Encyclopedia of Pop, Rock, & Soul, 1977
Harvard Dictionary of Music, 2nd ed., 1969
International Cyclopedia of Music and Musicians, 10th ed., 1975
Musician's Guide, 6th ed., 1980
New Grove Dictionary of Music and Musicians, 20 vols., 1980

Philosophy and religion

Encyclopedia of Philosophy, 4 vols., 1973
Encyclopedia of Religion, 1976, reprint of 1945 ed.
The Interpreter's Dictionary of the Bible, 5 vols. and supplement, 1976

Science

Cambridge Encyclopedia of Astronomy, 1977
Cambridge Encyclopedia of Earth Sciences, 1982
Grzimek's Animal Life Encyclopedia, 13 vols., 1972–1975
McGraw-Hill Encyclopedia of Science and Technology, 15 vols., 5th ed., 1982

Social science

A Dictionary of Psychology and Related Fields, 1974
Encyclopedia of Psychology, 2nd ed., 1979
Encyclopedia of Social Work, 2 vols., 17th ed., 1977; and supplement, 1983
Encyclopedia of the Social Sciences, 15 vols., 1974
International Encyclopedia of the Social Sciences, 8 vols., 1977; biographical supplement, 1979

Special dictionaries

Dictionary of American Slang, 2nd ed., 1975
Dictionary of Modern English Usage, 2nd ed., 1965
Dictionary of Slang and Unconventional English, 7th ed., 1970
Harper Dictionary of Contemporary Usage, 1975
Modern American Usage, 1966
New Roget's Thesaurus in Dictionary Form, 1983

Unabridged dictionaries

The Oxford English Dictionary, 13 vols., 1933
The Random House Dictionary of the English Language, 1966
Webster's Third New International Dictionary of the English Language, 1981

Compiling a working bibliography

A **working bibliography** is a record of sources you plan to consult for information about your topic. Since a working bibliography is open to change, most instructors suggest you keep it on index cards, thus making it easy to add or delete books and articles.

Keep the following points in mind when developing your working bibliography.

1. List each source on a separate 3″ × 5″ index card.
2. Arrange these cards alphabetically by author. (You may also find alternate arrangements convenient. For example, you may find it useful to organize the cards by subcategory.)
3. Include the name of the author, with the last name first. (If the book has an editor or a compiler rather than an author, indicate this.)
4. Include the complete title of the source.
5. Include the place and date of publication.
6. Include the name of the publisher.
7. Include the library call number.
8. Include any other pertinent information, such as volume number or edition.

When Tim Rogers was preparing a working bibliography, he first consulted the card catalog in his library. Then he looked at several indexes to periodicals. Finally, he read the articles on hypnosis in the *Encyclopaedia Britannica*, *Collier's Encyclopedia*, and the *Encyclopedia Americana*, checking the bibliography at the end of each article. As he worked, he kept adding titles to his working bibliography and eliminating titles that did not turn out to be relevant.

Here is one of Tim's bibliography cards. Notice that the book has two editors rather than an author.

154.7
F

Fromm, Erika, and Ronald E. Shor, eds
Hypnosis: Developments in
Research and New Perspectives.
2nd ed. Hawthorne, NY: Aldine,
1979.

Eventually, you will turn your working bibliography into the formal bibliography, or list of works cited, which appears on a separate page at the end of the paper. Before compiling your working bibliography, check with your instructor to determine which guidelines for bibliographic form to follow. Since many instructors choose the guidelines of the Modern Language Association and the *MLA Handbook for Writers of Research Papers* (1984), these are the guidelines used in the following examples. Consult the *Handbook* for situations that are not covered by these examples.

General guidelines

1. Always include the author's name (as listed on the title page), the complete title, and the complete publication information.
2. Separate these three parts with periods followed by two spaces.
3. If the book is not by an author, but by an editor or a compiler, indicate this with the abbreviation *ed.* or *comp.* (Use *eds.* or *comps.* if there is more than one editor or compiler.)
4. In the publication information, for books, you may use the shortened forms of publishers' names that are listed in the *MLA Handbook* or other standard sources. In the place of publication, use the two-letter zip code abbreviations of state names. In the publication dates for periodicals, abbreviate the names of all months except May, June, and July.
5. Include the page numbers for a periodical article; a work that is part of an anthology or collection; or an introduction, preface, foreword, or afterword.

Books

Book by one author

Anderson-Evangelista, Anita. <u>Hypnosis: A Journey into

the Mind</u>. New York: Arco, 1980.

Book by two authors

Luckmann, Joan, and Karen Creason Sorenson. <u>Basic

Nursing: A Psychophysiologic Approach</u>.

Philadelphia: Saunders, 1979.

Book by three authors

Glass, A. L., K. J. Holyoak, and J. L. Santa.

<u>Cognition</u>. Reading, MA: Addison-Wesley, 1979.

Book by more than three authors

Adorno, T. W., et al. <u>The Authoritarian Personality</u>.

New York: Harper, 1950.

More than one book by the same author

Erickson, Milton H. <u>Advanced Techniques of Hypnosis</u>

<u>and Therapy</u>. New York: Grune, 1967.

---. <u>Hypnotherapy: An Exploratory Casebook</u>. New

York: Irvington, 1979.

Book by a corporate author

Group for the Advancement of Psychiatry. <u>Symposium</u>

<u>No. 8: Medical Uses of Hypnosis</u>. New York:

Mental Health Material Center, 1962.

Edition after the first

Fromm, Erika, and Ronald E. Shor, eds. <u>Hypnosis:</u>

<u>Developments in Research and New Perspectives</u>.

2nd ed. Hawthorne, NY: Aldine, 1979.

Book in more than one volume

Wylie, R. C. <u>Theory and Research on Selected Topics</u>.

Vol. 2 of <u>The Self-Concept</u>. 2 vols. to date.

Lincoln: U of Nebraska P, 1979.

Selection from an anthology, collection, or critical edition

Hilgard, Ernest R. "Divided Consciousness in

Hypnosis: The Implications of the Hidden

Observer." <u>Hypnosis: Developments in Research</u>

<u>and New Perspectives</u>. Ed. Erika Fromm and Ronald

E. Shor. 2nd ed. Hawthorne, NY: Aldine, 1979.

45–79.

An introduction, preface, foreword, or afterword

Bryan, William J., Jr. Foreword. <u>Helping Yourself</u>

<u>with Self-Hypnosis</u>. By Frank S. Caprio and

Joseph R. Berger. Englewood Cliffs, NJ:

Prentice, 1963. 7–8.

Periodicals

Article in a monthly periodical

Moine, Donald J. "To Trust, Perchance to Buy."

<u>Psychology Today</u> Aug. 1982: 51–52.

Article in a weekly or biweekly periodical

Wykert, J. "Fromm's Last Interview." <u>Psychiatric</u>

<u>News</u> 16 Mar. 1980: 4.

Article in a journal with continuous pagination

Warner, Kenneth E. "The Use of Hypnosis in the

Defense of Criminal Cases." <u>International</u>

<u>Journal of Clinical and Experimental Hypnosis</u> 27

(1979): 417–436.

Article in a daily newspaper

Reinhold, Robert. "New Chief Shaking Up Prison System

in Texas." <u>New York Times</u> 22 June 1983, late

ed.: A8.

Unsigned article

"Notes and Comments." <u>New Yorker</u> 11 June 1984: 29.

Encyclopedias and other sources

Article in an encyclopedia

Garrett, Adele, and Milton V. Kline. "Hypnosis."

Collier's Encyclopedia. 1984 ed.

Government document

United States. Dept. of Commerce. Bureau of the

Census. "Population Profile of the United

States, 1977." Current Population Reports.

Series P-20, No. 303. Washington: GPO, 1979.

Other published material

Weitzenhoffer, A. M., and E. R. Hilgard. Stanford

Hypnotic Susceptibility Scale, Form C. Palo

Alto, CA: Consulting Psychologists Press, 1962.

Personal or telephone interview

Markus, John. Personal interview. 14 July 1982.

Writing a thesis statement and making a working outline

Once you have completed your preliminary research, you should formulate a plan for writing. Your first two steps in formulating a plan are to write a thesis statement and to prepare a working outline.

As in an essay, your thesis statement should express the idea you wish to develop in your paper. The formulation of this statement will help you focus your research. Word your thesis statement carefully, but at this point, do not worry about the style with which you express your main idea. Most likely, you will reword your thesis statement many times before you are satisfied with it. Tim Roger's initial thesis statement was the following: *Hypnosis has finally become respectable.*

Your working outline should include all the main points you wish to include in your paper. Of course, as you do more research, you may find you have overlooked some points and add them to your outline. At this time your outline need not be in perfect form, for it is certainly subject to change, but it should be complete enough to serve as a guide for your research and your note taking.

Tim Rogers developed the following working outline based on the research he had done so far. As he gathered more information about his topic, he added to his outline.

Hypnosis

Thesis Statement: Hypnosis has finally become respectable.

A. Early history

1. Ancient Egyptians

2. Early Christians

B. Mesmer

1. His theories

2. His contributions

3. His followers

C. Mesmerist surgeons

1. Eliotson

2. Esdaile

D. Attackers of Mesmer

1. James Braid

2. Ambroise–Auguste Liébeault

3. Hippolyte Bernheim

E. Sigmund Freud

1. His interest in hypnosis

2. His turning from hypnosis

F. Hypnosis today

1. Its uses

2. Its acceptance

Taking notes

Note taking is a way of keeping track of information that you think is important and that you may use later in your paper. Some people take notes on legal pads. A more efficient way is to use 4″ × 6″ index cards. The size prevents you from mixing up your note cards with your bibliography cards. The cards themselves allow you to arrange and rearrange your information as the need arises.

What information should you put on your note cards? First, each card should have at the top of it a heading indicating the category under which the information falls. Second, it should have a summary or paraphrase of the information or a quotation. Third, it should give the source of the information. Usually this need be only the author and the page number, since you will have the complete information on your bibliography card. If you are using more than one source by the same author, include the title or a shortened form of it.

Be sure to use a separate card for each piece of information. This will make it easier to arrange your notes when it comes time to write.

When Tim Rogers was working on his paper, he noticed how much easier it was to keep notes this way than on a legal pad. For example, instead of thumbing through pages to find all the information he had on Mesmer, he needed only to flip through his cards, pull out the ones that said *Mesmer* on the top, and put these together.

One method of taking notes is to write a summary of the information you wish to record. A summary presents the substance of the information in a condensed form. It does not use the words of the author but conveys the thoughts of the author in your own words.

Here is a summary card Tim Rogers wrote.

Mesmer – Contributions

Hilgard xi

By studying Mesmer's records of his cases, other scientists eventually gained a better understanding of hypnosis.

Compare the summary with the original.

> Mesmer accumulated empirical evidence that *something* was happening in his encounters with his patients. He called it "animal magnetism." His theory was not accepted, but his empirical findings led by slow steps to modern research on hypnosis and to its use in medical practice, dentistry, psychiatry, and clinical psychology. The name mesmerism (with a small *m*) still occurs in reference to hypnotism.
>
> E. R. HILGARD
> *Mesmerism: A Translation of the*
> *Original Scientific and Medical*
> *Writings of F. A. Mesmer, M.D.*

A second method of taking notes is to paraphrase the information. A **paraphrase** is a restatement of someone else's statement in your own words. A good paraphrase reflects your own style of writing and extracts important information but does not lose the original meaning of the statement.

Here is a paraphrase card Tim Rogers wrote.

Attackers of Mesmer - Bernheim

Estabrooks 128-129

Bernheim devoted the next twenty years to learning more about hypnotism, and because of his own reputation he was able to give this phenomenon a respectability it had never had before.

Compare the paraphrase with the original. Notice that Tim did not merely substitute synonyms or change the order of words of the original. He managed in his paraphrase to express the main idea of the original while using his own style of writing.

> . . . Bernheim immediately began a serious study of hypnotism and for the next twenty years devoted all his great talents to serious work along these lines. His position gave the subject respectable standing, and to his eternal honor, he never overlooked an opportunity of directing attention to Liébeault.
>
> G. H. ESTABROOKS
> *Hypnotism*

A third method of recording information is to write down exact quotations. You may find that the information you wish to record has been so well expressed or contains such precise facts and details that you wish to use the exact words of the source rather than summarize or paraphrase the information.

On the next page is a quotation card Tim Rogers wrote.

> *Hypnosis today – its acceptance*
>
> *Kagan 51*
>
> *"Over 40 percent of the graduate departments of clinical psychology, 35 percent of medical schools and 30 percent of dental schools now offer courses or lectures in hypnosis."*

With quotation cards, you must be extremely careful to record the exact words of the original and to transfer these words exactly if you use the quotation in your paper. (Review pages 157–158 for the use of punctuation marks with quotations.) Be careful not to overuse quotations in your paper, since too many quotations leave the reader with the impression that you did not truly master the material. Remember that a research paper expresses your understanding of a subject based on information gleaned from research. Even if you have written a quotation card, you can always summarize or paraphrase the information when you write your paper.

A fourth method of recording your information is to combine quotation and paraphrase. This method allows you to record the information in your own words while retaining a few particularly well chosen words from the original.

On the next page is a combination quotation and paraphrase card Tim Rogers wrote.

Be judicious in taking notes. Do not record everything you read, but only what you think will be relevant. Even when you write your paper, you will not use all your notes but will cull them, using only the notes that develop your thesis.

Making a formal outline

After you have taken notes, the next step is to turn your working outline into a formal outline. Your formal outline must include a formal statement of your thesis and all of the main points you will develop in your paper arranged in a logical sequence. Ask your instructor whether you should develop a topic outline or a sentence outline. (Review the procedures for outlining on pages 255–257.) Remember that your working outline is for yourself; your formal outline will be read and evaluated by your instructor.

Study the formal outline on pages 365–369 that Tim Rogers turned in with his research paper.

45c Writing the paper

The process of actually writing the research paper is much like that of writing an essay, except that you are relying to a large extent on source material outside your own mind. Using your formal outline, write a first draft, let it sit for a while, and then go back to it and begin the process of criticism and

Mesmer—his theories
Hilgard xiii

Mesmer realized that he did not need magnets to cure his patients. He decided that the "mysterious fluid" also resided in him. It was "something accumulated in his own body, which he named 'animal magnetism.'"

revision. In particular, consider your paper as a piece of research. Are you relying too heavily on one or two sources? Perhaps you need to do some more research. Do you seem to be using a great many quotations? Perhaps it would be more effective to summarize or paraphrase some of them. Does any section of the paper seem to need strengthening? Perhaps you could use some of the note cards you didn't use in the previous draft.

When Tim Rogers wrote his first draft, he started his paper with a paragraph dealing with current attitudes toward hypnosis as reflected in *Fate* magazine. His second paragraph dealt with attitudes toward hypnosis as reflected in *Psychology Today*. He later realized he was giving too much emphasis to this information; therefore, in his final draft, he combined this information in one paragraph with other information about current attitudes. The final draft of Tim's paper appears on pages 363–397.

Write or type your final draft according to the guidelines for manuscript form on pages 170–172, and don't forget to proofread it for spelling and punctuation. In addition, be sure to acknowledge all of your outside sources according to the guidelines described below.

45d Acknowledging sources

An absolute requirement in writing a research paper is that you must acknowledge all of your sources according to accepted guidelines. Plagiarism, or using the words or thoughts of others as though they were your own, is a serious offense, and you must be scrupulous about avoiding it in your writing. Acknowledge all quotations and all summaries and paraphrases of information that is not generally known and readily available from other sources. For example, since the information that Sally Ride was the first American woman to travel in space is commonly known and readily available, you need not acknowledge a source for it. Since information about how Sally Ride's performance during her first flight was evaluated by NASA is not commonly known or readily available, you do need to acknowledge your source for it. If in doubt about whether to acknowledge a source, always do so.

The traditional method of acknowledging sources uses superscript numbers in the text to refer the reader to notes identifying the sources. The notes are placed either at the bottom of the text pages on which the superscripts appear (footnotes) or together at the end of the paper (end notes). However, the most recent edition of the *MLA Handbook for Writers of Research Papers* recommends a newer method in which sources are briefly identified in parentheses within the text itself. These parenthetical acknowledgments refer the reader to the full source information contained in the bibliography, or list of works cited, at the end of the paper. The following guidelines are based on the *MLA Handbook*. Consult the *Handbook* for situations not covered by these guidelines.

At times, you may wish to refer to the entire work. In this case, give the author's name and the title of the work in the text itself.

In Hypnosis: A Journey into the Mind, Anita

Anderson-Evangelista traces the history of hypnotism.

Usually, however, you will cite references to particular parts of the work. In this case, you use parenthetical citations.

1. When citing a reference to the work of an author whose name is included in the text, place the appropriate page number(s) in parentheses after the author's name. (If the work is by more than one author, follow the rules for citing multiple authors listed above under the guidelines for bibliographic references.)

Anderson-Evangelista (1), musing on Egyptian art show-

ing trepanning, a surgical procedure providing access

to the brain, suggests that they may have used it as

an anesthetic during surgery.

Binet and Féré (11) report how young women were "so
much gratified by the crisis, that they begged to be
thrown into it anew."

Note: Textual punctuation marks, such as commas or
semicolons, come after the parenthetical information.

2. When citing a reference to the work of an author whose
   name is not included in the text, give the author's name
   and the page numbers in parentheses after the cited
   information.

The use of hypnosis spread from Egypt to Greece and
Asia Minor (Estabrooks 122); however, the early
Christians, fearing a demonic power behind hypnotism,
banned its use.

3. When citing a reference to a work listed by title rather
   than author, treat the title in the same manner you would
   treat the author. In a parenthetical reference to a work
   with a long title, use a shortened version of the title.

According to Contemporary Medical Uses of Hypnosis
(11-14), many dentists are now using this procedure to
reduce their patients' fear.

Hypnosis may help reduce bleeding (Contemporary
Medical Uses 16).

4. In general, cite only as much information as the reader
   will need to identify the source in the bibliography, or list
   of works cited.
5. Place a reference as close as possible to the material it

acknowledges. Try to place it at the end of a sentence or some other place where there is a natural pause, especially if the reference contains more than page numbers.

After you have written the final draft of your paper, you must prepare the list of the sources you used, giving the full author, title, and publication information for each work. The following guidelines are based on the *MLA Handbook*.

1. Start the list on a new page following the text of the paper. Number each page of the list in the upper right-hand corner, continuing the page numbers of the text. (For example, if the text ended on page 8, the first page of the list would be page 9.)
2. Type the title *Works Cited* centered one inch from the top of the page.
3. Double-space between the title and the first entry, and then double-space the entire list, within entries and between entries.
4. List the works alphabetically by author, or by title for works by anonymous authors. (Disregard *A*, *An*, and *The* in alphabetizing titles.)
5. If you have followed the guidelines for the working bibliography on pages 346–351, your sources are already listed in the proper form; simply copy the information for each source that you actually used in your paper.
6. Begin each entry at the left-hand margin; if an entry is longer than one line, indent the subsequent lines five spaces.

Even if you use the parenthetical method of acknowledging sources, you can still use footnotes or end notes to give additional information or commentary about points in the text. If you use end notes of this kind, they should be typed on a separate numbered page at the end of the paper (before the list of works cited) under the title *Notes*. Like the list of works cited, the end notes are double-spaced, but the indentation system is reversed: the first line of each note is indented five spaces, and any subsequent lines begin at the left margin.

All items are centered. Title is about ten lines from the top of the paper. The word *by* is about seven lines under the title. The student's name is about two lines under that. The course name, instructor's name, and date are at the bottom of the paper.

Hypnosis

Its Long Road to Acceptance as a Healing Tool

by

Tim Rogers

English 303

Ms. Helgenson

April 17, 1984

Notice how Tim revised his thesis statement from the one on page 352.

Ask your professor whether you should prepare a topic or a sentence outline. Then follow the format for outlining detailed on pages 255–257.

Thesis: After a long and checkered history, hypnosis has gained acceptance as a tool for healing.

I. Possible attitudes toward hypnosis

    A. A form of sleep

    B. A mysterious force

    C. A gateway to psychic experience

    D. A means of breaking bad habits

    E. A healing tool

II. Hypnosis in the ancient world

    A. First recorded use in Egypt

        1. Use for healing in sleep temples

        2. Possible use as anesthetic

    B. Spread to Greece and Asia Minor

    C. Ban by early Christians

III. Mesmer

    A. His theories

        1. Force stored in magnets

        2. Force within himself—animal magnetism

    B. The case of Franziska Oesterlin

    C. Controversy surrounding Mesmer

        1. Use of sensational techniques

        2. Suspicion of scandalous sexual activity

        3. International inquiry

    D. His contributions

        1. Worked in scientific tradition

        2. Collected empirical evidence

        3. Classified disorders

IV. Puységur

    A. His theory

        1. Followed beliefs of Mesmer

        2. Interested in psychic aspects

    B. His contributions

        1. Identified magnetic somnambulism

        2. Laid groundwork for concept of posthypnotic suggestion

        3. Identified power of suggestion

V. James Braid

    A. Scientific view of mesmerism

    B. Development of hypnotic technique

VI. Mesmerist surgeons

    A. John Eliotson

    B. James Esdaile

VII. A breakthrough for hypnosis

    A. Ambroise-Auguste Liébeault

    B. Hippolyte Bernheim

VIII. A setback for hypnosis

    A. Theories of Jean Martin Charcot

    B. Rejection by Sigmund Freud

  IX. Hypnosis in the twentieth century

    A. Use during World Wars

    B. Experiments to determine nature

  X. Scientific acceptance of hypnosis

    A. American Medical Association report

    B. University of North Carolina survey

Introductory paragraph establishes possible views toward hypnosis.

Source of quotation is cited.

Thesis statement presents view of hypnosis that Tim wants to discuss.

Hypnosis. What is it? Is it a form of sleep? Because its name is based on the Greek word for sleep, many people believe this. Is it a mysterious force with which we should not tamper? Years ago people seemed to think so. They formed their ideas of hypnosis from movies and books in which the sinister hypnotist used this strange power to make people commit evil acts against their will. Is it a gateway to psychic experience? Articles in magazines such as _Fate_, which publishes accounts of supposedly supernatural events, seem to support this view. For example, one column is by Mildred Strake Walker, who wrote _An Autobiography of After Death via Hypnosis_. Is it a means of breaking bad habits, such as smoking or overeating? Popular magazines such as _Psychology Today_ are filled with advertisements promoting this view of hypnosis. For example, one recent issue carried a full-page advertisement urging readers to "use hypnosis to lose weight—to stop smoking—or to lose any other habit" (June 1982: 84). While disagreement about its exact nature continues, today both the scientific community and much of the public have come to view hypnosis in still another way. After a long and checkered career, hypnosis has gained acceptance as a tool for healing and the relief of pain.

All pages after the first are numbered in the upper right-hand corner.

Paragraph begins with topic sentence. The rest of paragraph details the first recorded use of hypnosis for healing.

Source for term "sleep temples" is cited.

Citations provide reference to sources of specific information.

Last sentence in paragraph provides bridge from information about ancient world to information about Mesmer.

Superscript numeral refers readers to note about Mesmer's name at end of paper.

Actually, this modern use of hypnosis in medicine represents a return to its first recorded use, in ancient Egypt. In "sleep temples" (Estabrooks 121), Egyptian priests put patients into trances and then suggested to them that various gods were visiting them to heal them or ease their pain. Often this suggestion brought about an effective cure. Indeed, the priests may have used hypnosis in even more startling ways. Anita Anderson-Evangelista (1), musing on Egyptian art showing trepanning, a surgical procedure providing access to the brain, suggests that they may have used it as an anesthetic during surgery.

The use of hypnotism spread from Egypt to Greece and Asia Minor (Estabrooks 122); however, the early Christians, fearing a demonic power behind hypnotism, banned its use. Like the black arts, hypnotism went underground, and it was not until the eighteenth century that it came back into public use.

In the 1770's, Dr. Franz[1] A. Mesmer, an Austrian physician, began using a remarkable technique to cure patients. Mesmer believed that many illnesses were caused by imbalances in bodily fluids resulting from the pull of the planets (actually, of the sun and the moon, which were

Sources for specific information are given.

then considered planets) (Hilgard xiii). These planets, he said, radiated magnetic forces which could be stored in magnets. By passing magnets over his patients, Mesmer believed he could restore their bodily harmony.

Later Mesmer found that he did not need magnets but could heal his patients merely by touching or passing his hands over them (Orne and Hammer 134). He decided that these cures resulted from a force called "animal magnetism" that was stored in his body. In fact, people witnessing Mesmer's cures claimed to see such a force, or fluid, moving from him into his patients (Anderson-Evangelista 2).

The case that first brought Mesmer into the limelight was that of Franziska Oesterlin. In 1773 she came to Mesmer suffering from pains in her ears and teeth, fainting spells, temporary paralysis, and a variety of other symptoms. At that time, no one could find any reason for her illness; today we would probably label her a hysteric (Schneck 3). Mesmer cured her by passing magnets over her body.

As Mesmer's fame grew, so did the controversy surrounding him. In 1778 he left Vienna for Paris, where his techniques became more and more sensational and drew more

Sources for quotations are given.

Topic sentence relates Mesmer to the thesis statement.

and more attention. He treated patients at his clinic, in which there was a large hall featuring his famous <u>baquet</u>, a receptable in which animal magnetism was supposedly stored (Schneck 7). Around the baquet stood the patients waiting to be cured. Into the midst of them would walk Mesmer, dressed in a brilliant robe, "passing his hands over his patients, fixing them with his gaze, and touching them with his iron wand" (Estabrooks 126). The atmosphere would become frenzied as patients at the height of their crises, or convulsive fits, fell to the floor and were healed.

The public feared for the safety of the participants and suspected scandalous sexual activity. Binet and Féré (11) report how young women were "so much gratified by the crisis, that they begged to be thrown into it anew." Finally, an international inquiry was held in Paris in 1784 (Hilgard xviii). Made up of scientists from many localities, it included Benjamin Franklin and the French chemist Antoine Lavoisier. This group declared that "animal magnetism" or "mesmerism" was quackery; as a result, Mesmer's techniques were banned in France.

Was Mesmer a quack, or did he provide the bridge by which hypnosis moved from the realm of religion and the

Sources for specific information are cited. Notice how citation for Hilgard lists multiple pages.

supernatural into the realm of science? Certainly, Mesmer saw himself as working in the scientific tradition and his work as building upon the findings of Isaac Newton (Mesmer 15). He accumulated empirical evidence, which others could later study. He categorized disorders as physical or "nervous." Before treating his patients, Mesmer interviewed them to determine the nature of their afflictions. Those with purely physical disorders he sent to physicians; those with "nervous" disorders—diseases that today would be considered psychosomatic or hysterical in origin —he treated with animal magnetism (Hilgard xi, xiii, xviii). Whyte (66) claims that the emphasis Mesmer gave to hysteria helped pave the way for the development of modern psychology.

One of Mesmer's disciples added another paving stone to the long road hypnosis was to follow to respectability. In 1784, while the Marquis de Puységur was mesmerizing a young man, he observed that the man fell into a trancelike state, which Puységur termed "magnetic somnambulism," instead of into a convulsive state (Anderson-Evangelista 4). While in this trance, the man developed a secondary personality and clairvoyance. It was the psychic aspect of the case that was of interest to Puységur, although it is

Sentence contains information from more than one source.

the nature of this "sleep–waking" state that is of interest to science (Schneck 8), since until 1885 only two
states of consciousness were recognized—the waking state
and sleep (Fromm 81). Two other aspects of this case are
significant. First, when the man came out of the sleep–
waking state, he could remember nothing of his experience
(Kingston 101). This event laid the groundwork for the
development of the concept of posthypnotic amnesia
(Schneck 44). Second, Puységur was able to bring about
this state by simple contact and spoken command, leading
him to conclude that what makes mesmerism operate is the
patient's mind and the power of suggestion (Kingston 104).
However, Puységur's emphasis on the psychic aspects of
mesmerism obscured the scientific aspects of his work.

Indeed, the sensationalism surrounding Mesmer and his
followers delayed any real scientific study of this phenomenon until the middle of the nineteenth century, when
James Braid, a Scottish surgeon, wrote a paper rejecting
the idea that mesmerism is caused by a magnetic fluid.
Instead, he claimed that its positive effects were the result of concentrated attention, and he considered suggestion only a device for causing the phenomenon, not an
explanation for it (Schneck 20). He invented the tech-

Superscript numeral indicates a source note at end of paper.

Sentence contains information from more than one source.

Notice that the name of the magazine is underlined.

nique, still widely used today, of bringing about the hypnotic trance by having the patient stare at a shiny object
(Estabrooks 127). In addition, in order to separate this
phenomenon from its sensational past, he coined a new term
for it: hypnotism (Hilgard xxi).

During the middle of the nineteenth century, several
doctors were using mesmerism effectively as an anesthetic
during surgery. Although their results were remarkable,
their work was tainted by their continued belief in the
"universal fluid" of mesmerism. In other words, they followed effective procedures, but they misunderstood why
these procedures worked. At the North London Hospital,[2]
John Eliotson used mesmerism to perform painless amputa-
tions (Kingston 106) and to treat "nervous disorders" such
as epilepsy (Schneck 11). However, he met with public
ridicule because of his insistence on the physical force
of animal magnetism. In fact, after he claimed that
nickel had unusually strong healing powers, Thomas Wakley,
the editor of the British medical journal Lancet, decided
to put his claims to the test. Substituting nonmagnetic
lead for Eliotson's nickel, he proved that patients could
be "magnetized" without the help of a magnet. On December
27, 1838, the practice of animal magnetism was outlawed

The source for the specific number of operations is cited.

from North London Hospital (Schneck 15).

The mesmerist surgeon James Esdaile performed the most remarkable feats while working in India. Using mesmerism to anesthetize his patients, he performed over 2,000 surgeries, 300 of which were major operations, with a mortality rate of only 8 percent (Anderson-Evangelista 6). However, ether and chloroform were soon introduced, and the need for mesmerism as an anesthetic faded away.

In 1864, after reading the work of Braid on hypnotism, a French physician, Ambroise-Auguste Liébeault, started practicing it among the poor in the city of Nancy. Believing that the trance was merely a means of helping his patients concentrate, he put them into this state and quietly suggested away many of their nervous disorders (Kingston 108). Liébeault's work would have been largely overlooked had it not been for the prominent physician Hippolyte Bernheim, a professor in the medical school at Nancy. Bernheim had been unsuccessful in treating a patient who later went to Liébeault and was cured. His professional jealousy aroused, Bernheim set out to expose Liébeault as a charlatan. Instead, after observing him work and examining his methods, he became convinced that Liébeault was a genius. Bernheim devoted the next twenty

years to learning more about hypnotism, and because of his own reputation he was able to give this phenomenon a respectability it had never before had (Estabrooks 128-129).

While Bernheim and Liébeault were fostering a scientific approach to hypnosis, a great Parisian neurologist, Jean Martin Charcot, was bringing back magnets (Kingston 108). Charcot believed not only that magnets were essential to hypnosis, but also that they could transfer illness from one person to another. This attitude seemed to throw hypnosis back into the realm of mysticism. Several influential people, among them Alfred Binet, the developer of intelligence testing, supported the view of Charcot over that of Bernheim (Estabrooks 130-131). However, Bernheim's view won out after Charcot died in 1893.

Charcot's interest in hysterics drew the attention of the young Sigmund Freud, who studied with Charcot in Paris and with Bernheim and Liébeault in Nancy. It was from these latter two men that Freud learned of posthypnotic suggestion, by which a subject can be made to act unconsciously in a certain way even after coming out of the trance (Estabrooks 142). It was also from them that he learned to use hypnosis to interpret dreams and to treat neuroses (Anderson-Evangelista 8). In his own practice,

10

Freud used hypnosis to help his patients recall painful events from their past, but because he encountered difficulty hypnotizing some of his patients, Freud eventually gave it up in favor of free association (Orne and Hammer 134).

With Freud's rejection of it, the scientific study of hypnosis declined. In the twentieth century, however, the two World Wars provided a laboratory for studying the effectiveness of hypnosis in treating combat neuroses—the "shell shock" of World War I and the "battle fatigue" of World War II. This work led to the suggestion that hypnosis is marked by a "dissociation of mental systems" similar to that found in the psychological disorder called multiple personality (Orne and Hammer 134). In other words, a hypnotized person can apparently carry on several independent trains of thought at the same time.

The period from 1930 to 1960 saw many experiments performed in laboratories under scientific conditions to determine the nature and effectiveness of hypnosis. With each new experiment, understanding of hypnosis grew. Although there is still uncertainty as to exactly what it is, there is certainty as to what it is not—a purely mystical experience. Erika Fromm (82) proposes that hypnosis

Final sentence restates the thesis statement.

is one of many altered states of consciousness that "constitute a continuum between waking awareness and sleep." In this state the mind is characterized by openness to suggestion, or "ego receptivity" (Fromm 93), and by focused attention (Fromm 99).

As understanding of the nature of hypnosis has increased, so too has its stature. In 1958 the American Medical Association issued a report on the use of hypnosis as an aid for healing (Kline and Garrett 445). Today it is being used effectively in medicine, psychiatry, and dentistry to treat or prevent physical pain, mental disorders, fears, and dental discomfort. A recent survey by a researcher at the University of North Carolina School of Medicine shows that "over 40 percent of the graduate departments of clinical psychology, 35 percent of medical schools, and 30 percent of dental schools now offer courses or lectures in hypnosis" (Kagan 51). Thousands of years after it began, hypnosis is again proving itself a beneficial tool for humankind.

Notes are placed on separate page. Title is centered.

Superscript numerals refer to numerals in text.

12

Notes

[1]Sources differ in regard to Mesmer's name. Some give his first name as Franz, some as Friedrich, some refer to him by his middle name, Anton, and some refer to him by his initials, F. A.

[2]The North London Hospital is also known as London's University College Hospital.

Works cited are placed on separate page. Title is centered.

Items are arranged alphabetically.

Each entry is typed flush to the left-hand margin. Subsequent lines are indented five spaces.

13

Works Cited

Anderson-Evangelista, Anita. _Hypnosis: A Journey into the Mind_. New York: Arco, 1980.

Binet, A., and C. Féré. _Animal Magnetism_. New York: Appleton, 1901.

Estabrooks, G. H. _Hypnotism_. Rev. ed. New York: Dutton, 1957.

Fromm, Erika. "The Nature of Hypnosis and Other Altered States of Consciousness: An Ego Psychological Theory." _Hypnosis: Developments in Research and New Perspectives_. Ed. Erika Fromm and Ronald E. Shor. 2nd ed. Hawthorne, NY: Aldine, 1979. 81–103.

Hilgard, E. R. Introduction. _Mesmerism: A Translation of the Original Scientific and Medical Writings of F. A. Mesmer, M. D._ By F. A. Mesmer. Trans. and comp. George Bloch. Los Altos, ÇA: Kaufmann, 1980. xi–xxiii.

Kagan, Julia. "Healing Through Hypnosis." _McCall's_ Apr. 1979: 51–52.

Kingston, Jeremy. _Healing Without Medicine_. New York: Doubleday, 1979.

Kline, Milton V., and Adele Garrett. "Hypnosis." _Collier's Encyclopedia_. 1984 ed.

14

Mesmer, F. A. "Physical—Medical Treatise on the Influence
of the Planets." Mesmerism: A Translation of the
Original Scientific and Medical Writings of F. A.
Mesmer, M. D. Trans. and comp. George Bloch. Los
Altos, CA: Kaufmann, 1980. 1—22.

Orne, Martin T., and A. G. Hammer. "Hypnosis."
Encyclopaedia Britannica: Macropedia. 1984 ed.

Psychology Today. June 1982: 84.

Schneck, Jerome M., ed. Hypnosis in Modern Medicine. 3rd
ed. Springfield, IL: Thomas, 1963.

Whyte, L. L. The Unconscious Before Freud. New York: St.
Martin's, 1978.

46 Business writing

Some of the most important writing you will do is writing that helps you get a job. The two basic writing skills you will need to use in looking for a job are preparing a résumé and drafting a business letter.

46a The résumé

A résumé is a summary of your experience presented in an easy-to-read format. Think of your résumé as your sales case to prospective employers. It must catch their eye, be brief and to the point, give them pertinent information, and persuade them to consider you for the job.

Writing a résumé involves planning. Before you start, take a good look at yourself. What are your strengths? What assets would you bring to a job? What particularly valuable experience have you had? What successes have you had? Why should someone hire you? Until you can answer this last question for yourself, it is unlikely that you will be able to sell yourself to a prospective employer.

Personal data

At the top of your résumé, include pertinent personal data: your name, your address, your telephone number. If you have a home address and a school address, list both. If you have a phone number where you can be reached during the day and one where you can be reached during the evening, list both. Do not include information such as your age, your marital status, your height, or your weight.

Educational background

List all the schools you have attended since high school, starting with the most recent. In other words, list these schools in reverse chronological order. Provide your years of attendance and the degrees you received. If you have not yet received a degree but will receive one by the end of the semester, include this information. If you did not receive a degree but accumulated a certain number of credits, include this information. Provide your major and your minor field of study. Do not provide names of particular courses you completed unless they are particularly pertinent to the job for which you are applying. (It is usually more effective to include this information in a cover letter.)

Work experience

List the jobs you have held. For each job, provide the dates of employment, the title of the position you held, the name and address of the company, and a brief description of your responsibilities.

For your job descriptions, do not use full sentences but fragments beginning with, wherever possible, strong action verbs. For example: *Directed playground activities for group of thirty 3–5-year-olds.* Do not exaggerate, but do emphasize your accomplishments. If you were totally responsible for one aspect of the job, say so. If you directed a campaign that resulted in a 10 percent increase in sales, say so. Help your prospective employer see how this experience is relevant to the job you want.

References

Most prospective employers will expect you to provide references—names of people who can vouch for you. If your college has a placement office, you can have all your letters of reference on file there. Then on your résumé list the address of the placement office. If your references are not on file, on your résumé state *References furnished on request.*

Other information

Keeping in mind that although your résumé should be brief—usually no more than one page, certainly no more than two—you might want to include additional information. Have you received scholarships or other awards? You can list these under *Awards.* Have you participated in activities that are directly related to your career goals? You can list these under *Activities.*

SAMPLE RÉSUMÉ

Jane Sullivan
404 Allen Street
Richmond, Kentucky 40475
(555) 256-7782

GOAL
A staff position with the office of a public official or with an administrative agency.

SKILLS
Ability to write effective advertisement and newsletter copy.
Ability to communicate pertinent information in face-to-face and telephone discussions.
Strong clerical and typing skills (40 words per minute).
Strong organizational skills.

EXPERIENCE
April–November 1986
Vice-chair of campaign committee to reelect Kentucky State Representative Linda Schmidt (who was reelected with 59% of the vote). Wrote copy for campaign newsletters, direct-mail letters, and advertisements; organized polling; campaigned door-to-door and by telephone.

May–August 1985 and May–August 1986
Worked as office assistant for Cloister Homes Realty Co. Filed records, composed property descriptions, answered phone, typed letters, coordinated multiple-listing service.

April–November 1984
Member of campaign committee to elect Richard Hughes as Kentucky State Senator. Duties included polling and door-to-door and telephone campaigning.

EDUCATION
September 1983 to May 1987
Attended Eastern Kentucky University
B.S. with honors; GPA 3.55
Major: economics
Minor: public administration

REFERENCES
Representative James Schmidt
State Capitol Building
Frankfort, Kentucky 40321

Other references furnished on request.

46b The business letter

A business letter is of necessity a formal letter. When writing a business letter, take extra care to follow standards for correct English usage and to obey the conventions of business letter form.

Type your letter single spaced on good-quality unlined 8½″ x 11″ paper. Be especially neat. Do not cross out or erase. If you make mistakes, use one of the "invisible" correction methods or retype the letter. Type on only one side of the paper. Leave adequate margins on the left and right sides. Center the letter vertically on the page.

Return address

In the upper right-hand corner, type on three lines your address and the date. Do not include your name. Of course, if you are using letterhead, you need only the date.

Inside address

At least two lines below the return address but starting at the left-hand margin, type the name, the title (on a separate line), and the full address of the person to whom the letter is addressed.

Salutation

Two lines below the inside address, type the salutation. Make every effort to find out the exact name of the person to whom you are writing, and be sure to spell this name correctly. However, if you cannot find the name, you have several options. (1) Unless you know the sex of the person, address the person as *Dear Sir or Madam*. (2) Address the person by position: *Dear Director of Personnel*. (3) Address the company: *Dear Michigan Trust Company*. If you are writing to a woman and you do not know whether she is married or is using her married name, address her as *Ms.*: *Dear Ms. Balducci*. Use a colon at the end of the salutation.

Body

Start the body of the letter two lines below the salutation. Type the body single-spaced, with a double space between paragraphs. If you use a block style, do not indent paragraphs. If you use a semiblock style, indent each paragraph five spaces.

Complimentary close

Two lines below the last line of the body, type your complimentary close: Sincerely yours, Truly yours, Yours sincerely. Place a comma after the close. Align it vertically with the return address. Sign your name under the complimentary close, and type your name under your signature.

SAMPLE LETTER—BLOCK FORM

return address →   598 Brookside Ave.
Ridgewood, NJ 07480
March 15, 1985

Loretta Jameson
Director of Personnel
Fairfax County Schools   ← inside address
111 Main Street
Fairfax, VA 22030

Dear Ms. Jameson: ← salutation

In <u>The New York Times</u> of March 14, you advertise an
opening for a teacher of English in the Fairfax County
Schools. I am very interested in the position and hope you
will consider my application and the résumé that I have
enclosed.

I will receive my bachelor's degree from New York
University in June, with a major in English and a minor in
secondary education. For the last two years I have also
tutored groups of high school students in grammar and
usage. Students with whom I have worked have succeeded in
raising their grades and have, in many cases, voluntarily
increased the amount of reading and writing they do on
their own. Two of the classroom teachers of these students
have agreed to give me references, and I have included
their names and addresses on my résumé. If you would like
me to ask them to write directly to you, please let me
know.

I think my qualifications will match your needs, and I
would welcome an opportunity to present my credentials in
person. I can arrange to come for an interview almost any
time on short notice.

complimentary close →   Sincerely yours,

Christine O'Toole

Christine O'Toole

SAMPLE LETTER—SEMIBLOCK FORM

404 Allen Street
Richmond, Kentucky 40475
February 17, 1987

The Honorable Elmer T. Scofield
U.S. House of Representatives
House Office Building, Suite 527
Washington, D.C. 20515

Dear Mr. Scofield:

I would appreciate your considering my application for an internship in your office this summer. I will be graduating in June from Eastern Kentucky University, and I understand from your office staff that you will have several internship appointments open at that time. I would be honored to fill one of these positions.

Through two of my friends who are currently working in Washington for other Representatives, I have gained an appreciation of the duties and responsibilities of an intern. Attention to detail and willingness to work long hours with single-minded attention to a task seem to be prerequisites, and I have acquired some skill in both of these as a student and as a clerical employee for a realtor during my summer vacations. I am also familiar with and enthusiastic about politics as a result of my participation in the campaigns of State Senator Richard Hughes and State Representative Linda Schmidt. I am myself considering a career in public service and would like to learn firsthand exactly what such an obligation entails.

I have enclosed a copy of my résumé and the completed application forms I received from your secretary. May I call your office in about three weeks to inquire about my application? I would be very glad of an opportunity to demonstrate my qualifications in an interview, and I hope very much to work for you.

Sincerely yours,

Jane Sullivan

Jane Sullivan

GLOSSARY
OF
USAGE

GLOSSARY
OF USAGE

The items in this glossary reflect current usage among experienced writers. Use the glossary to check the appropriateness of your word choices.

a, an Use the article *a* before a consonant sound; use *an* before a vowel sound.

| a receipt | a history | a one-liner | a unit | a B |
| an idea | an hour | an officer | an umbrella | an F |

aggravate *Aggravate* means "to make worse." In formal writing, do not use *aggravate* with its informal meaning of "to annoy, irritate, or vex."

agree to, agree with Use *agree* with *to* when you mean "to grant or give approval." Use *agree* with *with* when you mean "to be in harmony," "to conform," or "to hold similar views."

The senator could not **agree to** to the amendment.
The senator could not **agree with** his colleague on the need for the amendment.

ain't   Nonstandard contraction. In general, avoid it in your writing.

all right   Always write *all right* as two words, not as *alright*.

allusion, illusion   An *allusion* is an indirect or casual reference to something. An *illusion* is a false or misleading perception or concept.

The poem is filled with many **allusions** to the Bible.
Five years in the theater stripped him of his **illusions** about the glamour of an actor's life.

a lot   Always write *a lot* as two words, not as *alot*. In general, avoid using *a lot* in formal writing.

A.M., P.M. *or* **a.m., p.m.**   Use these abbreviations only with figures.

Not: The lecture ends at eleven in the **A.M.**
But: The lecture ends at 11 **A.M.**

among, between   Use *among* with three or more people or objects. Use *between* with only two.

According to the will, the funds were to be divided equally **between** the two children.
He decided to leave his entire estate to his eldest son, rather than divide it **among** his six children.

amount, number   *Amount* refers to mass or quantity. It is followed by the preposition *of* and a singular noun. *Number* refers to things that can be counted. It is followed by *of* and a plural noun.

The **amount** of time he spent completing the job was far greater than the reward he derived from it.
The **number** of domestic animals that have contracted rabies is alarming.

an   *See* **a.**

and etc. The abbreviation *etc.* means "and other things" or "and so forth." Therefore, *and etc.* is redundant.

anxious, eager *Anxious* means "worried, uneasy, uncertain." In formal writing, do not use *anxious* for *eager*, which means "expectant" or "desirous" but carries no implication of apprehension.

> The doctor was **anxious** about her patient's condition.
> Since we have heard so many good things about them, we are **eager** to meet our new neighbors.

anyone, any one *Anyone* means "any person at all." It refers indefinitely to any person whatsoever. *Any one* refers to a specific person or thing within a group. Similar cases are *everyone, every one* and *someone, some one.*

> **Anyone** willing to work hard can get good grades.
> **Any one** of these plans is acceptable.

anyplace *Anywhere* is preferred.

anyways *Anyway* is preferred.

anywheres *Anywhere* is preferred.

as In general, use the stronger and clearer conjunctions *because, since,* and *while.*

> **Not:** We could no longer see the river from our terrace, **as** the new building blocked our view.
> **But:** We could no longer see the river from our terrace **because** the new building blocked our view.

as, like *See* **like.**

awful In general, use a more specific adjective such as *shocking, ugly, appalling,* or *great.* In formal writing, do not use *awful* as an intensifier meaning "very."

awhile, a while *Awhile* is an adverb meaning "for a short time." It is not preceded by the preposition *for. A while* is an article plus a noun. It is usually preceded by *for.*

> We asked our guests to stay **awhile.**
> They could stay for **a while** longer.

bad, badly Use the adjective *bad* before nouns and after linking verbs. Use the adverb *badly* to modify verbs or adjectives.

> Several **bad** strawberries were hidden under the good ones.
> The students felt **bad** about the loss.
> The dancer performed **badly.**
> The book was **badly** written.

being as, being that Use the more formal *because.*

> **Not:** **Being as** the sketch was signed, it was valuable.
> **But:** **Because** the sketch was signed, it was valuable.

> **Not:** **Being that** they needed money badly, they took a second mortgage on their home.
> **But:** **Because** they needed money badly, they took a second mortgage on their home.

beside, besides *Beside* is a preposition that means "next to." When used as a preposition, *besides* means "in addition to" or "except for." When used as an adverb, *besides* means "in addition" or "furthermore."

> She was buried **beside** her husband.
> **Besides** mathematics, there are no required courses.
> To keep warm, she wore a coat, a hat, and gloves—and a muffler **besides.**

between *See* **among.**

between you and I A common grammatical mistake. Write *between you and me.*

bring, take Use *bring* when you mean movement from a farther person or place toward a nearer one. Use *take* when you mean movement away from a nearer person or place toward a farther one.

> **Bring** me the book I left in the bedroom.
> **Take** this package to the post office.

bunch Do not use *bunch* to refer to a group of people.

burst, bursted, bust, busted *Burst* is a verb that means "to come apart suddenly." Its past and past participle forms are both *burst*, not *bursted*. *Bust*, a verb meaning "to come apart suddenly" or "to break," is considered slang. Do not use it or its past form *busted* in formal writing.

can, may In formal writing, use *can* to indicate ability and *may* to indicate permission. In informal writing, you may use them interchangeably.

Can the defendant answer the question? (Is he able to?)
May the defendant answer the question? (Does he have permission to do so?)

can't hardly, can't scarcely Avoid these double negatives. Use *can hardly* and *can scarcely* instead.

center around Use *center on* instead.

climactic, climatic *Climactic* refers to the climax, or highest point of intensity. *Climatic* refers to the climate, or characteristic weather conditions.

compare to, compare with Use *compare to* when referring to the similarities between essentially unlike things. Use *compare with* when referring to the similarities and differences between things of the same type.

Hart Crane **compares** the sound of rain **to** "gently pitying laughter."
The professor **compared** a poem by Hart Crane **with** one by Edna St. Vincent Millay.

contemptible, contemptuous *Contemptible* means "deserving contempt." *Contemptuous* means "feeling contempt."

She claimed that efforts to cut back funds for food programs for the poor were **contemptible.**
She was **contemptuous** of people who ignored the suffering of others.

continual, continuous *Continual* means "recurring regularly." *Continuous* means "occurring without interruption."

He was kept awake by the **continual** dripping of the faucet.
The nation was experiencing a period of **continuous** growth.

410

convince, persuade *Convince*, which is often used with *of*, means "to cause to believe." *Persuade*, which is often used with an infinitive, means "to cause to do."

> The physicist **convinced** his colleague of the correctness of his methods.
> The doctor **persuaded** her patient to undergo therapy.

could of Nonstandard. Use *could have*.

criteria, data, phenomena These words are plural and in formal writing take plural verbs. The singular forms are *criterion*, *datum*, and *phenomenon*.

deal As a word meaning "agreement," "bargain," or "business transaction," this word is informal and overused.

disinterested, uninterested *Disinterested* means "impartial." *Uninterested* means "indifferent" or "not interested."

> The jury paid special attention to the testimony of one **disinterested** witness.
> She did not finish the book, because she was **uninterested** in the subject.

done *Done* is the past participle of *do*. Do not use *done* as the past tense.

> **Not:** He always read the last page of a mystery first to find out who **done** it.
> **But:** He always read the last page of a mystery first to find out who **did** it.

don't Avoid using *don't*, which is a contraction of *do not*, in formal writing. Never use *don't* as a contraction of *does not*.

due to In formal writing, do not use *due to* to mean *because of*.

> **Not:** The shipment was delayed **due to** the bad weather.
> **But:** The shipment was delayed **because of** the bad weather.
> **Or:** The delay in the shipment was **due to** the bad weather.

eager *See* **anxious**.

enthused In formal writing, use *enthusiastic*.

etc. *See* **and etc.**

everyday, every day Use *every day* as an adverb. Use *everyday* as an adjective.

> During training, he took vitamins **every day**.
> He needed an **everyday** suit.

everyone, every one *See* **anyone.**

everywheres Nonstandard. Use *everywhere*.

exam In formal writing, use *examination*.

expect In formal writing, do not use *expect* to mean "to presume or suppose."

> **Not:** I **expect** the performance went well.
> **But:** I **suppose** the performance went well.

explicit, implicit *Explicit* means "stated forthrightly." *Implicit* means "implied" or "suggested."

> The warning was **explicit**: Beware of the dog.
> Although he never said a word, his threat was **implicit** in his action.

farther, further In formal writing, use *farther* to refer to geographical distance. Use *further* to refer to time, quantity, or degree.

> We were **farther** from home than we had imagined.
> The court demanded **further** documentation of his expenses.

fewer, less Use *fewer* to refer to things that can be counted. Use *less* to refer to a collective quantity that cannot be counted.

> This year **fewer** commuters are driving their cars to work.
> In general, smaller cars use **less** fuel than larger cars.

finalize *Finalize* is an example of bureaucratic language. Do not use it in place of *complete, conclude,* or *make final*.

fine *Fine* is informal and weak when used for the words *very well*. In formal writing, use a more exact word.

firstly, secondly, etc. Use *first*, *second*, etc., instead.

fix In formal writing, avoid using *fix* to mean "predicament."

flunk *Flunk* is informal. In formal writing, use *fail*.

folks In formal writing, avoid using the informal word *folks* for *parents*, *relatives*, or *family*.

former, latter *Former* means "the first mentioned of two." When three or more are mentioned, refer to the first mentioned as *first*. *Latter* means "the second mentioned of two." When three or more are mentioned, refer to the last mentioned as *last*.

> Anita and Jayne are athletes: the **former** is a gymnast, the **latter** a tennis player.
> The judges sampled four pies—apple, plum, rhubarb, and apricot— and gave the prize to the **last**.

funny In formal writing, avoid using *funny* for *odd* or *peculiar*.

further *See* **farther.**

get In formal writing, avoid using slang expressions beginning with *get: get even, get going, get on with it*, etc.

good, well *Good* is an adjective. *Well* is usually an adverb, but it can also be used as an adjective meaning "healthy."

> She looks **good** in that color.
> The baby looks **well** today.
> They work **well** together.

great In formal writing, do not use *great* to mean "wonderful."

had ought, hadn't ought Use *ought* and *ought not* instead.

hanged, hung Use *hanged* as the past and past participle form when referring to a method of execution. Otherwise, use *hung*.

> In the Old West, horse thieves were **hanged**.
> The clothing was **hung** out to dry.

has got, have got In formal writing, use simply *has* or *have*.

herself, himself *See* **myself.**

hisself Nonstandard. Use *himself.*

hopefully *Hopefully* means "in a hopeful manner." Avoid using *hopefully* to mean "it is hoped" or "let us hope."

> **Not:** **Hopefully** it will not rain again this weekend.
> **But:** **Let us hope** it will not rain again this weekend.

illusion *See* **allusion.**

implicit *See* **explicit.**

imply, infer *Imply* means "to suggest or hint." *Infer* means "to draw a conclusion." A writer or speaker implies something; a reader or listener infers it.

> He **implied** that he knew someone had cheated.
> From his remark I **inferred** that he is worried about her.

in, into *In* indicates position. *Into* indicates direction of movement.

> When the sergeant came **into** the barracks, she found several of the new recruits still **in** bed.

infer *See* **imply.**

in regards to Use *in regard to* or *regarding* or *as regards.*

into *See* **in.**

irregardless Nonstandard. Use *regardless.*

is when, is where Do not use these constructions in giving definitions.

> **Not:** Improvisation **is when** actors perform without preparation.
> **But:** Improvisation **occurs when** actors perform without preparation.
> **Or:** Improvisation **is** a performance by actors without preparation.

> **Not:** An aviary **is where** a large number of birds are housed.
> **But:** An aviary **is a place where** a large number of birds are housed.
> **Or:** An aviary **is** a house for a large number of birds.

its, it's *Its* is the possessive case of the pronoun *it*. *It's* is a contraction of *it is* or *it has*.

The cat was cleaning **its** paws.
It's too late to submit an application.

kind of, sort of In formal writing, avoid using *kind of* and *sort of* as adverbs. Use instead the more formal words *rather* and *somewhat*.

Not: His description was **kind of** sketchy.
But: His description was **rather** sketchy.

Not: She left **sort of** abruptly.
But: She left **somewhat** abruptly.

kind of a, sort of a When using these expressions to mean "type of," delete the *a*.

What kind of fabric is this?
What **sort of** person was he?

lay *See* **lie**.

lead, led *Lead* is the present infinitive form of the verb. *Led* is the past tense and past participle form.

learn, teach *Learn* means "to receive knowledge." *Teach* means "to give knowledge."

We can **learn** from the mistakes of history.
History can **teach** us many lessons.

leave, let In formal writing, use the verb *leave* to mean "to depart (from)." Use the verb *let* to mean "to allow to."

Paul Simon wrote about the many ways to **leave** a lover.
The natives would not **let** themselves be photographed.

less *See* **fewer**.

let *See* **leave**.

liable *See* **likely**.

lie, lay *Lie* is an intransitive verb that means "to recline." Its past and past participle forms are *lay* and *lain*. *Lay* is

415

a transitive verb that means "to place." Its past and past participle forms are both *laid*. (See also page 64.)

Although he **lay** in bed for hours, he could not sleep.
Please **lay** the book on the table.

like   In formal writing, do not use *like* as a conjunction. Instead use *as, as if,* or *as though.*

Not: The headlines claim that it looks **like** peace is at hand.
But: The headlines claim that it looks **as if** peace is at hand.

like, such as   Use *like* to introduce a direct comparison with one example. Use *such as* to introduce a series.

She was determined to be a great dancer **like** Maria Tallchief.
She admired innovative choreographers **such as** Twyla Tharp, Paul Taylor, and Laura Dean.

likely, liable   *Likely* indicates probability. *Liable* indicates responsibility or obligation.

The Kremlin asserted that changes in the makeup of the government were not **likely** to lead to changes in U.S.-Soviet relations.
The court determined that the driver of the truck was **liable** for all damages.

lose, loose   *Lose* is a verb. *Loose* is an adjective.

In what year did Nixon **lose** the election to Kennedy?
Loose talk can cause much trouble.

lot   *See* **a lot.**

lot of, lots of   In formal writing, use *a great deal of, much, plenty of,* or *many* instead.

may   *See* **can.**

may be, maybe   *May be* is a verb phrase. *Maybe* is an adverb meaning "perhaps."

His findings **may be** accurate.
Maybe they will find a solution.

may of, might of, must of   Use *may have, might have,* or *must have* instead.

more importantly, most importantly   Use *more important* and *most important* instead.

most   In formal writing, do not use *most* to mean "almost."

Not: The survey predicted that **most** everyone would vote.
But: The survey predicted that **almost** everyone would vote.

myself, yourself, himself, herself, etc.   Pronouns ending in *-self* or *-selves* are reflexive or intensive. In formal writing, do not use them in place of *I, me, you, he, her,* etc.

Not: My friend and **myself** are campaigning actively.
But: My friend and **I** are campaigning actively.

nice   In formal writing, replace this weak word with a more exact one—*attractive, appealing, kind,* etc.

not hardly   Avoid this double negative. Use *hardly* instead.

nowhere near enough   Colloquial. In formal writing, use *not nearly enough* instead.

Not: The concessions the company made its employees were **nowhere near enough** to avoid a strike.
But: The concessions the company made its employees were **not nearly enough** to avoid a strike.

nowheres   Nonstandard. Use *nowhere.*

number   *See* **amount.**

off of   Use *off* without *of.*

Not: During the tremor the paintings fell **off of** the wall.
But: During the tremor the paintings fell **off** the wall.

OK, O.K., okay   Avoid these expressions in formal writing.

people, persons   Use *people* to refer to a large group collectively. Use *persons* to emphasize the individuals within the group.

The committee is investigating ways in which **people** avoid paying their full taxes.
The group thought it was near agreement when several **persons** raised objections.

percent, percentage   Use *percent* after a specific number. Use *percentage* after a general adjective indicating size.

> The poll showed that 75 **percent** of Americans supported the President's foreign policy.
> The poll showed that a large **percentage** of Americans supported the President's foreign policy.

persuade   *See* **convince.**

phenomena   *See* **criteria.**

P.M.   *See* **A.M.**

quote, quotation   *Quote* is a verb. *Quotation* is a noun.

> During her speech she **quoted** from one of Blake's poems.
> She began her speech with a **quotation** from one of Blake's poems.

raise, rise   *Raise* is a transitive verb meaning "to lift." Its past and past participle forms are both *raised*. *Rise* is an intransitive verb meaning "to go up." Its past and past participle are *rose* and *risen*. (See also pages 65–66.)

> Inflation is **raising** the cost of living.
> The cost of living is **rising.**

real, really   *Real* is an adjective. *Really* is an adverb.

> What is the **real** value of the dollar?
> Mortgage rates are **really** high this year.

reason is because   Use *that* instead of *because* or rewrite the sentence.

> **Not:** The **reason** for the patient's lethargy **is because** his diet is inadequate.
> **But:** The **reason** for the patient's lethargy **is that** his diet is inadequate.
> **Or:** The reason for the patient's lethargy is an inadequate diet.
> **Or:** The patient is lethargic because of an inadequate diet.

respectably, respectfully, respectively   *Respectably* means "in a manner deserving respect." *Respectfully* means "in a manner showing respect." *Respectively* means "in the order given."

The tenor performed his aria **respectably**, but his voice cracked during the duet.

The defendant **respectfully** asked permission to address the court.

Baghdad and Damascus are the capitals of Iraq and Syria, **respectively**.

rise *See* **raise.**

sensual, sensuous Both of these adjectives mean "appealing to the senses," but *sensual* describes something that arouses physical appetites, while *sensuous* describes something that leads to aesthetic enjoyment.

The censors claimed that the dancing was too **sensual**.

The painter was praised for the **sensuous** quality of his still lifes.

set, sit *Set* is a transitive verb that means "to put or place." Its past and past participle forms are both *set*. *Sit* is an intransitive verb that means "to be seated." Its past and past participle forms are both *sat*. (See also page 64–65.)

The stagehands **set** the chairs on a raised platform.

The actors will **sit** in the chairs during the rehearsal.

shall, will The distinction between *shall* and *will* is fading. However, for strictly formal writing, use *shall* with first-person pronouns and *will* with second- and third-person pronouns to indicate simple futurity. Reverse the order to indicate determination, duty, or need.

Simple futurity

I **shall** see you at the theater.

He **will** meet us at the theater.

Determination

We **will** find a solution to this problem.

They **shall** not defeat us.

should of Nonstandard. Use *should have*.

sit *See* **set.**

someone, some one *See* **anyone.**

sometime, some time Use *sometime* as an adverb to mean "at an indefinite or unnamed time." Use *some time* after a preposition.

The announcement will be made **sometime** next month.
He has been retired for **some time** now.

sort of   *See* **kind of.**

sort of a   *See* **kind of a.**

suppose to   *See* **use to.**

sure, surely   *Sure* is an adjective that means "certain." *Surely* is an adverb that means "undoubtedly" or "certainly."

The expedition was **sure** to succeed.
The expedition was **surely** a success.

sure and, try and   In formal writing, use *sure to* and *try to* instead.

Not: Be **sure and** pay attention to the speaker's body language.
But: Be **sure to** pay attention to the speaker's body language.

teach   *See* **learn.**

that, which   Use *that* to introduce a restrictive clause. Use *which* to introduce either a restrictive or a nonrestrictive clause. (In order to maintain a clearer distinction between *which* and *that*, some writers use *which* to introduce only a nonrestrictive clause.)

Is this the manuscript **that** he submitted yesterday?
This contract, **which** is no longer valid, called for a 30 percent royalty.

theirself, theirselves   Nonstandard. Use *themselves*.

these kind, those kind; these sort, those sort   Since *kind* and *sort* are singular, use singular adjectives: *this kind, that kind, this sort, that sort*. For the plural use *these kinds, those kinds, these sorts, those sorts*.

thusly   Use *thus*.

try and   *See* **sure and.**

uninterested   *See* **disinterested.**

unique   The word *unique* means "unequaled" or "unparalleled," a quality that is not capable of comparison.

> **Not:** He has the **most unique** sense of humor I have encountered.
> **But:** His sense of humor is **unique.**

use to, suppose to   The correct forms are *used to* and supposed *to.*

> **Not:** In *My Dinner with Andre,* Wally **use to** be a Latin teacher.
> **But:** In *My Dinner with Andre,* Wally **used to** be a Latin teacher.

wait for, wait on   Use *wait for* to mean "await" or "attend to." Use *wait on* to mean "serve."

> Many young actors **wait on** tables while they **wait for** the right role.

ways   Use *way* to mean "distance."

> **Not:** He lives only a short **ways** from London.
> **But:** He lives only a short **way** from London.

well   *See* **good.**

when, where   *See* **is when, is where.**

where   Do not use *where* for *that.*

> **Not:** I read in the magazine **where** flood victims were now receiving federal aid.
> **But:** I read in the magazine **that** flood victims were now receiving federal aid.

which, who   Use *which* to refer to objects. Use *who* to refer to people. (*That* usually refers to objects but at times may be used to refer to people.)

> The book, **which** was written by Nat Hentoff, is called *Jazz Is.*
> Nat Hentoff, **who** wrote *Jazz Is,* contributes articles to many magazines.

will   *See* **shall.**

-wise   Avoid using *-wise* as a noun suffix—*budgetwise, careerwise, marketwise.*

without   Do not use *without* for *unless*.

> **Not:** The director could not act **without** the committee approved.
> **But:** The director could not act **unless** the committee approved.
> **Or:** The director could not act **without** the committee's **approval**.

yourself   *See* **myself**.

GLOSSARY
OF
GRAMMAR

GLOSSARY
OF GRAMMAR

absolute phrase   A group of words containing a noun and a nonfinite, or incomplete, verb. It modifies the entire clause to which it is attached, instead of an individual word within the clause: ***His energy depleted,*** *the fighter conceded the bout.* (See also 43a.)

abstract noun   *See* **noun.**

active voice   *See* **voice.**

adjective   A word that modifies, or describes, a noun or pronoun. An adjective tells what kind, how many, or which one: *In **his latest** novel, **this prodigious** writer uses **several historical** studies to create **a realistic** portrait of **the** man often considered **our greatest** president—Abraham Lincoln.* (See also 2c.)

adjective clause   A dependent clause that acts as an adjective and modifies a noun or pronoun. Usually, an adjective clause begins with a relative pronoun (*who, whose, whom, that,* or *which*): *The king of England **who broke with the Catholic Church** was Henry VIII.* (See also 4b.)

adverb   A word that modifies, or limits the meaning of, a verb, an adjective, or another adverb. An adverb tells when, where, to what extent, or how: *This **extremely** absorbing book deals **quite successfully** with the way computers function **today** and the way they will affect our lives **tomorrow**.* (See also 2d.)

adverb clause   A dependent clause that begins with a subordinating conjunction (*although, because, while,* etc.) and acts as an adverb in the sentence: *The museum was closed **because it was being renovated**.* (See also 4b.)

agreement   The correspondence in form between a verb and its subject or a pronoun and its antecedent to indicate person, number, and gender: ***Each** of these women **makes her** position understood.* (See also 9 and 10a.)

antecedent   The word or words to which a pronoun refers. A pronoun must agree with its antecedent in number and gender: ***Jack** pledged his support for the project.* (See also 2e and 10a.)

appositive   A noun or group of words that renames, identifies, or gives additional information about the preceding noun or pronoun: *Typhoid Mary, **the notorious carrier of typhoid fever,** died in 1938.* (See also 18 and 43a.)

article   The indefinite articles are *a* and *an*; the definite article is *the.* Articles are classified as adjectives. (See also 2c.)

auxiliary verb   A form of *be* or *have* used to form perfect tenses, progressive forms of tenses, and the passive voice: *I **am** leaving. They **have** left. The money **had been** left in the safe.* (See also 2b).

case   The structural function of a noun or a pronoun in a sentence. English has three cases—subjective, objective, and possessive. The subjective case indicates the subject of a verb or a subject complement: *The* **umpire** *called a strike. The* **umpire** *was* **he.** The objective case indicates the object of a verb or of a preposition: *Connors returned the* **serve** *to* **McEnroe.** *He returned* **it** *to* **him.** The possessive case indicates possession: *The* **team's** *overall performance was disappointing.* **Their** *overall performance was disappointing.* Nouns and most pronouns have the same form in the subjective and the objective cases; an apostrophe and *s* or an apostrophe alone is added to form the possessive case: *investor's, investors', anybody's.* The pronouns *it* and *you* have special possessive forms: *its, your* or *yours.* The following pronouns have different forms in all three cases.

Subjective: I, he, she, we, they, who
Objective: me, him, her, us, them, whom
Possessive: my, mine; his; her, hers; our, ours; their, theirs; whose

(See also 2a, 2e, and 11.)

clause A group of words with a subject and a predicate. A clause may be independent or dependent. An independent (main) clause is structurally independent and can stand by itself as a simple sentence: *The President honored the Unknown Soldier.* A dependent (subordinate) clause is not structurally independent and cannot stand by itself as a simple sentence. Therefore, it must be joined to or be part of an independent clause: **Although newspapers strive for accuracy,** *they sometimes make mistakes.* **What you see** *is* **what you get.** Dependent clauses, which can function as adjectives, adverbs, or nouns, usually begin with a subordinating conjunction or a relative pronoun. (See also 4.)

collective noun *See* **noun.**

comma splice An error that occurs when a comma is used to separate two independent clauses not joined by a conjunction. (See also 7.)

common noun *See* **noun.**

comparative, superlative Forms of adjectives and adverbs used to make comparisons. The comparative form is used to compare two things; the superlative form is used to compare more than two. The comparative and superlative of most one-syllable adjectives and adverbs are formed by adding *-er* and *-est* to the base, or positive, form: *long, longer, longest.* The comparative and superlative of most longer adjectives and adverbs are formed by placing the words *more* and *most* before the positive form: *beautiful, more beautiful, most beautiful.* (See also 2c, 2d, and 12c.)

complement A word or group of words that completes the meaning of a verb. The four types of complements are direct objects, indirect objects, predicate nominatives, and predicate adjectives. (See also 1a, 1b, and 1c.)

complete predicate *See* **predicate.**

complete sentence *See* **sentence.**

complete subject *See* **subject.**

complex sentence *See* **sentence.**

compound A word or group of words that is made up of two or more parts but functions as a unit. Compound words consist of two or more words that may be written as one word, as a hyphenated word, or as separate words but that function as a single part of speech: *hairbrush, well-to-do, toaster oven.* A compound subject consists of two or more nouns or noun substitutes that take the same predicate: ***Chemistry*** and ***physics*** *were required courses.* A compound verb consists of two or more verbs that have the same subject: *The doctor **analyzed** the results of the tests and **made** a diagnosis.* (See also 1a, 1b, and 2a.)

compound-complex sentence *See* **sentence.**

compound sentence *See* **sentence.**

concrete noun *See* **noun.**

conjunction A word or set of words that joins or relates other words, phrases, clauses, or sentences. There are three types of conjunctions: coordinating conjunctions, correlative conjunctions, and subordinating conjunctions. Coordinating conjunctions (*and, but, for, nor, or, so,* and *yet*) join elements that have equal grammatical rank. Correlative conjunctions (*both . . . and, either . . . or, neither . . . nor, not only . . . but also, whether . . . or, just as . . . so*) function as coordinating conjunctions but are always used in pairs. Subordinating conjunctions (*after, as long as, because, if, since, so that, unless, until, while,* etc.) join subordinate, or dependent, clauses to main, or independent, clauses. (See also 2g.)

conjunctive adverb An adverb that functions as a coordinating conjunction to join independent clauses: *The movie received many excellent reviews;* **consequently,** *people across the country lined up to see it.* (See also 2g.)

coordinating conjunction *See* **conjunction.**

correlative conjunction *See* **conjunction.**

dangling modifier An introductory phrase that does not clearly and sensibly modify the noun or pronoun that follows it. (See also 16d.)

degrees of modifiers *See* **comparative, superlative.**

demonstrative pronoun *See* **pronoun.**

dependent clause *See* **clause.**

direct object *See* **object.**

double negative A construction, considered unacceptable in standard modern English, that uses two negative words to make a negative statement. (See also 12d.)

elliptical clause A clause in which a word is omitted but understood: *He works harder than his partner [does].* (See also 4b and 11.)

expletive The word *there, here,* or *it* used to fill the position before a verb of being but not to add meaning to the sentence: ***There*** *are several excellent reasons for taking this course.* ***Here*** *is one of them.* ***It*** *is wise to register early.* (See also 1a and 9.)

fragment *See* **sentence fragment.**

fused sentence Two independent clauses written without a coordinating conjunction or a punctuation mark between them. (See also 7.)

gender The classification of nouns and pronouns as masculine (*man, he*), feminine (*woman, she*), or neuter (*skillet, it*). (See also 2a, 2e, and 10a.)

gerund *See* **verbal.**

gerund phrase *See* **phrase.**

imperative *See* **mood.**

indefinite pronoun *See* **pronoun.**

independent clause *See* **clause.**

indicative *See* **mood.**

indirect object *See* **object.**

infinitive *See* **verbal.**

infinitive phrase *See* **phrase.**

intensive pronoun *See* **pronoun.**

interjection A word that expresses emotion and has no grammatical connection to the sentence in which it appears: ***Oh,*** *how happy he was!* ***Wow,*** *that was painful!* (See also 2h).

interrogative pronoun *See* **pronoun.**

intransitive verb *See* **verb.**

inverted word order A change in the normal English word order of subject-verb-complement: *In the doorway stood Tom.* (See also 1a and 9.)

irregular verb   A verb that does not form its past tense and past participle according to the regular pattern of adding -*ed* or -*d* to the present infinitive: *begin, began, begun; draw, drew, drawn; put, put, put.* (See also 8.)

linking verb   *See* **verb.**

main clause   *See* **clause.**

misplaced modifier   A modifier placed so that it seems to refer to a word other than the one intended. (See also 16e.)

modal   A verb form used with a main verb to ask a question, to help express negation, to show future time, to emphasize, or to express such conditions as possibility, certainty, or obligation. The following words are modals: *do, does, did; can, could; may, might, must; will, shall; would, should,* and *ought to.* (See also 2b.)

modifier   A word or group of words that limits the meaning of or makes more specific another word or group of words. The two kinds of modifiers are adjectives and adverbs. (See also 2c and 2d.)

mood   The aspect of a verb that indicates the writer's attitude toward the action or condition expressed by the verb. In English there are three moods: the indicative, the imperative, and the subjunctive. The indicative expresses a factual statement or a question: *The weather **is** fine today.* ***Will** it **rain** tomorrow?* The imperative indicates a command or a request: ***Buy** your tickets today.* ***Will** you please **be** quiet.* The subjunctive indicates a wish, an assumption, a recommendation, or something contrary to fact: *She wished she **were** home. If she **were** mayor, she would eliminate waste from the city budget.* (See also 2b and 14.)

nominative case   *See* **case.**

nonessential element   A modifying phrase or clause that does not limit or qualify the noun it modifies. Since a nonessential element is not necessary to the meaning of the clause in which it appears, it is set off with commas: *Hurlyburly,* ***which was written by David Rabe,*** *conveys the confusion and aimlessness of modern American life.* (See also 18h.)

noun   A word that names a person, place, object, or idea. Proper nouns name particular people, places, objects, or ideas: *Gertrude Stein, Spain, Corvettes, Puritanism.* Common nouns name people, places, objects, and ideas in general, not in particular: *poet, country, cars, religion.* Concrete nouns name things that can be seen, touched, heard, smelled, or tasted: *portrait, mansion, chorus, garlic.* Abstract nouns name concepts, ideas, beliefs, and qualities: *honesty, consideration, fascism, monotheism.* Collective nouns refer to groups of people or things as though the group were a single unit: *committee, choir, navy, team.* (See also 2a and 9.)

noun clause   A dependent clause that acts as a noun in a sentence. It functions as a subject, an object, or a predicate nominative: ***That an agreement would be reached before the strike deadline*** *seemed unlikely.* (See also 4b.)

noun phrase   A noun and its modifiers: ***The sound of the orchestra playing Mozart*** *filled the air.* (See also 3b.)

noun substitute   A pronoun, gerund, clause, or other group of words that functions as a noun in a sentence. (See also 2e and 2i.)

number   The quality of being singular or plural. (See 2a, 2b, 2e, and especially 9 and 10.)

object   A noun or noun substitute that completes the meaning of or is affected by a transitive verb or a preposition. A direct object specifies the person, place, object, or idea that directly receives the action of a transitive verb: *The three heads of state signed the **treaty.*** An indirect object tells to whom or what or for whom or what the action of a transitive verb is performed: *They gave the **refugees***

food and clothing. An object of a preposition is the noun or noun substitute that the preposition relates to another

part of the sentence: *The cat is sleeping under the* **table.** (See also 1c, 3a, and 11a.)

objective case *See* **case.**

parenthetical expression An expression that comments on or gives additional information about the main part of a sentence. Since a parenthetical expression interrupts the thought of the sentence, it is set off by commas: *Music,* **I** **believe,** *is good for the soul.* (See also 18.)

participial phrase *See* **phrase.**

participle *See* **verbal.**

parts of speech The eight groups into which words are traditionally classified based on their function in a sentence: noun, verb, adjective, adverb, pronoun, preposition, conjunction, and interjection. (See also 1.)

passive voice *See* **voice.**

past participle *See* **verbal.**

personal pronoun *See* **pronoun.**

phrase A group of words lacking a subject and a predicate that often functions as a single part of speech. (See also 3.)

positive degree *See* **comparative, superlative.**

possessive case *See* **case.**

predicate The part of a sentence that tells what the subject does or is. The simple predicate is the main verb, including any auxiliaries or modals: *The rice* **was** *lightly* **flavored** *with vinegar.* The complete predicate consists of the simple predicate and all the words that modify and complement it: *The rice* **was lightly flavored with vinegar.** (See also 1b.)

predicate adjective An adjective that follows a linking verb and describes the subject of the verb: *Lestrade's solution was too **simplistic***. (See also 1c.)

predicate nominative A noun or noun substitute that follows a linking verb and renames the subject of the verb: *The model for Nora Charles was **Lillian Hellman***. (See also 1c.)

preposition A function word used to show the relationship of a noun or pronoun to another part of the sentence. (See also 2f.)

prepositional phrase A phrase consisting of a preposition, the object of the preposition, and all the words modifying this object: *The narrator **of the story** is a young man who lived **with the writer** and assisted him **in his work***. (See also 3a.)

pronoun A word that stands for or takes the place of one or more nouns. A personal pronoun takes the place of a noun that names a person or a thing: *I, me, my, mine; you, your, yours; he, him, his; she, her, hers; it, its; we, us, our, ours; they, them, their, theirs*. A demonstrative pronoun points to someone or something: *this, that, these, those*. An indefinite pronoun does not take the place of a particular noun. It carries the idea of "all," "some," "any," or "none": *everyone, everything, somebody, many, anyone, anything, no one, nobody*. An interrogative pronoun is used to ask a question: *who, whom, whose, what, which*. A relative pronoun is used to form an adjective clause or a noun clause: *who, whose, whom, which, that, what, whoever, whomever, whichever, whatever*. An intensive pronoun is used for emphasis. It is formed by adding *-self* or *-selves* to the end of a personal pronoun. A reflexive pronoun, which has the same form as an intensive pronoun, is used to show that the subject is acting upon itself. (See also 2e, 10, and 11.)

proper adjective An adjective formed from a proper noun: ***Machiavellian** scheme, **Byronic** disposition, **Parisian** dress.* (See also 33.)

proper noun   *See* **noun.**

reflexive pronoun   *See* **pronoun.**

regular verb   A verb whose past tense and past participle are formed by adding *-d* or *-ed* to the present infinitive: *analyze, analyzed, analyzed; detain, detained, detained.* (See also 2b.)

relative pronoun   *See* **pronoun.**

restrictive element   A modifying phrase or clause that limits or qualifies the idea expressed by the noun it modifies. Since a restrictive element is necessary for the basic meaning of the clause in which it appears, it is not set off with commas: *The woman **wearing the blue suit** just received a promotion.* (See also 18.)

run-on sentence   Two or more complete sentences incorrectly written as though they were one sentence. (See also 7.)

sentence   A group of words with a subject and a predicate that expresses a complete thought. Sentences can be classified into four basic groups according to the number and kinds of clauses they contain. A simple sentence contains only one independent clause and no dependent clause: *The relationship between the United States and the Soviet Union needs to be improved.* A compound sentence contains two or more independent clauses but no dependent clause: *The senator worked hard for passage of the bill, but his efforts proved futile.* A complex sentence contains one independent clause and one or more dependent clauses: *Although the two nations were technically at peace, their secret services were fighting a covert war.* A compound-complex sentence contains two or more independent clauses and one or more dependent clause: *Voter confidence in the administration grew as interest rates went down; however, it quickly faded when interest rates started to rise.* (See also 1 and 5.)

sentence fragment   An incomplete sentence written as a complete sentence. (See also 6.)

simple predicate   *See* **predicate.**

simple sentence   *See* **sentence.**

simple subject   *See* **subject.**

squinting modifier   A modifier that, because of its placement, could refer to either the preceding or the following element in a sentence. (See also 16f.)

subject   The part of a sentence that answers the question "who?" or "what?" in regard to the predicate, or verb. The simple subject is the main noun or noun substitute in the subject: *Women's **fashions** from the 1950's are becoming popular again.* The complete subject is the simple subject together with all the words that modify it: ***Women's fashions from the 1950's** are becoming popular again.* (See also 1a.)

subject complement   *See* **complement.**

subjective case   *See* **case.**

subjunctive   *See* **mood.**

subordinate clause   *See* **clause.**

subordinating conjunction   *See* **conjunction.**

superlative degree   *See* **comparative, superlative.**

tense   The time expressed by the form of the verb. There are six tenses: (simple) present, present perfect, (simple) past, past perfect, (simple) future, future perfect. Each of the tenses has a progressive form that indicates continuing action. The present tense is used to write about events or conditions that are happening or existing now: *She **writes** a column for the local newspaper.* The present tense is also used to write about natural or scientific laws, timeless truths, events in literature, habitual action, and (with an adverbial word or phrase) future time. The present perfect tense is used to write about events that occurred at some unspecified time in the past and about events and conditions that began in the past and may still be continuing in the

435

present: *She **has written** a series of articles about child abuse.* The past tense is used to write about events that occurred and conditions that existed at a definite time in the past and do not extend into the present: *The researcher **studied** voting trends in this district.* The past perfect tense is used to write about a past event or condition that ended before another past event or condition began: *They **had studied** the effects of television on voting trends.* The future tense is used to write about events or conditions that have not yet begun: *They **will consider** her proposal.* The future perfect tense is used to write about a future event or condition that will end before another future event or condition begins or before a specified time in the future: *By next month, they **will have considered** all the proposals.* (See also 2b, 14, and 15.)

transitive verb *See* **verb.**

verb A word that expresses action or a state of being. An action verb expresses action: *The ballerina **danced** beautifully.* A linking verb expresses a state of being or a condition. It connects the subject of the sentence to a word that identifies or describes it: *Vitamin C **may be** effective against the common cold.* A transitive verb is an action verb that takes an object: *The fleet **secures** the coasts against invasion.* An intransitive verb is an action verb that does not take an object: *After deregulation of the industry, prices **soared.*** (See also 2b.)

verb phrase A phrase made up of the present participle or the past participle plus one or more auxiliaries or modals: *Jesse Jackson **had proved** himself an effective negotiator. The gymnasts **have been practicing** regularly.* (See also 2b and 8.)

verbal A grammatical form that is based on a verb but that functions as a noun, an adjective, or an adverb, instead of as a verb, in a sentence. There are three types of verbals: participles, gerunds, and infinitives. The present participle and the past participle of most verbs can function as adjectives: *One of the most memorable figures in* Alice in Wonderland *is the* **grinning** *Cheshire cat. The lawyer demanded a* **written** *contract.* A gerund is a verb form spelled the same way as the present participle but used as a noun in a sentence: ***Walking*** *is good for your health.* The present infinitive and the present perfect infinitive form of a verb can function as a noun, as an adjective, or as an adverb: *In* A Chorus Line, *the overriding ambition of each of the characters is* **to dance.** *Cassie was glad* **to have gotten** *the part.* (See also 2i.)

verbal phrase   A phrase consisting of a verbal and all its complements and modifiers. There are three types of verbal phrases: participial phrases, gerund phrases, and infinitive phrases. A participial phrase functions as an adjective in a sentence: *The image of a garden* **filled with poisonous flowers** *dominates "Rappaccini's Daughter."* A gerund phrase functions as a noun in a sentence: ***Exercising in the noonday sun*** *can be dangerous.* An infinitive phrase functions as a noun, an adjective, or an adverb: ***To make the world safe for democracy*** *was one of Wilson's goals.* (See also 3c.)

voice   The indication of whether the subject performs or receives the action of the verb. If the subject performs the action, the verb and the clause are in the active voice: *Herman Melville* **wrote** *"Bartleby the Scrivener."* If the subject receives the action or is acted upon, the verb and the clause are in the passive voice: *"Bartleby the Scrivener"* **was written** *by Herman Melville.* (See also 2b and 14.)

INDEX

The italicized page numbers refer to the Glossary of Usage and the Glossary of Grammar.

WRITING A FIRST DRAFT

1. Write the first draft well before the finished essay is due. A week in advance is desirable; a twenty-four-hour lead is essential. *Don't wait until the last minute—ever.*

2. Write the first draft as rapidly as possible. You want to capture ideas rather than form.

3. Ignore spelling and punctuation questions as you write. If you are uncertain of one or the other at any point, mark the place and write on. Any signal will do. Use a wavy line under the doubtful place or circle it, but don't stop to look things up. Do that *after* the first draft is complete.

4. Minimize your investment. Cut regular-size sheets of paper in half and start every paragraph on a new half-page. The less writing you have on a piece of paper, the easier it will be to move that writing around in the essay or to discard it altogether.

5. Write double or even triple space. Leave room to insert.

6. Cross out; don't erase. And when you cross out, let what you have crossed out show through. You might want to go back to that wording later.

7. Be sloppy! Discourage yourself from even *thinking* of the draft as finished work.

8. Write the draft where you cannot be interrupted. You want a free, sequential flow of ideas. Work in a place where you can stop and pace the floor if you have to, but not where friends can drop in and knock an hour off your concentration.

9. Don't worry about intriguing openings and watertight conclusions. Keep your mind on your thesis, the main points supporting it, and the details that support the main points. Lay a foundation and leave architectural refinements for a later stage.

10. If you find your first draft wandering from your thesis or suggesting more interesting developments, stop. Weigh the merits of starting over to get back to the thesis against the possible value of constructing a new thesis. *At this stage nothing is permanent.*